BY THE BANKS OF
THE BROKENHEAD

One life — and one summer —
on the Canadian prairie

To Aunty Eleanor
+ Uncle Don,
I hope this book
makes you smile +
remember (especially
you Uncle Don ☺)
love, Karmel.
Hong Kong, Jan/86

OTHER BOOKS BY KARMEL SCHREYER

Empress Emi-poo (Chameleon Press, 2004)

A Singing Bird Will Come: Naomi in Hong Kong (Great Plains, 2002)

Naomi: The Strawberry Blonde of Pippu Town (Great Plains, 1999)

FRONT COVER PHOTOS

from top left, clockwise:

circa 1973: (back) John James Schreyer, (front) Lisa Schreyer, Jason Schreyer, Karmel Schreyer, Elizabeth Schreyer.

circa 1912: (from left) Peter Schreyer, John James Schreyer, Caroline Schreyer Sr., Anton Schreyer Sr.

circa 1941: (from top) Leonard Schreyer, Eleanor Schreyer, Elizabeth Schreyer, Edward Schreyer.

2003: (from left) Emi, Blaise.

BY THE BANKS OF THE BROKENHEAD

One life — and one summer —
on the Canadian prairie

by

KARMEL SCHREYER

and incorporating the journals of
JOHN JAMES SCHREYER

Chameleon Press

A Chameleon Press book

BY THE BANKS OF THE BROKENHEAD
ISBN 988-98362-3-8

© 2006 Karmel Schreyer

Published by Chameleon Press
23rd Floor, 245–251 Hennessy Road, Hong Kong
www.chameleonpress.com

Typeset by Alan Sargent

Printed in the United Kingdom, the United States and Hong Kong
First printing 2006

Supported by

Hong Kong Arts Development Council

The Hong Kong Arts Development Council fully supports freedom of expression. The views and opinions expressed in this publication, and the entire contents thereof, are those of the author and do not represent the stand of the Council.

This memoir is dedicated to the memory of my grandparents:
Elizabeth Schreyer (née Gottfried)
(b. 1902, Galicia, Austro-Hungarian Empire — d. 1990, Beausejour, Manitoba)
John James Schreyer
(b. 1897, Brokenhead, Manitoba — d. 1977, Beausejour, Manitoba)
Amelia Schulz (née Kelm)
(b. 1900, Friedenstal, Bessarabia — d. 1984, Winnipeg, Manitoba)
Jacob Schulz
(b. 1901, Friedenstal, Bessarabia — d. 1983, Winnipeg, Manitoba)
who gave me my roots.

And to my parents:
Lily Schreyer (née Schulz), and Edward Schreyer
who gave me my wings.

People must know the past to understand the present, and to face the future.
— Nellie McClung

It is the wise parent who gives her child roots and wings.
— Chinese proverb

PREFACE

A river runs through it. . . .

In my sixth-grade geography class one day, our teacher asked us to name some rivers. As geography was my favourite subject, and being an eager student in any case, my hand shot up. There was a moment of panic when I watched the teacher turn to me and say my name. Suddenly I was blank. So many important names had been jockeying for position in my mind — Amazon, Nile, St. Lawrence, Red — that not a sound issued from my mouth. The class was silent, waiting for my reply. I had to clear my head and think fast.

"Brokenhead," I blurted. The choice surprised me, but it would do. I sat back in my chair, relieved — and self-satisfied, too. Yes, a good choice; not the most famous example of course, but serviceable.

The silence in the classroom continued. My teacher's eyes widened a little; his somewhat bored gaze morphing into a surprised stare. I wondered what was wrong with him. Then, slowly, he shook his head and grinned. It was a wide grin — and a rare occurrence. As if taking his cue, a few of my classmates snickered. I felt only a little embarrassed by this. Mostly, I was curious and perplexed. What, I wondered, was my teacher grinning at? I knew my answer was correct; Brokenhead was indeed the name of a river. In fact, so important was this river that mention of its name was often preceded by the words 'the' and 'mighty'; the tone used, reverential. As a child, I had heard my father speak of it in this way many times.

I realize now that this was just another example of my father's unusual sense of humour. But even if I had known it then, I am not sure that things would have unfolded any differently. . . .

This is the story of one life (my grandfather's) and one summer (my own) well lived by the banks of the Brokenhead.

CHAPTER 1

Arrival

MY FATHER, ANTON SCHREYER, and my mother emigrated from Galicia, Austria on the 19th day of April 1896, and arrived in Canada on the 11th day of May, at the port of Quebec. They brought with them four daughters and four sons (I was their next child, John James – and not yet born):

Caroline, age 21 years Anton, age 15 years
Elizabeth, age 17 years Jacob, age 13 years
Margaret, age 9 years   Joseph, age 7 years
Catherine, age 4 years   Peter, age 9 months

They arrived at the Winnipeg Canadian Pacific Railway Station on May 18th. My father left the family at the Immigration Hall and took the train for Beausejour the next day. He had an uncle there and was in a hurry to settle down. He had been a farmer in Austria, and that's what he wanted to do in Canada.

In the meantime, my mother was left at the Immigration Hall and did not know when he was coming back. There came a man to the hall while she was giving the children their dinner. He asked if they were all her children and where her husband was and when he was coming back. He told her that if they had $600.00 they could buy 80 acres just a half-mile north of the Canadian Pacific Railway (CPR) station. He went with her and showed the place to her. They met the family that wanted to sell, and my mother was very happy. She felt that if my father came back before these people sold the farm they would buy it, but my father came back a week later and by then the man had sold the farm.

In the earlier years, a family could stay at the Immigration Hall for 10 days to two weeks at the most. The time was up for my father's family, so he bought tickets from the CPR agent in Winnipeg for Beausejour. When the family arrived at Beausejour – there being no place to stay – he rented a team of oxen and a wagon and drove about four miles from town where his uncle had a small shack. The small children and my parents slept in the shack while the older children slept on the wagon.

The next day they got as far as Ladywood, which was nine miles from the town of Beausejour, and there they stayed in the school at night. In the daytime they had to stay outside and hide from the rain beside the wall that was dry. In other words; if the rain came from the south they stood under the north wall, if it came from the west they stood under the east wall.

In the meantime, my father applied for a homestead. He got the land but did not want to live on it as it was too far from the main road. The best places, close to town, were taken up by people that came from England. There were about 36 families living by the road and along the Brokenhead River. None of these river settlers had ever ploughed land. They were not farmers; they lived mostly by fishing and hunting.

That's where my father bought his land from an English settler. He bought 120 acres at $2.00 an acre. There was a small shack on the land and about 100 acres of solid timber – mostly poplar and about 80 to 100 feet tall – and 20 acres of slough grass. The shack was a building of the dimensions 20 by 15 feet. There was room for a stove and one bed, so my mother and father started building another house so that all of the family could be protected from the rain, and especially from the mosquitoes. . . .

– John James Schreyer

WE – MY HUSBAND DARREL, our two young daughters Emi and Blaise, their nanny Emelyn, and myself — are standing on the gravel drive leading to the house. It is white with green trim, small, and plain. This house — where my father was born — is the final stop in a long, convoluted, and occasionally stressful journey, via Japan and the United States, from China. Hong Kong has been my home for the last eight years, and the only one my daughters have ever known.

When feeling dramatic, I say that we have fled our home, that we are fleeing China. It sounds bizarre — romantic to some, perhaps — but it was in a sense the truth. We had left Hong Kong propelled in part by an epidemic: two months before, a malady called Severe Acute Respiratory Syndrome (SARS) had taken hold there, infecting dozens of people daily. Each night, all of Hong Kong would listen to the news, waiting to hear the number of new cases, how many people in hospital, how many of us had died from SARS that day. At the time, the way the disease was spread remained a mystery, but we did know that you could catch SARS if you lived in the same apartment block or the same neighbourhood as an infected person, if you stayed in the same hotel or rode the same aircraft.

People began to go about wearing masks, which was disturbing to see — and to do. Restaurants, movie theatres and playgrounds were deserted. The government shut down the schools. Rumours spread of Hong Kong being declared an infected port, and people rushed the supermarkets, emptying the shelves of rice and other necessities. By then I had decided that the panic and paranoia were as contagious as the disease, and just as much of a health hazard. We were not the first to go, but in those first few weeks, as the fear among us and within us grew, I began to make plans to get my family out of Hong Kong.

Many of our neighbours, long-time fellow expatriates and born-and-bred Chinese Hongkongers alike, escaped to beaches on remote islands in Thailand and Indonesia. Others, whose jobs had brought them only temporarily to Hong Kong, flew back to homes in Australia or elsewhere. After living there for so long, I had been working on plans for a lengthy family break away from the treadmill, but these were plans I had been thinking of carrying out a few years down the road, when my girls were a little older. Fate, however, had brought these plans forward.

Only a few months before SARS crept into Hong Kong from China, dengue fever was the disease we were told to watch out for. We heeded the public service announcements on television that warned us to be on the lookout for mosquito breeding grounds: stagnant water in plant pots, tires in playgrounds and empty Coke cans. I wryly thought that this gave us something in common with family and friends in Manitoba, whose readiness to combat the giant prairie mosquito had been made all the more vigilant with to the appearance of the West Nile virus the year before. Was West Nile the lesser of the two evils, or were we jumping from frying pan to fire? I had no idea, but in any event it felt better to be closer to family.

It was May when the time finally came to leave our home. By then the SARS crisis in Hong Kong had begun to abate only to become more of an issue in Toronto. But on the flight to Canada, I read that Bovine Spongiform Encephalopathy— BSE or 'Mad Cow Disease' — had been found in a cow in Alberta, and was the new thing causing panic in Canada. We transited the airport in Minneapolis under a 'code orange' terrorist alert. When we cleared immigration, to our surprise Emelyn was led away to join a group of other dark-skinned people. She was being quarantined, so to speak, on the basis of her Filipina race. I asked the two elderly female attendants if we could go with her, and while they looked at each other as if it was the first time such a request had been made, they didn't say no. On the flight to Winnipeg, I began to wonder if we would be let into Canada. I dreaded having to write the words 'Hong Kong' on my entry card: would some functionary at the airport in Winnipeg look at our passports and quarantine *us?*

But now, standing before this simple farmhouse, I put the troubles of the world far back in my mind. It is an incredible morning; clear and bright. A typical May morning in Manitoba, I suppose, but I can't get over it. Intoxicated by the fresh air, I shake my head to see if the crystal clarity around me is just an illusion. It isn't. I smile at the hunch that, here at the farm, banishing bad thoughts isn't going to be hard. The cool mid-May breeze is sweeping gently past us and whistling in the trees. It really is.

Yes, this little house is a world away from all our troubles. It'll be a nice place to raise my children — if only for a summer.

Which brings me to the second thing this old farmhouse means to me. It has to do with my plan, dreamed of and constructed in my mind since the day Emi was born and brought forward by disease and pestilence. I want to give my daughters their birthright: their Canadian roots, comprised of me and everyone who came before me here in Manitoba (their Yorkshire roots being, of course, their father's domain). I want them to know who they are. This project is going to be my legacy. I am old enough to know that at the end of the day, it may well be the best of all I have to give them.

But there is another more personal reason for this enterprise. I've moved around too much, and am feeling rootless and stateless myself after years of backpacking around the world and summer jobs in Thailand and Mexico, stints in France (learning French), Italy (studying Renaissance art and history), Australia (university), Japan (teaching English), Seattle (teachers' college), Indonesia (studying women's cooperatives), and finally settling down as an expatriate Canadian living in Hong Kong when it was still the last jewel in the British crown (publishing — and marriage). Since I embarked on that most important journey — motherhood — four years ago, I understand that home is where the heart is, and my two hearts are named Emi and Blaise. But where will *their* home be? Asia? Europe? Canada? My roots are a part of theirs, and for that reason, I am going back myself.

I hope this crazy idea of living on the family farmstead in the Rural Municipality of Brokenhead, Manitoba, with my proper British husband and my two city-slicker Hong Kong-born-and-bred daughters is also going to help me find out, or remember, who I am. I struggle to put out a flicker of nervousness. I want it to work, but I am not sure what to expect.

Several summers ago, I heard of an interesting manuscript somewhere in the family: my grandfather — my father's father, John James Schreyer — had written a record of his family's life from the time they arrived from Beckersdorf — in what was then a part of the Austro-Hungarian Empire and is now eastern Ukraine — over a hundred years ago. I eventually found a yellowed and dog-eared sheaf of papers, typewritten by my cousin Bev before anyone in the family had a computer. My grandfather's memoirs tied in nicely with books that I loved to read, about expats finding their way in their new surrounds. It started with *A Year in Provence,* then Italy, with *Under the Tuscan Sun.* I read more as the genre expanded: *Apricots on the Nile* (Egypt), *On Rue Tatin* (Northern France), *The Olive Farm* (Italy again) — all written, it seemed, around a dwelling . . . and food.

I would read these books and scheme and dream about my family's future. Upon marrying my Yorkshireman, I began reading the British monthly *Country Living* — which conjured up images of a genteel life among Yorkshire moors and dales. Living in a cramped Hong Kong apartment, I dreamed of a Yorkshire barn conversion. But the novelty of yearly visits to England were worn away by the continual cold and rainy weather, and so I began dreaming more of endless prairie skies, and a horizon as far as the eye could see. As much as I appreciated my new home on the far side of the Pacific, I looked forward to that far horizon, not one crowded out by mountains, obscured by rain, or smothered by smog wafting over the border from China.

As my family expanded and my daughters grew, the ideas for my motherly mission took shape, and I felt drawn to places closer to *my* home. I began reading — and rereading — prairie literature: Martha Ostenso's *Wild Geese,* Frederick Philip Grove's *Fruits of the Earth* and *Settlers of the Marsh,* Gabrielle Roy's *The Road to Altamont,* Robert Stead's *Grain, The Empire Builders,* all sorts of things by Margaret Laurence and Nellie McClung, as well as my childhood favourites that I can't wait to read to my own girls: Laura Ingalls Wilder's *Little House on the Prairie* books and Lucy Maud Montgomery's *Anne of Green Gables.* I looked up archival material on the Internet, and browsed through websites about Beausejour, Manitoba, and the Rural Municipality of Brokenhead, where the family farm is located. I made lists of things to think about, places to visit, and things to do when we would arrive in Canada. . . .

There is silence, it seems to me, as we stand facing our home for the summer, but no doubt Emi — and maybe even my dear husband, or Emelyn — is talking, perhaps a comment on the flat landscape, wondering where the mountains have got to, or a remark suggesting disappointment with the new living situation. Perhaps they have already taken in their new home with a glance — plain as it is — and have swivelled their heads towards the big red barn or the old chicken coops, which offer more visual interest. I take no notice: I am wrapped up in my own thoughts. Even I can't help but think that the house seems at first glance ordinary and nondescript; neat, but so much smaller than it had seemed when I spent my summers in it as a child. Disappointment starts to creep up inside me and I mentally stomp on it. I remind myself to focus. I am ready to cross the threshold of a sacred place, to open the door to a long-lost part of my life, to look for more, and to share the treasures with my family. My great-grandfather Anton, his son John James, and *his* son, my father, Edward, have lived on this land and in this house and, over one hundred years after it all began, I am bringing my daughters to it.

So here we stand at the doorstep of this simple farm home. Emi knows her own 'Grandpa Schreyer' (my father) was born here. This grandpa had once been the premier of this province, and governor general of the country we are now in — but my little girls know nothing about all that. And I am not inclined to get into it, either. I have always been aware that part of the reason I find myself living in Asia — on the other side of the planet, as I sometimes refer to it — was to get away from all that. What my daughters do know was that we are in Canada, at Grandma and Grandpa's farm by the Brokenhead River, near the town of Beausejour. They are expecting a summer full of fun and adventure.

I imagine my great-grandfather's family as they stood at this spot in 1896 (my grandfather John James would be born a year later) full of hope and sensing promise; happy and relieved to have finally arrived, eager to put the troubles of the past behind them and move forward. I imagine that's how they felt, because that's how I feel right now. For me, this place is going to be my family's house of dreams — our own little house on the prairie.

I unlock the door and lead my family inside.

CHAPTER 2

Promise

IT TOOK MY FAMILY about a month to get their home ready so as to be able to live in it. The biggest problem was to get the building materials, as the stores in town did not carry nails. If anyone needed nails or items such as windows, you would have to go by train to Winnipeg. That was the reason it took so long to get the house done. The roof was no problem, as my dad knew how to build straw roofs and done right they were as good as a shingle roof.

In the meantime, my dad wanted to do some ploughing for a garden. It was getting late in the fall before freezing. He needed a team of oxen and a plough. There was one German farmer that had about 40 head of cattle. They roamed all over the place and he had steers that were about six years old that were not trained to pull, as they had never had a harness on their backs. The farmer had a team that he worked with, and that my father wanted to rent, but the man wanted too much for a day, so my father decided to buy his own team. He bought a team of young oxen, untrained, but he had worked with oxen all his life and so it did not take him long to train them. He rented a plough and also a mower. He cut enough grass and put up enough hay for two oxen and a cow for the first winter and ploughed about an acre of land for the next year's garden.

Their closest neighbours were about a half-mile away when my father bought the farm. They were a German-speaking family who had lived some years in Ontario as farmers. My dad and mother were very happy that they had such people close by, as they could speak to them and get some information about how to make a living here in Manitoba and what to do. They were told that the only way for a farmer to make a living in winter was to take a sharp axe and go cut down those big poplars that he had on his farm and cut them into four-foot lengths, then take his oxen and sleigh and haul it into town. There the storekeeper will trade you for flour, sugar or whatever you need. My father thanked their neighbours for the advice but was still not convinced that the storekeeper would trade all those things just for wood. Our neighbour lady came over next day to show my dad how cordwood should be cut, so in a couple of days my dad took a cord of wood to town and got the things he needed. He was very happy. He was glad he had so many acres of heavy bush, and he told my mother that the family was not going to be hungry as long as this bush stands. I may mention that in the same year they built a barn for the oxen and about two cows.

The winter was very cold here. In Galicia the climate was mild, and some of the immigrants wanted to go back to Austria but did not have the money for the fare, so they had to stay and make the best of everything. Some started to work and saved their money for the return trip. But by getting paid 75 cents a day they never saved enough. So most of them stayed and began working, cutting cordwood in winter and going to the southern part of Manitoba working for Mennonite farmers. Most of them saved some money and in a few years got a homestead or bought some land, and most of them became more acclimatized to life in Canada.

My dad and his family began to enjoy the cutting and hauling of wood. My dad would cut a cord one day and haul it to town the next. It was only six miles to Beausejour, but with oxen it was an all-day trip. He was getting more ambitious and was cutting cordwood every day and made his oldest son, also named Anton, haul the wood to town. The boy was still young – only 15 years old. One day, my brother was driving along with a load of cordwood when someone with a team of horses passed him, driving the oxen off the road. The load of wood was thrown to the side and the boy fell with the wood and broke his leg.

My dad did not take him to the doctor for some time, there being no doctors around. The boy had pain but still could limp, and he told his parents that he was getting better. But my parents noticed that he was in great pain so they finally took him into Winnipeg. The doctor examined his leg and found that it was broken in two places and that it was too late to do anything about it as gangrene had already spread to all parts of the body. He died a week later and was buried at St. Mary's Cemetery at Winnipeg. And so ended my family's first year in Canada.

— John James Schreyer

I AM SHAKEN as I finish re-reading this entry in my grandfather's journal. Not even a year in Canada, and already my great-grandfather's optimism and hope for his family was being tested by the death of his eldest son and namesake. Perhaps this was the price my great-grandfather paid for buying the promise of the New Land. Was it worth it? I wonder if he regretted coming here after losing his eldest son.

I find that my carefully laid plans are quickly unravelling. It seems that the farmhouse, recently, and very graciously, vacated for the summer by the present tenant Cousin Greg, in order to accommodate the whim of Cousin Karmel, is not quite ready for its new inhabitants, some of whom are prone to crawling on carpets, and generally getting into mischief in every corner. As my girls and I explore the house, it doesn't take long to realize that it will take a bit of work to get the house in order, although I won't be needing to make a trip into Winnipeg for nails. It appears my bachelor cousin is an avid poker player, judging by the state of the dining room table and its assortment of ashtrays, beer cans and poker chips, and I wonder if he had had an all-nighter just yesterday. But he didn't mention anything when I picked up the key from him at the Co-op supermarket in Beausejour, where he works, on our way over.

"We need to buy some bleach," Emelyn says from the kitchen. I hear Darrel laugh. I look down at Emi, who is standing by my side, closer than usual. She is holding my hand tight as well. She looks up at me and wrinkles her nose.

"Stinky."

We move on into the living room. Blaise, in my arms, looks at me and also wrinkles her nose, imitating her sister. But unlike Emi's childlike expression, Blaise's reveals a set of big square teeth, with several large gaps, simultaneously comical and scary. Emi and I laugh.

My father had warned me earlier about the lack of air-conditioning and the unreliable plumbing in the farmhouse. But I had waved that all aside, determined that a leaky faucet, or even no hot water, was not going to make me abandon my mission. As it turns out, after inspecting the kitchen and bathroom sinks, I am pleased that the water pressure is fine, with plenty of hot water — a little rusty-smelling perhaps, but serviceable. The faucets drip, but I can deal with that, too.

"We can get things cleaned up in a day. Bring the car full of bed linens from Mom and Dad's and books and toys for the girls, and move right in tomorrow," I shout over my shoulder, sounding cheerful.

But the rest of my family has other ideas. Darrel, who up to now has said nothing against the idea of living in an old farmhouse, has looked around the place and begins voicing his own desire to spend more time in Winnipeg during his two-week vacation with us. This would allow him to set off for a game of golf with his father-in-law at a moment's notice, he tells me, by way of justification.

Emi and Blaise, too, I know, are thrilled to be staying at Grandma and Grandpa's house just outside of Winnipeg, helping them water the flowers, eating bacon and eggs together at breakfast, going to Kildonan Park for a romp, or to the Half Moon — a famous old hotdog stand along the Red River — for lunch. Emi is especially keen to ride the secondhand bicycle her grandmother's friend Judy had thoughtfully provided, and the asphalt driveway at my parents' house is the perfect place for her to learn; the farmhouse having only gravel. I had been hoping that we could spend at least a few days together as a family in the farmhouse before my husband returns to Hong Kong, but I have to admit that the lack of enthusiasm is understandable. After all, my husband is not the one embarking on a voyage of self-discovery, and I remind myself that this endeavour is supposed to be a mother-daughter project, anyway. As for my girls, at the ages of three-and-a-half years and 16 months, I can hardly expect them to appreciate the significance of what I am trying to accomplish.

And so ended our first week in Canada, still in the exurbs of Winnipeg. But all is not lost; we will head out to the farm again in a day or two to get started on the vegetable garden — a symbolic part of our new farm life — and return every few days, depending on the weather, to water it. I will take my girls to the farm 'officially' when their dad returns to Hong Kong. The change in scenery may even divert their attention away from their father's absence. In the meantime, I continue to prepare for the mission. Back at my parents' home, I mention to my mother and father about my plans for a vegetable garden at the farm, and they are intrigued.

"But don't think you can just plant a garden — just like that — without knowing how to do it," my father cautions me in his usual understated way. Both my parents suggest that Uncle Leonard is the man to see. He will tell me all I need to know. What I *do* know, from reading Nellie

McClung — Canada's first 'renaissance woman': author, feminist, political leader, and avid gardener among other things — is that mid-to-late May is the best time to put in a vegetable garden. I don't have much time to spare.

"Leonard has already planted a few things," my mother tells me. Her voice registers something akin to awe, and I take it to mean that Uncle Leonard is bravely pushing the envelope, in some agricultural way.

I head across the Red River to St. Andrews, where several of my aunts, uncles, and cousins live, to see Uncle Leonard. He is mowing the lawn when I drive up. After a bear hug, I follow him into his garden, and he shows me thick rows of chives, neat lines of spring onions just poking through — radishes, too. We walk the length of the enormous garden plot. It looks industrial size. There is row upon row of sprouting melons, corn, cabbages, beets, turnips, carrots, peas, beans, with not a weed in sight. I am awed and impressed — and a little intimidated. Perhaps even jealous.

Uncle Leonard lifts some seed boxes off the stakes that mark the rows, to show me diagrams of how deep and how far apart to plant the seeds. "Plant the rows far apart, you've got the room there at the farm," he tells me. "That way you can just till between the rows. Makes it easy."

Uncle Leonard certainly did make it look easy, and very tidy. Dad had mentioned that this brother had always been a gifted gardener, and that he would often win ribbons for his produce in junior farming competitions.

"Yes," Uncle Leonard says when I ask him about his special passion. "I was a member of the gardening club. I won quite a few ribbons for my marrows."

He hasn't shown me any seed packets with marrows, and I don't have the nerve to ask him what a marrow is. How come 'marrow' isn't on my list of things to plant? Nellie McClung loved to talk about onions and potatoes and peas, but if she ever mentioned marrows, I hadn't read about it.

"Uncle Leonard, we have to go back to Hong Kong at the end of August. Will we be able to eat any of the things we grow?" I ask. I don't mind leaving a garden full of vegetables for my urban relatives. In fact I imagine that this will be our 'thank you' to them all — especially Cousin Greg. But I am hoping that the girls and I will be able to sample some of the fruits of our labour.

Uncle Leonard surveys his garden with pride as he replies, "You plant now, and you'll have food ready to eat by mid-July." He looks at me. "Just a second," he says, and walks off to his shed, returning with a spade and a big burlap bag. He digs up some chives, and I help him fill the bag with four big chive-laden clods of earth. "Plant these before they dry out. I've got a bag of seed onions you can have, too."

I accept the gifts, realizing that the garden idea has now passed the point of no return. Up until this moment, the idea of weeding hasn't even crossed my mind. My uncle leads me across his yard to the other side, to another large plot of black earth: the potato patch. But these potato plants are already a good 18 inches high, and it is not even the 24th of May — the day Nellie McClung always set out to plant her beloved Early Rose potatoes! Uncle Leonard begins to instruct me on the finer points of planting potatoes; cutting the seed potatoes in half if they are big, planting the pieces with the eyes down, and making a little hill around them when they sprout to avoid them growing 'green' — and therefore inedible. Dad is right, there is more to growing a vegetable patch than I ever realized.

At that moment, I see my uncle's daughter-in-law and neighbour, Donna, in the yard next door, and after thanking my uncle I head over there. Donna's daughter, my second cousin Christy, is inside the house and we all sit down for a chat. They are surprised to see me so soon; they had heard about my farm project, but they didn't expect to see me in May. I tell them about my plans for a vegetable garden, and how it is necessary to be here for the planting season — which starts in late May, I add knowingly. I don't mention SARS.

When I mention that I have come over to visit Uncle Leonard for some gardening advice, Donna laughs, then asks, "Did he tell you about the potato bugs? Those darn bugs, you have to put a powder on them to get rid of them, or squish them one by one with your finger and thumb. They are big — and ugly!" she says with disgust. "That's why Leonard moved the potatoes to this side of the lot, away from the rest of his garden. Closer to ours."

I'm puzzled. Why didn't Uncle Leonard warn me about that? Is he trying to sabotage my efforts? Afraid of the competition? Or maybe he's trying to keep things in a positive light. But soon Donna, Christy and I are busy talking of other things, getting caught up on the news of the whole big extended family and the generation after me, of which my two daughters are the youngest. But while my children are still in diapers (at least at night) I soon learn that some of my cousins' children are already approaching their thirties and are off seeing the world; working on Dutch cruise ships, dating New Zealanders and Romanians. I make a mental note to avoid encouraging my daughters to work on cruise ships if I want to keep them near me in my old age. My Uncle Leonard, for one, is lucky enough to have two of his three sons as neighbours. But I should talk: I left my parents' home for a job teaching English in Japan 15 years ago, and have come back for only a few weeks each year ever since.

My parents have already asked me, in an oblique way, if Darrel and I were considering moving to Canada after Hong Kong. But a mixed marriage (Canadian-British) is one of the hazards of living abroad as a single woman, which makes such easy-sounding questions difficult to answer. I would like to raise my daughters in Manitoba, but it is not so simple. Or maybe it is, and I just haven't figured that out yet.

I offer congratulations to Christy. Her upcoming marriage was one of the first bits of family news my mother had mentioned upon my arrival in Canada a week ago. What she had forgotten to tell me was that my second cousin and her new husband would be moving to Japan within days after the wedding, and would likely be living not far from the place where I spent two years of my life. I envy them their honeymoon, and for the chance to be in Japan together. Although my time there was a magical period in my life, I was alone — the only foreigner in the small farming town I had been posted to. In the beginning, with few language skills to help me, I had found life there lonely at times. "You newlyweds will have the best of everything," I tell Christy.

After promising to come to the bridal shower, I head back across to Uncle Leonard's home, past the potato patch and its latent scary monsters. I chat with my Aunty Elsie about her other children and grandchildren, in particular the family living in Seattle (another one who flew the coop). We talk about her golf game, and make arrangements for a game with my husband. Then I head home, chives and seed onions in the trunk of the car, and tips from a prize-winning gardener in my head. My mind fills with images of mother and daughters making neat rows in the dirt, popping the small seed onions into holes, and watering them together. I feel confident that this garden idea of mine is going to work.

My girls will learn about things they have never imagined in the concrete jungle that is their home in Hong Kong. A wave of emotion washes over me as I remember Blaise walking barefoot on the grass in my parents' backyard earlier in the day. She had lifted her feet up high with each step and looked at them, puzzled. Then it dawned on me that it was probably the first time those bare little feet had ever felt the cool green softness of grass.

Tears well up and I grip the steering wheel tightly with one hand, run the back of my hand across my eyes with the other. *What has become of us?*

CHAPTER 3

Roots

IN 1897, MY FAMILY'S second year in Canada, we planted one half-acre of potatoes and one quarter-acre of other vegetables such as cabbage, carrots, beets and turnips. The vegetables were planted in the latter part of May and all came up by the 1st of June. The potatoes were still not up or to be seen out of the ground as they had a very heavy frost on the 6th of June and all other plants were killed by frost and had to be replanted. Our neighbour had an acre of barley and that day it was frozen flat. We also had planted three-quarters of an acre of oats, and since the plants had not been above ground at the frost, it turned into a very good crop.

June 6th was an eventful day in 1897 for my parents and brothers and sisters and me. It was the day I was born: son number five and what a day! There were no doctors around and neither a midwife. My mother asked the neighbour's wife to come and help her when the time came. She promised to come but said that she could not be of much help as she knew nothing of midwifery. When that time came my mother sent one of the children to call the lady. My mother told her what to do and in a few minutes I was yelling at the top of my voice.

By this time my parents had two cows and more milk and butter than we could use. My mother gave me a lot of milk and said that I was doing real good. So after about four months, I was baptized and given the name John. The family now had two oxen and two cows and two calves and two small piglets.

I might mention that our German neighbour had first come from the United States where he had farmed for four years. Then he sold his farm there and emigrated to Ontario in the year 1891, before coming to Manitoba. By the time my parents arrived he had over 40 head of cattle, about 20 hogs, sheep, and chickens. All the settlers came to buy livestock and eggs from him. He was the only farmer that had something to sell, until the Austrian settlers came. The summer was not too bad for the settlers, but the mosquitoes and the bull flies were a real menace.

The other big event in this year was that my father was told he could be a British subject in four years time. There were two men that came to our house to tell him. So when the next federal election came in 1900 he could vote and did vote Liberal. When the Conservatives found out that there was a new vote they tried to bribe him but he was a Liberal and stayed with them until 1940, when I got him to change to CCF (the Co-operative Commonwealth Federation). In the earlier years, most of the farmers' vote went Liberal. I would say not so much for the Liberals as for Sir Wilfred Laurier, who is still the best prime minister Canada ever had.

– John James Schreyer

IT IS BECOMING CLEAR to me that my grandfather's journal is seasoned with politics as much as the day-to-day concerns of a pioneer farmer. This comes as a bit of a surprise: I search my memories, and do not recall my grandfather talking about politics — even when his son was the premier of the province. Growing up, I believed that only my *mother's* father, Jake Schulz, was the politician of that generation in my family; the founding president of the Manitoba Farmer's Union, and later the CCF Member of Parliament for the riding of Springfield back in 1957 and '58.

As an expatriate living in Hong Kong for the last eight years, and before that as a freshly-minted graduate teaching English in Japan, I developed a reticence about politics. Expatriates are often reminded that it's not our business; we get into collective trouble when one of us dares to meddle in local affairs. But there is a provincial election campaign going on right now in Manitoba, and my interest is rekindled. A drive along the bays and crescents of residential North Kildonan — in the north-east quadrant of Winnipeg — is a drive down memory lane. As a child, I would accompany my parents, canvassing door-to-door, to help my father get re-elected in Rossmere constituency. Over the last several weeks my mother has been volunteering in this same riding. My father, mindful of his position as a former governor general, gets involved only if somebody or something triggers his indignation, which can unleash great energy still.

In this campaign, though, my father has been helping out in the Beausejour and Lac du Bonnet areas for rather more social reasons: it's where he grew up. I am tempted to join the excitement, but I know my place; right now, it's with my daughters. The election is in its final week, and the media are predicting a landslide for the New Democratic Party, (which grew out of the ccf). I'm pleased, because such an outcome would surely not put a damper on my summer plans. An ndp defeat at the polls, however, would put a little gloom over the grandparents, for a few days at least. My interest in this campaign surprises me a little, but when politics and public service are things you grow up with, the interest is not something you can simply shut off.

But back to more pressing matters: my 'mission' in general; the vegetable garden in particular. For all my grandfather's talk in his memoirs about the farm and farming, he didn't give any details regarding planting. So I turn to Nellie McClung again. To continue the list of her accomplishments: she was one of Canada's first female senators, a teacher, novelist, columnist, businesswoman, farmer, transplanted Manitoban to boot, and a source of good advice — almost as good as Uncle Leonard. She is one of my heroes. One of my mother's heroes, too.

Nellie was a suffragette, championing the right for women to vote. And until she got involved in politics, women in Canada were not legally considered persons. It's funny — and sad — how we learn to take things for granted. The workplace in Hong Kong has given me great opportunities: I am busy writing for magazines and newspapers, writing textbooks for students in Asia, not to mention working on my novels — and all with the flexibility that a fully-connected home office gives me. Moreover, as is common in Hong Kong, I am fortunate to be able to employ a full-time helper, our dear friend Aunty Emelyn, so that I can raise two young children and enjoy the satisfaction of both motherhood and my career at the same time. Women of my mother's generation laboured under a glass ceiling and against social attitudes that are now considered quaint, anachronistic, or worse. What will my daughters take for granted that I have found to be a struggle?

But today is not a day to ponder over such matters. Today, my daughters and I are going to start our garden. We will go to the farm and plant Uncle Leonard's chives and onions that have been sitting in the burlap bag in the trunk of my car. My husband is still here to help us, and my parents are taking a day off from the campaign to lend a hand as well. My girls are happy that Grandma and Grandpa will be joining us at the house where Grandpa lived when he was a little boy and where we will spend the summer.

We all crowd into my rented vehicle and make our way to the farm, only 30 minutes from my parents' house in Winnipeg — even when sticking to the speed limit. As we approach Beausejour, I see a familiar sign: *Welcome to the Rural Municipality of Brokenhead: Home of former Governor General of Canada Ed Schreyer.* I've passed this sign hundreds of time, it seems, over the years. Boring.

But things are different now; I want to point it out to Emi. She is old enough to begin to understand certain things. And an explanation to Aunty Emelyn is also in order, I think; she is aware that my father used to be a politician. But many heads of state in her home country of the Philippines were corrupt dictators or debauched former actors, and I wonder what she might be thinking.

"See that sign, Emi? It's got Grandpa's name on it. Because he comes from this place. Isn't that neat? Your Grandpa's name on a big road sign." Emi cranes her neck in the back seat for a better view. In the rear-view mirror I see her looking intently at the sign as we pass it.

A few minutes later, we are turning into the gravel drive. "We're here," Emi says joyfully. I am surprised and touched that she feels attached to this place already.

"Yay!" says Blaise, imitating her sister.

Nellie McClung loved her onions. In her book of essays, *Leaves from Lantern Lane,* she remembers her childhood in Manitoba, and the popularity of onions. As a student at Northfield School, she and her classmates all ate onions 'most of us by choice, the others in self-defence'. Of onions, she wrote:

> My heart has always inclined toward onions since the days in Manitoba, when I had to weed the garden before I went to school, and the onion rows gave some return for my labours. Young carrots, beets, turnips, while great in promise, made no immediate contribution, but a dozen young onions, when washed in the creek and wrapped in a bit of the *Brandon Times,* and put in a dinner pail, helped to season the noon-hour.

"Let's hope we love onions half as much," I mutter under my breath, as I heave the burlap bag out of the trunk and lug it to the large rectangle of freshly-tilled soil next to the barn. Cousin Greg was kind enough to till the plot for us before we arrived to save us time, borrowing a rototiller from *his* cousin, Terry Baker, who lives on the neighbouring farm a half-mile south. Cousin Greg tilled a huge patch, easily 20 metres by 10, and I wonder if we are going to have the energy to plant the whole thing. I am a little disappointed, too, by the amount of weeds already growing nicely where are onions and chives are going to go. Never mind, I tell myself, this is all a part of the exercise.

My father starts pacing out the rows and hammering in stakes, and Emelyn and I set to with string. Emi and Blaise can't wait to help me place the small dry, brown onions into the crumbly earth. "Uncle Leonard has given us enough onions to plant the whole garden," I say to no one in particular, but we stop at three rows before transplanting the thick green chives.

As the task progresses, and as my daughters' interest in gardening wanes in the heat of the day, Grandma is pulled into service as baby-sitter. I stand to stretch between rows and see my mother and her grand-daughters sitting in the grass in the shade of the barn, absorbed in the art of dandelion-necklace making. It has been dry in the Rural Municipality of Brokenhead — dry everywhere in Manitoba, actually — and later I find myself lugging big tin watering cans from the farmhouse bathtub over 100 metres away. Emi insists on helping me carry these heavy cans but ends up getting soaked instead, and I mutter to myself that next time we come to the farm we will borrow a hose from my parents' place and do it right.

But with Emelyn, Darrel, my parents, myself — and the girls — on the job, we have planted the onions and chives, and staked out the rest of the garden in under two hours. Peas, beans, beets, leeks, carrots, potatoes and corn will be planted next week. We reward ourselves with a picnic lunch and a rest in the shade of the trees that line the driveway, and after taking another look around the farmhouse to see what we will need to make our stay a little more comfortable, we head back to Winnipeg.

*   *   *

I have promised my daughters and Darrel and Emelyn a special treat this weekend: a road trip to Brandon. I am excited myself, not just because the scenery is what I love, but because I will enjoy getting behind the wheel and just motoring down Manitoba's long, quiet highways. Few people own cars in Hong Kong, and the mode of transport in Discovery Bay is bus and golf cart.

"We get to go to Brandon with Grandma and Grandpa, to help Grandpa do his job," I explain to Emi. "Grandpa is the Chancellor of Brandon University, and he has to do a *convocation.*" I enunciate the last word carefully, and she takes the bait.

"What's *convocation?*"

I smile. She is always asking questions. Usually her questions are preceded by the words 'I want to ask you a question'. She picked that up in school. "Convocation is when Grandpa gives students their special papers. Grandpa will be wearing a big funny, floppy hat and costume," I tell her, and she is eager to see her Grandpa in them — we all are. The robes for the Chancellor of Brandon are wonderfully elaborate; deep blue and gold, and apparently very expensive, paid for personally by my father's predecessor once removed, who obviously felt that a most expensive garment befitted the office — even if the university's budget didn't agree.

We arrive in Brandon with little time to spare before the ceremony, and I sneak my family into the basement of the hall, where my father had hurried off moments before and where a large group of officials are 'robing up'. I am looking for a photo opportunity. I notice that the lieutenant governor of Manitoba has come for the occasion, and has some nice robes of his own. In fact, the whole place is a riot of hues; all the deans of faculty are in attendance, wearing colours that indicate their particular fields, as well as chancellors from other universities, who have come to lend additional *gravitas* to the occasion. I feel a little nervous and out of place. I catch my father's eye through the crowd and wave my camera. He makes his way through the crowd to stand for photos like the indulgent grandfather he is, then beckons me to follow him. I see we are heading over in the direction of the lieutenant governor and my face heats up. I know what my father is going to do.

Sure enough, after introductions, my father launches into the story of how, as a child, I had just been introduced to the lieutenant governor of the day, Bud Jobin, and then referred to him later that day as 'the left-handed governor'. My father loves that story and tells it as often as he can. Red-faced, I tell His Honour, Lieutenant Governor Liba, how pleased we all are to make his acquaintance, then make a hasty retreat with my own entourage to the seating hall. I think I can hear the left-handed governor's laughter.

We take our seats in the packed auditorium, looking at a stage filled with empty chairs, as well as three large, ornate 'thrones' front and centre; one is bigger than the other two. "Grandpa gets to sit in one of those big chairs," I tell Emi, who is seated on my knee. Emi nods, then spies her grandmother filing into a row of chairs in the middle of the auditorium with the other spouses of the robe-clad dignitaries.

"Grandma! GRANDMA!" Emi shouts. My daughter's voice fills the hall and I shush her, but my mother turns and sees us across the room and beams, then points us out to the woman walking next to her, who also smiles our way. My mother is clearly pleased to be the grandma in question. When your granddaughters live on the other side of the planet, even a moment such as this can be a gift, I realize. Then the bagpipers begin to play, and the graduands are led to their seats at the front of the auditorium, followed by the assorted dignitaries who take the stairs to the stage. My father and the vice-chancellor enter the hall together looking, in their matching robes, like elegant medieval twins. Lieutenant Governor Liba, in his red and white robes and hat, is the last to enter the hall and he takes his seat next to my father to the tune of a vice-regal salute.

"Hey — why does *he* get to sit in the biggest chair?" Emi asks — loudly — just as the sound of the bagpipes fade.

I pull Emi tightly to me, trying to distract her so she won't ask the question again; I see a few people around us smiling and know that she has been heard. "Never mind," I whisper hoarsely into her hair. "Grandpa wanted to sit beside the other man, the one in the matching costume." She settles down, and I watch her wide eyes scan the colourful people on stage. I can tell she is impressed by the pageantry — as is Aunty Emelyn. Unfortunately, my daughters' attention spans collapse soon after, and Darrel and I feel obliged to leave the hall before seeing my father give the students their special papers.

Since it is not yet noon, we have the day to explore southwestern Manitoba, and we decide to go to Souris, a lovely town on the Souris River. Darrel takes the wheel; he is excited to partake in this unique type of highway freedom, as we head south on a highway that is dead straight all the way to the United States' border. I love this part of Manitoba, with its gently-rolling hills. It is a relative contrast to the flat land that stretches westwards from Beausejour. But nevertheless, it is that flat land which tugs most at my heart: the land that looks like it was made by God and a rolling pin.

"What do you think of all this, Emelyn," I ask with a self-satisfied grin on my face. "I'll bet you've never seen wide open space like this before."

Emelyn nods and laughs. "No, I haven't." She pauses. "I am wondering . . . where are the mountains?"

My grin fades. "We have mountains, too, in Manitoba," I reply somewhat indignantly. "Look!" I say, and point straight ahead down the highway. "Those are the Turtle Mountains." Emelyn looks; I can tell she is not convinced. I study the Turtle Mountains for a moment. They are mere lumps on the horizon. "We have everything in Manitoba," I add, not so forcefully this time. Darrel chuckles.

The girls are asleep when we get to Souris, so I take pictures of Emelyn walking across the famous suspension bridge, and go to the local souvenir shop to buy some postcards, then it's on to Boissevain to see the giant turtle. These are the things you do when you have kids in the car. Before I left Hong Kong, I did some research on the Internet to see where I should take my family for a road trip, and came across a most intriguing website that detailed all the larger-than-life items that can be spotted on the highways of Manitoba. Deloraine boasts of being home to the world's largest cookie jar; Altona, the world's largest Van Gogh painting of Sunflowers; Boissevain, the turtle of course. These are just a few examples. I take photos of Emelyn and Emi and Blaise in front of the big turtle, as well as a nearby big bear next to a souvenir shop — the first photos in our collection entitled 'Emi's Roadside Big Things'.

After Boissevain, we stop for lunch in Killarney, buying some food at the supermarket and heading for the park by the lake for a picnic. I look around for the little leprechaun I remember from my childhood and find it sorrowfully dilapidated. Then, with prairie literature in my mind, I take over the driving and steer us north to Ninette and Pelican Lake, where the author Robert Stead once lived; then to Wawanesa, Nellie McClung's first home in Manitoba, and where she presumably fell in love with onions and potatoes. We drive all the way to Glenboro for a photo-op with Sara, the giant roadside camel, and finally to Spirit Sands at Spruce Woods Provincial Park for a peaceful and magical walk in the dunes of a genuine desert. We take Emi and Blaise for a swim in the hotel pool when we return to Brandon, and by then the girls are sufficiently exhausted to sleep soundly through the night, a rare occurrence.

The next day, we head back to Winnipeg along a circuitous route; via Manitou (where Nellie McClung taught school for a while). We pass through the rolling landscape of the Pembina Hills, and I remember a pivotal scene in Gabrielle Roy's *The Road Past Altamont*.

"Can you believe it Emelyn, we're in the Pembina Mountains." I emphasize the word 'mountains'; it is a teasing aside to Emelyn, but also a direct quote from Roy's novel, and I am enjoying my own private literary joke.

Emelyn laughs at my gibe, but Emi springs to life. "Where?" asks Emi. "Where are the mountains? I want to see the mountains!" Coming from

Hong Kong, she is familiar with mountains — or, at least, steep, green hills of major significance.

"Over there," I tell her, pointing to the Pembina Hills. I am serious now.

Emi is getting a little cranky from the drive. "Where? WHERE? I can't SEEEE!" she shouts impatiently. Her impatience is a little annoying, but mostly I am embarrassed. Darrel and Emelyn are both giggling. So is Blaise.

The car quiets down again, and as we drive through towns named La Rivière and Pilot Mound, I can't help but think how much more interesting this landscape may seem to some than the complete flatness of the land west of the Brokenhead River. And yet, for others — people from Hong Kong, or British Columbia, for instance — even this gently rolling landscape may seem dull and desolate. Perhaps only the strong can see and appreciate the stark beauty of the prairies. My daughters will learn to love it, I tell myself. I will make it happen.

The girls need to expend some energy, so we stop at a folk festival in the next town. Emi squeals and runs to join the children lined up for face-painting, coming away with a Barbie-pink face framed in red hearts and blue flowers. We buy ice cream and relax on the grass in front of the outdoor concert. Later, I buy a dwarf sunflower in a pot to put in my mother's flower garden, and then I tell Emi and Blaise it's time to head back to Grandma and Grandpa's place in Winnipeg.

Our first summer road trip complete, I email some more photos to Emi's schoolteacher back in Hong Kong; Emi with Aunty Emelyn under the big camel outside of Glenboro, Emi and Blaise in front of Boissevain's giant turtle; Emi with a Barbie-pink face. I survey the growing number of photos on the computer screen with satisfaction. It's hardly been a week and already my two daughters — and the rest of us — have had many wonderful Manitoba experiences.

CHAPTER 4

Something good

GETTING BACK TO HOME again, there was always so much to do. There was more hay to make – so that the oxen and cows had enough for the winter – and more land to break and to plough, which was a very slow process. There was ever so much deadwood that had to be thrown on a pile. It would take about two weeks before it was dry enough to burn. Cutting the trees down had to be done by hand. The roots had to be cut away so that it was possible to plough. It took weeks of hard work to clear a couple of acres. Back then, the forests made man and wife cry. The family did clear about two acres a year, besides making hay and building a small log barn.

That same year, 1897, was the year of the big fire. The fire was started by a CPR locomotive. There was tall grass, about five to six feet tall. It started west of Beausejour, around a train stop called Sebright. It was in the first or second week in October. My dad and mother noticed smoke around four o'clock in the afternoon. The wind was coming from the southwest, which meant that with a wind speed of 20 miles an hour, they would not have much time to get away. It took about 15 minutes when they already noticed the flames. They carried all the possessions they could out of the house and placed them on the ploughed land. The bed, pillows and other goods in the house would still have burned.

But when the fire was still a mile away, there came three settlers. They, and my dad and two brothers, started back setting fire all along the trail and from the ploughed land towards the big fire. By the time the big fire came, this fire had already gone about 200 yards and it went out like a light. The big fire then turned north and south, burning a lot of hay.

It also burned a lot of spruce bush, and a family of five children and two women. Their husbands had not been back from working; they had gone working for the Mennonites, threshing. We were lucky; we had no damage, except one corner of our feather quilt was burned.

The family were all excited and scared. I was the baby, about four months old. My sister told my mother just before the fire came that she would take me to the river and keep me close to the water. The biggest fire was on the other side of the river. The spruce bushes burned like candles at night. The fire did a lot of damage, but it also did some good. The homestead that my dad had; there was a lot of shrubs and spruce on it. After the fire, with very little work of clearing, we could plough about 20 acres of land, and it was not long that we could plough around 80 acres, while earlier on, it would have taken about 20 years to clear 100 acres. Still, it was a lot of work. We, as children, had no time for playing. I was about five years old when we were told to pile the dead wood. We would start at about eight o'clock in the morning and throw the dead wood on the pile until it was too far to carry the wood or too high to throw it on the pile. Then we'd start another and that was going on until haymaking time.

The winter of 1897 was uneventful; there was the usual cutting and hauling of cordwood to town. But there were more immigrants. They arrived during the summer and could not find work. The men would work for their board for the winter. We had one such man that cut cordwood, and the year after married my sister. My sister worked in the City [of Winnipeg] for the winter. My sisters needed clothes and had to earn money to buy them. One of my sisters worked outside the City. The people she worked for had two cows which had to be milked, the house cleaned, and the family washing and ironing. All for the sum of $5.00 a month. The other had to do only housework and was paid $7.00 a month. There were no days off at that time, but they were happy they had a job and could buy their clothes.

– John James Schreyer

IT'S MONDAY, and my daughters and I are heading back to work — finishing the garden. Darrel and Emelyn are with us, as well as my daughters' Grandma and Grandpa. I am determined that no one should feel roped into helping me with this project, but I sense that my parents are enjoying the rare opportunity to work at the farm. So is Emelyn; she grew up on a rice farm in a place called Dupax del Sur, seven hours south of Manila, and loves being on the land. As for my husband, I am wondering if he'd rather be on land of a different sort, like a golf course.

The drive to the farm is becoming increasingly familiar and even Emi knows where we are heading now, and what to expect: Ashfield (although there is hardly anything there to mark it except an old Gospel Hall. Robert Stead used to teach there, I think); Garson (a town made famous by Carol Shield's Pulitzer Prize-winning novel *The Stone Diaries*) and Tyndall. Emi is excited when we approach the sign with Grandpa's name on it.

Finally the water tower comes into view, telling us we are nearing Beausejour, and looking for all the world like a giant multi-coloured golfball on a tee. During this drive, however, I see something new; a sign pointing to a farmer's market. The name rings a bell: Sebright. Funny how I had never noticed it before. My grandfather's story is making me see things differently.

Work — always the work. I had never pictured prairie pioneers clearing the land of trees in order to do the task we all know them for: growing wheat. Necessity made them lumberjacks as well as farmers. I survey the landscape we are passing through on the way to the farm. It is quite treeless but for the occasional planted rows of windbreak surrounding each farmstead. "I've driven this route for years, Dad, and I never realized until now that the land here is not its original state."

My father, in the passenger seat, nods. "You know, this land here in Brokenhead District cannot really be termed 'prairie'," he explains. "The *real* prairie — the vast, treeless lands further west — had already been settled by the time your great-grandfather Anton arrived in 1896. The Brokenhead region is typical of the land abutting the vast tree-and-rock landscape of the Canadian Shield." It is a point of pride with him, and he repeats the thought. "The Brokenhead River area is a part of a very special place in Canada, where shield meets the plains," he sums up in his usual, poetic way.

Of course, these days, such widespread altering of the landscape would be unthinkable. I understand, now, that my great-grandfather Anton and his children — and his *grand*children, too — cleared the land for fuel, but also, of course, to make way for crops; they were farmers after all, and needed room to grow.

And a forest fire would help by clearing the land — if it didn't burn down your house in the process, or kill you. This clear-cutting meant survival. I wonder if this is why one of my father's favourite pastimes, when I was growing up, was burning off the dead grass in our yard each spring. I remember hanging out with him all day in the crisp air, glad to be with him, inhaling the unmistakable smells of spring: melting snow and burning grass, delighted in the fact that my father was enjoying himself on a rare day off from being the premier of Manitoba. I am pretty sure that one is not allowed to do that sort of thing anymore in what were at that time the rather rural exurbs of Winnipeg (and which have now grown very suburban).

My family had a very close call with a bush fire once — although my father was not the cause of it. It happened in Australia, when my father was the high commissioner to Australia and we were living at the official residence, located on a street in Canberra called Mugga Way, a so-called 'embassy row'. Our backyard abutted a greenbelt area called Red Hill, although, in Canberra, 'greenbelt' is definitely a misnomer, as Red Hill was covered in tall brown grasses and dotted with grey-brown eucalyptus trees. As was common in the summer, some bushfires were burning around Canberra, and this time the one that started on Red Hill grew out of control. My father soon became quite anxious and started hosing down the roof of the house and the bushes in the backyard, making us do the same by bucket brigade. I was determined not to be nervous, until I heard a eucalyptus tree explode up on Red Hill, just 200 metres from where I was standing. I watched, terrified, as flames roared, shooting 20 metres into the dry, crackling air. I could see the staff at the residence of the Indian ambassador next door doing as we were. When I went inside to get a drink and escape the morbid heat, I noticed that someone had placed suitcases by the front door. Through the living room window I saw people lingering on the sidewalk in front of our house, rubbernecking. I ran back to my post.

"Why haven't they called up the military?" I heard my father shout angrily. It was true; there was no one from the fire services on the scene and things were really getting quite frightening by this time. But neither the fire services nor the military ever showed up and, by some miracle, the huge bushfire burned out about 20 metres from our backyard. The Turkish ambassador wasn't as lucky; his garage burned to the ground. And I heard tell that the Argentine ambassador's residence was saved partly due to the efforts of those living at the nearby residence of the British high commissioner. This was real diplomacy, given that the Falklands War must have still been rather fresh in their minds. By another odd coincidence, my father was trying to help secure a deal that would see the government of Australia buy several Canadian-made water bombers.

*   *   *

There has been a little rain, it seems. Grandma quickly gets the girls busy making dandelion necklaces again, and teaching them how to make whistles from blades of grass, while the rest of us toil in the garden. There hasn't been any rain since we were last here, and the soil is dry. Although Cousin Greg has tilled it, it is full of stones and dead brown grass — and of course the green weeds. Our soil is not neat and black like the soil in Uncle Leonard's garden. Beausejour used to be called Stoney Plain, until the wife of a Canadian National Railroad engineer — French-Canadian, I am assuming — decided that the area was 'a nice place to stay'.

I survey the large plot that is going to be our garden and decide that Stoney Plain was indeed a suitable name. I look over at the rows of onions we planted earlier. Nothing. And the green chives are lying limply on the ground; no sign of them growing thick, like weeds, as Uncle Leonard had promised me they would. I try to hold back a twinge of disappointment. There will be work involved here, I remind myself, and I attack the project with determination, if not alacrity. We will have a garden full of vegetables, that we will harvest and eat ourselves. No more supermarket fare for this family!

I am looking forward to the vegetables of my youth: broccoli instead of *bok choy,* cauliflower instead of *choi sum.* To be fair, these are delicious, too, stir-fried in a wok with some tofu and chicken, and a dash of soy sauce and ginger, but I am hungering for Western cuisine. We'll grow cabbage, carrots, beets and turnips, just like my great-grandparents did in 1897, in a place where I know they don't use night soil. My great-grandparents grew potatoes too, that prairie staple, but after the potato bug warning I decide we will keep them out of our garden. Emelyn brings out the packages of seeds that we'll be planting. One in particular catches my eye; the same one that Uncle Leonard had shown me last week in his garden. "Look here. Chinese cabbage. I thought it looked nice here in the picture. I thought I'd give it a try. It's coming up already," he had said at the time. I smile: *bok choy* after all.

As we set to work in the good earth of Manitoba, I am grateful for the opportunity to show my daughters how to plant food. A little food-related self-reliance is a good thing, even in this day and age. And with so many hands, we have in no time planted a dozen rows of carrots, peas, beans, corn, and *bok choy* (no turnips, it turns out). But just when I think we are done, as I stand and do what I think is my final stretch, my father speaks up. "I thought it would be nice to plant potatoes." I see he is already carrying four bags of seed potatoes from the trunk of the car. I am surprised, not to mention disappointed by the prospect of more work, and I start to feel like my garden project is being hijacked. But filial piety overrides. Damn the beetles, too! We will plant potatoes. Nellie McClung planted her beloved Early Rose potatoes on the 24th of May, and we won't be much more than a week behind. This is doable.

My father and I pick a spot under a tree that offers a little dappled shade, dump out the seed potatoes and start cutting them into pieces. It was from Nellie (and Uncle Leonard) that I learned potatoes don't grow by seed; they grow when you cut seed potatoes into chunks. It's best to put the pieces into the ground with eyes down — Nellie says three pieces to a hill. This my daughters and I can do, I am sure. Even though Nellie, having been the designated 'dropper' in her day, complained that the task caused her to feel as if her back would break, Emi and Blaise and I have fun doing the dropping. I make a game of it because I can tell they have had their fill of dandelion necklaces by this point, and I am aware that making a game of this is a luxury my grandfather's generation never had.

We all laugh when Blaise plops herself down on the ground between the rows, and I don't care about the dirt on her pants. I watch her, holding my breath with a sense of wonder as she giggles, looking at her own fat fingers as they squish themselves into the soil. I am grateful for this moment, and I look at Emi, whom I suddenly realize is, at the grand old age of three-and-a-half, far too old to have never had this experience. I hold her hand and bring her over to her little sister and then — why not — we all plunk ourselves down in the dirt, and dig in the soil with our hands. We feel the earth, watch it drop through our fingers. We make mounds and dig holes for favoured pieces of our seed potatoes. We spy bugs of all description. There are ladybugs (which Emi calls ladybirds, the British term) galore. I even find a worm and pick it up myself. I don't think I ever held an earthworm in my fingers as a child; I was probably too afraid. Blaise, reaches for the worm in my fingertips. I look at my two girls and I am reminded once again how they are each a part of me and how, at this moment, it is the older who has proven to be the more cautious with bugs, just like her mother. I hesitate for a moment, then drop the worm in Blaise's hand to see what she will do. She smiles — and squeezes. Emi and I simultaneously voice our disgust, which just makes Blaise laugh. I gently pry open the fat fingers, rescuing the worm to another patch of soil, so it can continue to do what worms do.

When the planting is finished, my girls and I join their grandparents in the shade of the trees and survey our work. There is little yet to see, but for a row of evenly-spaced stakes with envelopes placed over them, and a couple of rows of wilted chives. But already I feel a sense of anticipation, of hope and promise. Emi, too, is aware that something good is going to come of all this; that this is the garden I have been talking about for so long, where she will be growing vegetables this summer. I think about my grandfather, and wonder if his family planted their vegetable garden on this very spot, next to the barn. His birthday, June 6th, is just a few days away now. He would be 106 years old. It had been frosty on the day he was born. Looking up and around me now, with the sky so big and blue and perfect, I tell my grandfather, John James, that things are absolutely grand this year. We won't be needing to replant after any frost. No, sir, there won't be any frost tonight. I am sure of it. I hope so.

In an essay entitled 'Where can safety be found?' Nellie wrote of her feelings working in the garden as a world war was being waged in Europe: "In times of perplexity, people crave the comforting rightness of the soil, the honesty of sowing the seed, and caring for it." However, she went on to say that the idea that there was sanctuary in nature was a delusion. Right now, I can't agree. As far as I am concerned, this farm in the Rural Municipality of Brokenhead, and the sanctuary it is offering me and my daughters, is very real.

CHAPTER 5

Community

IN THE SPRING OF 1898, my family had about four acres broken at home and about ten on the homestead. They planted most of it to wheat and about two acres to barley and oats. We now had three cows and two oxen and three hogs and my mother set about three clucks to hatch some chickens. The biggest problem was to get eggs. The storekeeper had some so my mother bought about four dozen. She also bought three hens for setting. She placed 15 eggs under each hen. The hens sat for three weeks. When they got through there was six chicks between the three of them.

In the summer of 1898, there was another influx of immigrants. Altogether there had been about 35 families, but this spring and summer it increased to about 65, mostly from Austria, Poland, and Russia. The Austro-Germans, Poles, and Ruthinians (as we called them at that time) settled in districts like Green Bay, Golden Bay, Greenwald and Thalberg, which had been strictly German and had their own churches and schools. The Austrians – whether German, Polish or Ukrainian – had their own church, too, and it was the day's majority of churchgoers that got the catechism in their language. At that time, there were two pupils to a desk. Later, when I was in school, I happened to sit with a Ukrainian youngster who was taking up that language to read and write. I did not take it up, but since I sat in the same seat and used the same desk, I learned to read and write Ukrainian as well as he did, and I can still read and write in that language. We had our instruction in German, too, but not for long, as the Ukrainian and Polish children soon had us outnumbered three to one.

The winter of 1898 saw more activity. More people settled, more oxen teams on the road. The settlers seemed to make a fair living by cutting cordwood and hauling it to the stores. But cash to pay for your tax was an impossibility. Sometimes the settler had a reserve with the storekeeper of about five or six dollars, but could not give him five cents as everything was in trade, whether it was wood, butter, eggs, or meat. The storekeeper got his goods from the wholesaler and traded it for the goods the farmers brought to him. I remember my dad had to pay his tax, which was only $6.00. He had $3.00 so had to go to Winnipeg to borrow another $3.00 in order to pay his taxes. It took a few years to change that as settlers began raising more cattle and calves. The drovers would come out on the farms and buy the calves, and if there were hides and eggs or a hog at that time, they would buy those, too.

1899 marked the beginning of four important events. The first was the marriage of my sister Caroline to a man that came from Austria on the same ship. He was cutting wood for my dad, and his name was Joe Engel. He was a very hard worker and when he was married, it did not take him long to have the most land in the district. The next important event was that the people wanted a new church, a place to worship in. They all got together and they agreed to work a day or two; a day would be considered one dollar, and so on. Those that had teams of oxen were to bring the logs from the bush. The trees were felled and hewed from both sides, ready to be put on the wall. A man and a team were considered three dollars a day. There were two teams besides my dad's, and the carpenter was a Mr. M. Modzewski who received $1.50 a day and help. And so, in about two years time the people had a new church, completed in 1901.

Another important event was the building of the new school at Cromwell, the Bachmann School No. 1117. It was started in 1899 and completed in 1900. There were about 15 children in attendance in the first year. Our first teacher was Wm. Cooper who came from Killarney, Manitoba. He stayed with us for three years. I was his pupil in 1902 and at that time I was five years old. My sister and older brother started school in 1900.

The last of the events for that year was that my youngest brother was born, on the 3rd of September, 1899. He was the second child born to our family in Canada – and the last – and they named him George. They waited to have him baptized in the new church. There was also another barn built for the hogs, as we had no more room in the first barn, and we now could keep about four hogs that winter.

The year 1900 started off with my second sister, Elizabeth, getting married on the 4th of January. The first of the brothers-in-law went on his own farm, so now we had another to help around our farm and cut cordwood until spring, at which time he and my sister went on their own farm, and started clearing land. He knew a farmer close to the City who wanted to sell his cows cheap, so he bought them. He had no money to ship them, so he tied them together and drove them as oxen. But the cows were not trained and they gave him a rough time. He was tired out and lay on the ground to rest and got rheumatism. He was a young man and was bothered by it all of his life.

Another big event was that the Municipality of Brokenhead was created in 1900, comprising townships 12, 13 and 14, and the south half of townships 15 in ranges No. 7 and 8 east, and the east half of townships 13 and 14 in range No. 6 east. There was no money to build roads in those times. And so the year 1900 started a new century and a new era – with the election of Sir Wilfrid Laurier to his second term as Prime Minister of Canada.

— John James Schreyer

TODAY IS ELECTION DAY in Manitoba. I had asked my parents if Emi could go with them to the voting booth, at my old middle school down the road, but these long summer nights are keeping my children up late and by the time they had woken this morning, their grandparents had already gone to do their civic duty. More than once during the day I hear my mother on the phone, reminding people to get out and vote, or asking people if they know of anyone who might need a ride to the polls. I realize that I can't recall ever having voted. I guess I wasn't in the right place at the right time, or for enough time to meet the residency requirements. This didn't stop me from working on campaigns, though; when I lived in Vancouver to attend Simon Fraser University, I volunteered to canvass for the NDP candidate in my riding in the provincial election, and was surprised to learn that canvassing was done only by phone. It had made me think about how the wonderful Halloween custom of going door-to-door was losing out, in the name of safety, to neighbourhood parties. It is reassuring that people still do door-to-door canvassing here in Manitoba, just as I can still take my girls door-to-door at Halloween, down the one street in our Discovery Bay neighbourhood with houses rather than apartment blocks.

But I have no electoral duties today. I just send my good luck wishes to several candidates whom I know personally, including a close family friend named Dave Chomiak — the province's minister of health — and a young man named Rob Altemeyer whom I met ten years ago, while researching women's cooperatives on a study tour to Indonesia through the auspices of the World University Service of Canada. The New Democratic Party, it seems, does not need my help in any case; all predictions suggest a sizable victory, perhaps even the largest ever. So my daughters and I head outside to Emi's new, secondhand bicycle, and Blaise and I watch as the owner rides triumphantly around the drive. After about ten minutes of cheering, both Blaise and I are ready to move on to other things, but Emi is showing no signs of boredom. My eyes wander to the garage, and I think about the sign above the doorway: CROMWELL SCHOOL. The sign is from the very school my grandfather wrote of, although it has been painted several times over. I have no idea how it ended up here.

I am reminded, too, after reading this entry from my grandfather's journal, just how incredibly brilliant the children of these prairie pioneers — and the pioneers themselves — were. Polyglots all of them. When my father spoke of his own father and grandfather, it often included a mention of how many languages they could speak, and how clever 'Old Anton' must have been to be able to pick up English so quickly after his arrival in Canada, already 46 years old. When my father speaks of this, the pride in his voice is apparent. And whenever I come to visit, it is not unusual to hear my father talking with my brothers in their own secret language; a patois of mixed-up English, French, German, Ukrainian and Russian.

My great-grandfather brought his family westward, to the frontier of a new country. I like to think that I am continuing the journey in the same direction — to the Orient. After English and French, it is not Ukrainian, but Japanese, that I can speak, and I sometimes feel compelled to throw a little Japanese into the dinner-table conversation when I visit, just to baffle the guys. And to bring the sibling rivalry up a notch, I might throw in my trump card and have Emi sing *Happy Birthday* or *Jingle Bells* to us in Cantonese.

A child is never too young to start learning a second or third language, and many of my neighbours' children in Discovery Bay are well on their way to speaking at least three languages: Cantonese, English, and now, since the handover of Hong Kong back to China in 1997, Putonghua. As it turns out, Emi's second language doesn't seem to be Cantonese or Putonghua, but Tagalog, the main language of the Philippines, and just one of the four languages that Aunty Emelyn speaks. One day, about a year ago, Emi came bounding up to me and proceeded to count to ten in that language. Now when I come to Manitoba, I am impressed by the sizable Filipino community here, and I think Emi would be well-served to keep on learning Tagalog. My father had had campaign literature in Ukrainian and Polish and German printed up on his first few campaigns. But today, Manitoba is as much Asian as central European.

My husband Darrel is heading back to Hong Kong in two days, and while the girls help Aunty Emelyn water Grandma's flower garden, I sit in a dusty, hot storage shed, among stacks of cardboard boxes. I need to pack a suitcase for Darrel to take back with him; it is going to be filled with things I have squirrelled away over the years — when the idea of being a mother was the dream I hardly dared to dream. I feel increasingly guilty that my parents are still expected to store my boxes of stuff, as if I were a student at university, and I am determined to make a big dent in them this year. My poor husband, he'll be carrying 20 kilos or more of items I've collected that will be just perfect for playing dress-up: a poncho from my travels to Mexico, and a funny Norwegian hat from a kids' camp I went to in Thailand, for example.

The task that was at first daunting has become delightful. I find the tiny Japanese kimono with matching pink slippers that I was hoping I'd find — a gift from Mr. Hayashi, the Japanese consul-general posted to the three prairie provinces when I was a little girl. It was from him that I learned Japan even existed. He would often come to visit us at our home, the only diplomat posted to Winnipeg who felt, I suppose, that visiting the premier's children was all in a day's work. Mr. Hayashi opened the door to Asia for me, which led me to where I am now; a mother and wife in Hong Kong (and author, too: my first young-adult novel was set in Japan). I will be forever grateful to him.

Also among the piles of memories, I find a green velvet box with an official-looking emblem on the lid. I open it and pull out a bolt of burgundy silk with a gold-embossed pattern. I find an envelope hidden within the folds and the note inside reads: *With the compliments of Begum M. Zia-ul-Haq*, the wife of the former president of Pakistan. This particular president's reputation was rather unsavoury: coup-plotter, dictator, jailer and executioner of brave men. I put the silken fabric down and move on, soon finding a lovely embroidered white suede vest with black fur trim, and a delicate embroidered blouse, sheer as gossamer. Emi and Blaise will love these, I think with satisfaction. They will be oversized, of course, but for dress-up purposes, a little belt or a few safety pins will do the job. These items of clothing are gifts from an evil couple: the former president of Romania, Nicolae Ceausescu, and his vice-president/wife, Elena.

Brushing away the occasional mosquito, I sit among the boxes and remember the state visit I made with my parents to that country, back when the Cold War was still being waged. I recall a Romanian soldier having no problem pointing his gun at me when I was taking a stroll on the grounds of the estate where visiting foreign dignitaries were housed. Without a hint of a smile, he motioned with the firearm for me to turn back in the direction of the house. My father's aide-de-camp, one of whom always accompanies the governor general on official visits, had whispered to me about the rooms being bugged, and to be careful of what I said. Being a teenager at the time, I thought this was all very intriguing stuff. I now wonder what the government of Canada was doing sending its representatives to such places. While visiting my parents one Christmas years later, and watching what amounted to the televised execution of the Ceausescus, live on CNN, I put the question to my father, who smiled a little awkwardly and talked about CANDU nuclear reactors, but also mentioning that, back in the early eighties, Canada's government did not have the intelligence on the Ceausescu regime and all its atrocities, which is now common knowledge.

I look up and see a bicycle hanging on the ceiling. I had one just like it; a gift from Chun Doo Hwan, the former president of South Korea, who made a state visit to Canada when my father was governor general. He and his wife had given all my siblings and me lovely, lightweight Korean-made racers. Mine had been an indispensable mode of transport during my university days, and I was sorry to have to sell it for a song when I moved to Japan. Say, what's with all the despots, and their tragic fates, I wonder. Three different ends to the meanies: airplane crash under mysterious circumstances; impromptu Christmas Day firing squad; imprisonment (it seems Chun got off lightly). I think I'm embarrassed on the Canadian government's behalf; I assume that we hobnobbed with these guys because there were some deals to be made, like selling CANDU reactors to Romania. Why did my father go along with it? Did he have a choice? I try to answer this myself as I paw through another box, and I am relieved to come across a white silk scarf. It is a gift from the Dalai Lama — and redemption.

I would love to linger over these memories and questions, but time is limited, so I speed up the rummaging. Next, I come across a small porcelain figurine, very delicate. The girl is kneeling, with a dove in her hands. The dove has broken off, but I am relieved to see that it is in fact a separate piece and can easily be glued back on. Emi will love this, I think; she so loves delicate things. It was a gift from President Ronald Reagan when he made a state visit to Canada in 1981. I remember that he instantly reminded me of my grandfather when I met him; tall and broad, with an easygoing manner and always a twinkle in his eye. The day before he was due to arrive in Ottawa, a classmate had thrust a *Time* magazine into my hands with Reagan's picture under the title MAN OF THE YEAR, along with the imperative that I was to procure an autograph. Later, at the gift-exchanging ceremony (usually the last item on the schedule during a state visit), I nervously held out the magazine for the president's signature.

"Excuse me, Mister President — Reagan — would you please sign this — for a friend?" I asked. My knees were weak. I still remember that.

President Reagan looked at me as he took the magazine — and the pen I was holding out to him. "And what is this — friend's — name?" he asked. He was smiling at me in a way that suggested to me he thought I might have been romantically linked to said person. It took a while for me to reply. For one thing, I never thought the president of the United States would ever have given me the time needed to write down my friend's name. For this reason, I hadn't bothered to ask my friend the spelling, and so was horrified to realize that I had no idea how to spell what was obviously a Polish surname. Mr. Reagan didn't know either, but my father was able to help us out. I stare at the doll in my hands and think about the man. President Reagan's life came to a sad end as well: perhaps in the most cruel way of all, by Alzheimer's.

Oh dear, I am spending far too much time in this dusty shed, but I press on. I pick up a small blue box and find inside it a round silver pillbox with an engraving of a crown and three plumes on the lid, along with the words *Ich Dien*. The design is the personal seal of the Prince of Wales — Prince Charles. It means 'I serve', but I think it's odd he would want to let us know this fact in German, not that being German is something one must hide. I know that the British royal family is descended from German royalty, and then wonder if my in-laws — who lived through the air-raids and were evacuated, with thousands of other children, to the countryside for safekeeping during World War Two — know this fact too. (I ask Darrel later in the day if he — and, more importantly for me, if his mother — is aware of this quirk in Her Majesty's DNA, and he is quick to tell me they most certainly are. What's more, he reminds me that Prince Philip and Princess Michael of Kent are also of German descent, and then he tells me not to worry.) I find another silver pillbox — this one is wider but not as deep — inside a red leather box; a gift from the King and Queen of Spain. What's with the pillboxes? I smile with a thought: a few more of these and I'll make my own coffee-table book. I'll call it: *Pillboxes: Confessions of a Vice-regal Hypochondriac.* No — not funny. I take a long look at the two silver pillboxes on my lap. Dress-up clothes and a delicate porcelain figurine of a kneeling girl holding a dove is one thing, but what am I supposed to do with sterling silver pillboxes? After a few moments, a brilliant idea enters my mind, the kind that only a new mother can have; these two silver boxes will be the perfect receptacles for baby teeth. They will be where the tooth fairy keeps her treasures.

I also find a lovely necklace of what looks like puka shells, much like the kind you could buy in any souvenir store around Pacific beaches, but these ones are a gift from a former governor general of the Solomon Islands, where I went with my father in 1985, when he was high commissioner to Australia — and by default (no country can afford to send a resident representative to every country in the world) Canadian ambassador to Papua New Guinea, New Caledonia, Vanuatu, and the Solomons. I know these shells were once considered legal tender in that country, and I think fondly of my few days in Honiara with my father, staying with the governor general, Sir Baddeley Devesi, in his tropical-island home with his wife and five rambunctious kids — more as a personal guest than as part of a visiting diplomatic entourage. I had begged my father to let me go with him, and for my considerable effort was rewarded by a tour around the island of Guadalcanal in the company of a local female police officer. I was asked to sit in a wicker chair in the back of a pick-up truck, while the young uniformed girl sat on the floor, smiling at me all the way. We stopped to look at an irrigation project funded with Canadian aid money, but what struck me most was seeing an old Japanese *kamikaze* airplane stuck in a tree, the rusted steel frame of a Japanese warship just a few metres off an idyllic beach, and an old cannon pointing out to sea; reminders that some of World War Two's bloodiest battles were fought there.

I wrap the puka shells in the kimono. All of this fabulous dress-up stuff will be heading to Hong Kong, I decide, and I end the hunt for interesting swag from my past to give to Emi and Blaise. These are the kinds of things one collects when your father is a premier/governor general/high commissioner/ambassador. As I survey the mountain of chachka, I think with glee that I will never have to buy another gift for either of my girls until they're at least 20. But I wonder when — and how — I can start to tell them the stories of how these things came into my possession. If only you could wrap up the memories along with their attendant emotions and feelings and simply hand them over. I leave the job unfinished; I've got as much as Darrel will want to take with him tomorrow. But I have enjoyed the chance to reminisce. There will be a few more boxes to rummage through next summer, and maybe I can ask Emi to help me.

At eight o'clock in the evening, the whole family gathers in front of the television to watch the provincial election returns — serious prime-time viewing for political families. Even Aunty Emelyn is watching with us, and we point out the candidates who are her fellow-compatriots from the Philippines. We tell her who to root for, which party are the good guys, and she gets into the spirit of things as if it were the final game in the world series of baseball, or an episode of *The Price is Right* (both are things Emelyn has quickly discovered on Canadian television). My father, however, is sitting alone at his desk in the next room, watching the election results from his own television, but once in a while he comes into the living room to comment on the results.

"Why doesn't Dad watch with us?" I ask my mother.

"Because he's nervous," she tells me. This makes me feel better. I thought perhaps it was because of the noise from Emi and Blaise, racing around the room and all over me, in the throes of their usual pre-bedtime hyperactivity. We clap and cheer when our friend Dave Chomiak is the first candidate to be declared a winner by the television commentators, and watch hopefully as the race appears tight in the two ridings where my parents had done most of their volunteer campaigning. As it turns out, neither of their candidates win, and neither does the NDP candidate whose sign was up on my parents' front lawn. The young man I know from our summer study tour in Indonesia, however, wins by a comfortable margin, and I feel sure that we will be hearing more about him in his new career as an elected official.

The next night, we go for Japanese food with family friends to celebrate the election victory. Dave Chomiak stops by with his son for coffee later in the evening. I am flattered that he has found the time — but if you can't take a break on the day after an election victory then when can you? I ask him if he expects to keep his portfolio, secretly hoping he'll take a break from the difficult and thankless task of being a health minister. He's got a family after all. But I know it's the way things are going to be: I don't remember seeing my father much at the dinner table when he was premier. I tease Dave, suggesting he ask his boss to make him Minister of Fun and Games. No, with the contentious issue of casinos, he jokes back, that portfolio would be too much work. Before long though, as parents do, we gravitate to the topic of our children and their schooling; what they are learning, what languages are they speaking: French and Ukrainian for his boys; Putonghua and Tagalog for Emi. Blaise isn't learning a foreign language; she has yet to learn English, I remind him.

It may be a cliché to say we live in a global village. But what I am realizing is that this is not a new phenomenon, nor a product of modern technology or higher living standards. As I read about my grandfather's life, I see many parallels. His little one-room school was just as much a global village as my daughter's school in Discovery Bay, which is filled with Chinese, Japanese, Thai, Canadian, Korean, American, Dutch, German, Australian, South African, Indian and various other children — and the combinations and permutations thereof. (Case in point: one of Emi's favourite classmates is a little boy named Johann Wong.) My grandfather was an open-minded man for his generation, and his open-mindedness towards others who are different than himself was born in that little one-room school. It's an open-mindedness that comes in part, I believe, from speaking another person's language — and I hope my daughters will feel this way as they continue on their global journey.

CHAPTER 6

Growth

1901 STARTED WITH MORE immigrants migrating to this district. People that were our neighbours in Austria became our neighbours here in Canada, and many more that were known to our parents in Austria lived around a ten-mile radius from our place. Most of the people settled on 40 acres of land, as most had just a few dollars to pay for land, which they bought from the first settlers, who were glad to get anything for their land as it had not cost them a cent. There were about 35 people taking their mail in Ladywood, and 25 in Cromwell. By 1909, there were over 500 at Ladywood and 150 at Cromwell.

In these years, there was a lot of land cleared and ploughed. But most of the settlers depended on making a living cutting and hauling wood, cutting railway ties, and delivering them to the CP Railway in town. There was only one general store, operated by a Mr. Gray, which was an old log building out of town. Part of the warehouse, which the storekeeper kept to store flour and other goods, is still standing. The place became Kanarowski's blacksmith's shop. With the influx of immigrants, there were two more stores built that year. Theodore Wyzikowski stayed and expanded his business, so that in a few years he was the main dealer in town. He later went into implement parts, and was the biggest dealer in the town of Beausejour.

The year 1902 was the year I started school. I was only five years old but was glad to go, as I wanted to be with the other children, although I was confused at first, as most of them were Ukrainian and I spoke German only. But I learned soon enough to speak their language as I had no other choice if I wanted to play with them. Our teacher left the same year and our next teacher for 1903 was a lady teacher, Miss Violet Wilton, who hailed from High Bluff, Manitoba.

In the year 1903, the arrival of immigrants was about the most of any year, and this kept up until 1914. Every morning during the spring and summer months when the train pulled into the station at about 9:30 in the morning, there were at least one or two arriving from Winnipeg. Most would go north from the town and it would take them about two hours to walk to our place, which was about six miles. There was a place called the Big Marsh which started one mile north of Beausejour and stretched northward two-and-a-half miles, and east to westward about five miles, so by the time they crossed the marsh they were good and hungry and tired. Most of them stopped to rest and were given a cup or two of cold milk and bread. My mother never let anyone go away hungry. She always had a big creamer of about three gallons of milk in the cold water.

That same year my dad and brothers traded our oxen and a cow and one heifer for two broncos. It took some time to train them. But when trained they could go to town faster and get home sooner. But you had to be early in the morning before the traffic arrived. If you were not on the road before nine in the morning, the oxen teams arrived at 9:30 and there were 60 or 70 teams at one time, including Barski's team: one horse and one ox. And then there would be more teams until one o'clock. By 1:30, the teams would be coming back which took till about eight or nine in the evening. Some stayed in town at the Hotel Bar and forgot that they had a team of oxen. A lot of them stayed at the bar until the bartender tossed them out. Most of the men that drove home earlier, if they had a 25-cent piece, could buy a 13-ounce bottle of rye or a 25-ounce of wine, so about three or four of them got together and they started drinking as soon as they left town. By the time they got to the Big Marsh their bottles were empty. There were thousands of bottles thrown into that marsh. If they had invested that money in cement, there would be a good road through that marsh.

The year 1904 brought more people into this district. There were two more stores built at Ladywood. Henry Gabel Sr. built his store across the road from the Ladywood School, and two businessmen from Winnipeg built a small store from hewed logs. They started their business to buy cordwood and also railway ties. Since it was nine miles closer, a lot of settlers would unload their wood and ties at this store. He would offer them one dollar less than they would get in Beausejour but they saved 18 miles so he always had his yard full of cordwood and ties, and all business was done on trade – no cash. There simply was no cash.

– John James Schreyer

IT IS JUNE 6th, and on our drive to the farm today I think about my grandfather's pride as he recounted the district's thriving growth. The Rural Municipality of Brokenhead had just been incorporated, and there was expansion and progress. Businesses were being drawn to the area, including farm-implement dealers. And all the while, the cutting continued, the clearing of the land. We Canadians were apparently nothing if not 'drawers of water, hewers of wood' and I wonder if, after all these years, this has changed significantly.

When I read this entry, I am reminded that my Uncle George, the oldest of my father's brothers — and my godfather — had owned a farm-implement business for a time. 'Schreyer Equipment' it was called, and I remember it to be a big grey box of a building with a big red Massey-Ferguson sign, located next to the Red River at Winnipeg's northern perimeter highway. I spent a lot of time on weekends there as a child. I vaguely remember what kinds of farming equipment were sold there, but I do have memories of lingering around the bubble gum and peanut dispensers at the back of the store, as my dad sat in the office behind a pane of glass, chatting with his brothers. Uncle Leonard worked there, too; my Uncle George had told me once that Uncle Leonard was his best salesman. If I was lucky, a cousin or two — those two uncles' children — would be there as well, earning a few dollars, and this would make the time go mercifully quickly. After all, a farm-implement store is a far cry from Toys'R'Us, or even Wal-Mart, and there were few things on the shelves — among such items as weed killer, tools, and mousetraps — to captivate the interest of an eight-year-old girl, at least not for very long. The building still stands, but it doesn't say 'Schreyer Equipment' anymore: it's a car dealership.

I get the impression that farm-implement dealerships have followed the trend of farming in general: smaller, family-owned farms have been given over to agribusiness. We have already done a lot of driving through southern Manitoba this summer — seen a lot of farm country — and I have become acutely aware of the signs that say 'Simplot' and 'Agricore'.

As I come to the junction of highways 44 and 12 and turn north for the final leg of our drive to the farm, I see such a sign.

When I lived in Japan ten years ago, one of the hot topics was the fate of the small, family-owned rice farms that are a cultural icon as much as a source of food. I lived just an hour from Tokyo; I could climb the hill behind my apartment and see the skyscrapers of the northern district of Ikebukuro. Yet only a ten-minute bike ride away were elderly Japanese rice farmers harvesting their small plots with hand-held scythes and the romantic image it presented took my breath away: a modern Asian version of Jean Francois Millet's 17th-century painting *The Gleaners*. I had a postcard of this painting, bought from the Louvre when I saw the original there as a teenager. Near my home in Japan, within sight of one of the world's largest metropolises, gleaners still gleaned.

I hadn't thought about what back-breaking hard work it was, even though I was familiar with the sight of old ladies walking the streets of modern-day Japan hobbled over, in some cases bent in half, the result of a lifetime of rice-farming. I just thought what I had seen on my bike-rides looked romantic and quaint, and I felt inspired to write a Letter to the Editor of the *Japan Times,* the country's largest English daily newspaper. It was published, and then translated into Japanese for the *Daily Yomiuri,* its Japanese sister newspaper. In the letter, I lamented the fact that these Japanese rice farmers' sons and daughters were not interested in carrying on the family farm, and that one day, the sacred task of seeding rice in Japan would perhaps be done by airplane, as it is in California.

It saddens me that there are no more Schreyers to farm the land by the Brokenhead, but I am glad that it is our long-time neighbours, the Bakers — the same family who grew up with my grandparents, aunts, uncles, and my father — who are farming our land today. This year they are growing wheat on our land, I see, and as I plonk Emi and Blaise in between the rows of green wheat near the chicken coops for the first in a series of 'my girls in the wheat' photos, it is already chest-high on Blaise. But the girls are not happy; the weather has taken a sudden turn and it is unseasonably cold. The sky is dark with clouds that promise rain. I knew this when we left Winnipeg, but I have decided to hope for the best; it is important that we come to the farm today, so Darrel can help one last time before he has to return to Hong Kong.

Our farm by the Brokenhead River has not been a working farm for years, but I do have memories of my visits as a child, and I remember some animals — dogs and a few chickens, maybe — and endless gardens filled with both vegetables and flowers and fruit trees, not to mention the wheat. The barn has now become a sort of neighbourhood storage shed, holding people's household items in between moves. The chicken coops are derelict, but their coat of red paint is hanging in there. And although the old fruit trees lining the drive are still bearing fruit, there hasn't been a flower garden here since the tenants before Cousin Greg (a family of young, new Bakers) moved away — and now there is not even a hint as to where that flower garden may have been.

But at least there is a vegetable garden again, at least for this summer, I think to myself proudly. My girls and I have come back to carry on the family tradition; to bring this farmyard back to life. But as I survey the rain clouds darkening the sky, I can tell that today will not be a great day for gardening. Within minutes of arriving at the farm, it starts to drizzle, although probably not enough to last the nascent veggies for the next three or four days. As I end my aborted attempt to take photos, I realize that I hadn't even thought to bring rain jackets for the girls. The cold is bone-chilling. Eight years of living on the Tropic of Cancer has thinned my blood. My husband and I decide to pack the girls back in the car and go for a drive around the area to kill time, waiting for the drizzle to lessen so we can go back and do a little weeding — or until the girls fall asleep, whichever comes first. Emelyn, eager to work in the soil, wants to stay behind.

I decide that we will take a closer look at the Brokenhead River, and we head north on the highway, in the direction of Lake Winnipeg. The first road sign says *Ladywood*. It is nothing more than a few buildings. There is a wooden structure that fits the mould of an old-time general store, but it is obviously not in use as such. I think it could even be the Gable's General Store that my grandfather wrote about. Across the road, almost hidden from view behind an overgrown hedge, is the derelict Ladywood School, and next to it, the Ladywood Roman Catholic Church. My father had told me recently that the church had been abruptly and unceremoniously closed down by the Archdiocese of Saint Boniface in 1998, despite a desperate attempt by the local parishioners to keep it going. But today there seems to be evidence of some life: a lawn ornament; an orange rooster. Heading further north, we pass by Ladywood's Saints Peter and Paul's Roman Catholic Cemetery, its grave markers just off the highway, with only a few planted pines to break the bleak landscape.

"You said your great-grandparents were in that cemetery," Darrel remarks quietly, so as not to disturb the girls who are in a semi-sleep state in the back seat.

"Did I?" I hadn't even remembered bringing my husband this way before. I am not even sure if my great-grandparents *are*, in fact, buried there, and I have never been in that lonely little cemetery, as far as I can recall. I drive on.

The next village, just a few kilometres on, was demarcated by another blue road sign: *Brokenhead.* Just one hundred or so metres farther down, I can see another road sign, on the other side of the road, with the words *Come again!* printed on the back. I look over my left shoulder as we pass it by. It says: *Brokenhead.* So the village of Brokenhead now amounts to about one house. There are others places like this, too. Cromwell, a mile south of our farm, has its own signs, indicating a derelict farmhouse and one residence, right at the intersection where Cromwell School had once stood. I had noticed all these signs in previous years, of course, and had wondered how a Department of Highways official finds the funds to put up these nice royal-blue signs to announce almost non-existent villages like these.

But now I am glad those signs are here. Those blue road signs stand for history. They stand for the people that came to live out their lives in the Beausejour-Brokenhead area, a booming area on the mainline of the Canadian Pacific railway at the beginning of the century. People had once come from Winnipeg, every day, to begin their lives anew here. But now there is no longer a train running to Beausejour. To add insult to injury, even the tracks were pulled up years ago. Ladywood School is spooky and derelict, hiding behind overgrown trees, and Cromwell School has disappeared altogether. But those signs stand to remind us of the more than 500 people in Ladywood and 150 people at Cromwell who were picking up their mail in these places in 1909. I know it now. I will remember this and tell my daughters.

A few metres beyond the Brokenhead sign is one that reads: *Brokenhead Cemeteries.* It points to the river, just a hundred metres from the road at this point. The thick row of trees, which indicate the presence of water in landscapes like this, is our guidepost, and we turn down the path, a bumpy ride that wakes up Blaise. We watch a young man in jeans and T-shirt riding a lawn mower inside the chain link fence, obviously not bothered by the rain and chill. I think that this cemetery, situated as it is next to the lush tree growth along the banks of the Brokenhead River, is a much finer resting place than the barren, windswept one by the highway, where my great-grandparents are alleged to be buried.

The drizzle continues, and I turn the car around. One of the girls is whimpering, and soon the other starts. It is time to go to Beausejour for ice cream; hardly suitable on a day like today, but the girls don't know that. We drive back through Brokenhead and Ladywood, pick up an exhilarated Aunty Emelyn, and get into Beausejour in less than 10 minutes, and I remind myself that the trip would have been an all-day undertaking by ox-cart.

I wonder where the Big Marsh is that my grandfather wrote of. I wonder where the place is where my great-uncle lay injured, when he was thrown off his wagon and crushed by logs, but all I see now are acres and acres of fields, wonderfully green and even, low on the ground; brand new and full of promise. I have no idea what these fields will become; wheat is not the only thing grown in these parts, and I am not able to identify some of the other crops I see. And then, as if to answer my questions, I spy a row of small signs at the side of the road, in front of the *Agricore* sign, as we drive through the junction of highways 44 and 12 south towards Beausejour. The smaller signs are, in fact, serving as labels for the mini-plots of grain growing behind them. Agricore has been kind enough to provide a road-side lesson in grain identification for the dilettantes driving by, and I make a mental note to pass it more slowly next time.

We sit happily on the porch of the ice-cream parlour, a converted house, safe from the rain. When we had been sitting in this same spot a week earlier with my parents, my father had mentioned that this ice-cream parlour used to be the Kanarowski's place, and that he had lived here with that family for a time as a young boy, since it was easier for him to go to school if he lived in town. Lucky him; as the youngest child, with so many older siblings working on the farm already, it had been decided that my father — the youngster Eddie — would get the education. And from there his life headed in a different direction. When my father had mentioned this, I thought it was a pity that he should be separated from his family at such a young age, but perhaps my grandfather couldn't spare the horse that would have allowed Eddie to stay on the farm and go to school from there each morning. I remember that my mother went to school by horse — a good three miles — in western Manitoba. Since arriving in Canada, I have already tried to get Emi on a horse, but she has so far refused. She is a Hong Kong born-and-bred city-slicker, after all.

The drizzle continues steadily as we head back to Grandma and Grandpa's house in Winnipeg. I am a little put out by the fact that the morning's objective was not fully accomplished; that things didn't go according to my plan. But I tell myself that the weather was doing the job of watering my garden for me, which is something to be grateful for. "Rain, rain, go away," Emi sings out from the back seat. I join in for a few bars, then confuse Emi by telling her to always pray for rain, because that's what farmers do — and we're farmers now.

That evening, during dinner back at my parents' home in Winnipeg, I raise my glass in a toast. "It's a special day, Dad. Do you know what day it is?" I ask.

My father smiles, and I can tell by the look on his face that he is being coy. He pretends not to know, but when he starts to speak I know what he is going to say. "June 6th. Do you mean my father's birthday?"

I smile back my answer, and to mark the occasion, I have on hand a small photo of my father's family, taken in 1941, which I found in a box in the storage shed. My grandfather is on the right-hand side, his family around him, his father and mother seated in the centre. My own father is seated between the elderly couple; he is a five-year-old in overalls and hair in his eyes. But first, I read the entry from my grandfather's memoir about the day of his birth. There is silence as I read my grandfather's thoughts; everyone at the table listens attentively. Then Emi interrupts, mindful that she is not the centre of attention at this moment, and wanting to put things right.

"Whose birthday is it? Is it your birthday, Mummy?" she asks. I hand her the photo to distract her, and she studies it. "Who's that?" she asks, pointing to the big man in the picture.

"Ask Grandpa," I reply.

She hands the old photo to her grandfather. My father's eyes light up. He smiles and leans over. "That's your great-grandpa Schreyer, Emi," he says.

The little girl looks confused. She studies the photo suspiciously and answers back, *"That's* not *Grandpa Schreyer."* She looks up accusingly at my father. *"You* are Grandpa Schreyer."

"I said, your *great-*grandpa Schreyer," my father corrects Emi gently.

Emi looks pleased. She believes she has been understood. "Yes — *you* are Grandpa Schreyer." And then, after a pause, she looks up at her grandfather beatifically. "You are *great,* Grandpa Schreyer."

Amid laughter, we pass the photo of John James Schreyer and his family around the table, and remember him all over again. It's 106 years ago on this day and how the world has changed; it took a day to go to town six miles away, and now we can make return trips to outer space. But through the changes, some things can endure, in one way or another. For one thing, a garden is growing on a farm not far from the Brokenhead River.

Happy Birthday, Grandpa.

CHAPTER 7

Journey

THE YEAR 1905 SAW ANOTHER BUSINESS coming to Beausejour. B. Pereles and son opened a general store on the corner of Park and Third. The store had dry goods, groceries and hardware. They started cutting prices on all items and it did not take them long to put the others out of business. They started another store and then built the Beausejour Hotel. But when they finished building it they sold the hotel to Sam Berger. Pereles and Son also had a licensed liquor store in Beausejour, and later were also operating a hardware store and lumberyard.

On the farm scene, the farmers now were planting more grain and so some of the farmers bought machines to do some custom threshing, such being Bill Troutan and Bill Mechinski and a few more farther to the north. Most of them that had the steam also used them for cutting or sawing lumber for the people in the district as most of the people needed lumber for houses, barns, granaries, and other buildings.

1905 was also the year that the council of the Municipality of Brokenhead started building on the main highway leading into Beausejour. Until then, the road was built of corduroy, and if one piece of a stick was broken, the wheels of the wagon would get stuck until you unloaded whatever you were hauling, and so the wood had to be taken out and filled in with clay. It took about 10 years to complete the two-and-a-half miles of road through the swamp, and was done a little each year until all of the wood was removed and good solid clay brought to replace it. Some of the work was done by statute labour. The councillors could not get enough money as there was only money for the most essential works. There was always some work done before a provincial election but the party in power made sure that it was no more than four or five days before the election. As soon as the election results were known, the foreman of the job told the farmers to go home as there was no money left, and that has been going on ever since the old parties were in power.

The year 1906 brought another two businessmen to town. J. Huntly, who was a Massey Harris dealer, and Joseph Shaw, who was the dealer for J.I. Case. There were now four implement dealers in town. More grain was planted, and more machinery was needed, and there was quite a lot of building in town. There seemed to be good prospects of jobs, as a brick plant was started in Beausejour as well. It was to be operated by the Turner Brothers of Beausejour and some other business from the east.

A glass factory was started in the year 1907, by Joseph Keilbach, a farmer and dealer in hay. The building was put up in Beausejour next to the brick plant. There was a lot of equipment needed, which had to be imported from Montreal. Glass blowers had to be hired out of the province and they came mostly from Montreal, too. It took two years to get it started, but it never worked. There was not enough capital, so the owner sold it to an eastern firm and they closed the whole thing down, and the building was dismantled, and that was the end of the glass factory. The same fate awaited the brick plant. It, too, was closed down after four years.

Other events for 1907 were that my sister Margaret was married May 20th, and I, for the first time, went with my parents to the City of Winnipeg, to see the exhibition. The industrial exhibition was on from the 1st of July to the 15th. There were exhibits of horse in all classes; cows, bulls, hogs, poultry. There were peacocks, parrots and all kinds of feathered birds. There were displays of different farm equipment, steam engines, and gasoline tractors. At that time, there was no road-building or industrial equipment of any kind. I, as a boy, enjoyed the merry-go-round and the Ferris wheel and the acrobats. We also went to shop at Eaton's. They had bands playing in the store. There were streamers strung across the aisles and the theme on the goods and all over the store was 'Three Years Old Today'. After two days in the City we were glad to board the train to Beausejour and home. While waiting for the train to start I glanced through the window of the car and noticed that there were still four cows grazing not far from the CPR station.

By 1907 there was a lot of acreage sown, the most of any year, and it was a fair harvest. There was more farm machinery purchased, and the farmers bought a lot on credit and signed notes. They had high hopes but it did not turn out very good. The notes were mostly payable in the fall, so the farmers had to sell their wheat in order to pay their debts. As soon as the farmers started delivering their wheat, the price would drop as much as 10 to 15 cents a bushel. But when the farmers had no grain left, and the members of the grain exchange had the grain in their hands, then the price went up as high as 25 to 35 cents a bushel and that was how the exchange exploited the farmers.

They yet had another way to beat the farmer. They told the farmer to sell his grain on the market, then buy it back and hold it till next spring at which time the grain would at least go up to 25 or 30 cents a bushel. Buying on the grain exchange, there had been a practice that anybody could buy a 1,000 bushels or 2,000 or 10,000. You would go to your broker and put a deposit of five cents a bushel, and it would cost another ¼ cent on commission for the dealer for his trouble. The grain had to be bought from a member of the grain exchange. You could buy and sell. If you thought that the grain would go up, you bought; if you thought it would go down, you sold. So if you bought wheat to go up, the dealer would sell in order to protect himself.

They had another racket. If there was a lot of grain held by the farmers in the exchange, they would all sell in order to freeze the farmers out. Even if you could put more money in to protect yourself, the exchange would devalue the market so fast that the farmers had no chance of protecting themselves. In the end, they got all the grain at a premium. And the grain exchange still existed until a large majority of all the farmers voted to have the wheat board be the sole agency for wheat, and later for coarse grain, too.

Getting back to local events; for the first time since the Parish of Saints Peter and Paul was founded, the Archbishop of the Diocese of St. Boniface, Archbishop Adélard Langevin, came to bless our new church in Ladywood. There was a parade and there were 30 riders on horseback, dressed up with all kinds of streamers. There were about 40 boys and girls to receive their first communion, and there were more than 80 people – young, and some older people – receiving confirmation at the same time. My brother Peter was amongst the 40 who received first communion and confirmation.

– John James Schreyer

I TAKE MY HUSBAND to the airport this morning at an ungodly hour to say goodbye, and we've left the girls in bed. It isn't a good goodbye. He leaves on a dreary-weather note, not pleased about the idea of spending the next 26 hours transiting through the United States and Japan, nor the next seven weeks alone in humid Hong Kong. We don't say much on the way.

I hate long goodbyes, especially when I know that my girls are waiting for me at the house, wondering where their parents have gone. So, after a curbside farewell, I drive out of the airport with music blasting from the radio to divert my feelings. I head to a nearby hotel to pick up an application for the Manitoba marathon, but discover that the office is not open until noon. I stare though the window of the locked door, at the darkened office inside. If I can't sign up now, I won't be able to enter the half-marathon, since we will be heading to the farm tomorrow. It's cold today and I'm not dressed for the weather — and not looking forward to moving to the farm if the weather is going to be like this. I shake my head; it's 8:58 in the morning and today is well into being a bad day.

Then I hear a noise that makes my breath catch. I haven't heard that sound in so long ... it's the sound of wild geese, that summoning trumpet-call. *As if they know something about being lonely.* My husband is gone, and I want to rush back to my parents' home and hug my girls. The geese are directly overhead, flying north, and I am glad to see that they still fly in V formation, as they did when I was a kid, and that some things will never change.

I drive home through town, past the spot where the Eaton's building once stood, where my grandfather went on his first thrilling visit to the big city of Winnipeg — when the Eaton's store was celebrating its third birthday with nothing less than a marching band. Eaton's is gone now, and what marks the spot is a huge construction pit where a sports and entertainment complex called True North will be built. I smile at the reminder of a joke a friend once told me: that there are two seasons in Manitoba — winter and construction.

I think I am beginning to understand why roads have always been such a big deal to my dad. They have always been one of his passions, and I suspect if he had ever had to choose between being premier of Manitoba or minister of highways, he may have chosen the latter. When he was premier, our summer holidays invariably involved long road trips. Where we went on those family vacations often depended on where the latest stretch of highway, leading to the resources and the remote communities of Manitoba, was under construction. One summer, we ended up in the wilds of northern Manitoba, following the giant road-building equipment — tractors and trailers and bulldozers so huge one could imagine that they were God's Tonka Toys. My dad would be puffed up with pride, telling us where the road would eventually lead, and when it would be completed, and what communities would now be accessible by land. For the three bored kids in the back seat, this information was of little consolation. As the only car on the road, we couldn't even amuse ourselves with a game of 'punch-buggy' (punching your sibling every time you saw a Volkswagen).

But those road trips with my family though rural and northern Manitoba are now some of my fondest childhood memories. My father would be hunched over the wheel after a long day of driving while my mother stoically kept him company, all the while trying to keep the three youngsters in the back seat occupied. If there was an election coming up, it meant even more time on the road. I remember potluck dinners in community halls and church basements in towns named Birtle, Camperville, Gypsumville, Ashern, and country bands playing an evening of music that the older folks wanted to dance to. And in between, all that driving. But my father didn't mind. As the self-appointed minister of highways — at least in his own mind — he enjoyed checking out how construction was progressing on what we termed 'Dad's roads'. He was able to talk his way past construction foremen and be the first vehicle driving down unfinished roadways with regularity. After a time — and especially in the south where the land was so flat — the miles of long quiet highways seemed endless. By then we had had our fill of forests, fields, and farms.

But not at night. Night time brought mystery with it. My parents knew that their kids could be entertained for hours by listening to the radio and trying to see what distant radio stations we could find. I was always impressed and excited when we heard a radio DJ identify himself to be from an American radio station. Although these American stations were usually in North Dakota, I didn't know that at the time, and I felt like a ham radio operator communicating with people in far distant countries.

My parents would let me fiddle with the dial for as long as they could bear the intermittent static and in this way we whiled away the miles.

But even more than scanning the airwaves, I loved lying in the back seat of the car, with my head resting on the back dashboard, looking up at the stars. I would search for the constellations that I had studied in school: Big Dipper, Little Dipper, Cassiopeia (the Broken W), Orion. Orion interested me the most, perhaps because it was the easiest for me to find. I didn't know then how special the sky in rural Manitoba was, how fewer and fewer places on this planet can offer people a glimpse of a jewelled midnight tapestry made from a million points of light. In Hong Kong, the stars don't come out at night. A combination of mist from the sea and the lights of the city prevents the stars from twinkling for us there. From our living room window in Discovery Bay, the famed Hong Kong skyline, 12 kilometres away, shines with a stronger, competing light — and is a different kind of beauty. It's easy for people in Manitoba to take their sky for granted. I know I did.

From road works to celestial wonders — and things in-between — my reminiscences have cheered me up considerably by the time I arrive back at my parents' house, and I am excited about the idea of showing my girls the night-time sky out at the farm. Maybe we will even try finding the voice of a DJ from a radio station in some exotic, far-flung place — like Fargo.

CHAPTER 8

Settling in

THIS YEAR, 1908, BROUGHT ANOTHER federal election, in which the Liberals were victorious, and so Sir Wilfrid Laurier won his fourth term as Prime Minister of Canada. There were by now a lot of settlers in the Beausejour-Brokenhead District, and about 1500 voters. The Liberals had their whisky at one place while the Conservatives had theirs at another. It did not matter much whether someone voted Liberal or Conservative; when they finished one place, they claimed that they voted for the party that still had liquor left. In one polling station alone there were more than five gallons of liquor consumed.

Another important event in 1908 was that Beausejour and district got its first bank. It was called the Northern Crown Bank, but later changed to the Royal Bank of Canada. We got another teacher, too, by the name of William Czumer. He was a grade-nine permit teacher, but he had order and discipline and most of the children learned more by this teacher in one year than with other teachers in two. He was Ukrainian-speaking, and so his class of 26 children were instructed in that language. He taught at our school for three years to good effect, even if we all ended up speaking English with Ukrainian accents regardless of our different backgrounds.

The year 1909 put an end to the era of oxen teams. There were only a few teams on the road; it was now mostly horses. The Rural Council of Brokenhead Municipality had borrowed money for making roads and digging ditches in the early years, but very little had been done. All was done by horses and small scrapers, and that was slow work, so the council decided to buy a dragline, a machine that could be used in swampy places. But when it was tried it was absolutely useless. They drove it off the road and it was standing for years. In the meantime, the money that was borrowed for drainage was spent and no benefit was derived.

In 1909 my brother Jacob got married, to Florence Weise. Also, Archbishop Sheptytsky for the first time visited the Ukrainian Catholic Church at Ladywood. Another event was that the glass factory started making bottles and walking sticks, and washboards, but had to close down after one year's time. There was also the public auction of all the school sections; the price being $10 to $11 per acre. This went to provide more local revenue for the schools.

The first event in 1910 was the provincial election; the Conservatives winning the election, with Rodmond Roblin as the premier. Also, for the first time, we had rusted wheat. The wheat was the Red Fife variety. There was a new wheat called Marquis, which some farmers claimed was rust-proof, but it was not available in large quantities until 1912. It was a better wheat; not too tall, stronger straw and harder to thresh, but it yielded a lot better than Red Fife. This wheat, the Marquis, lasted until 1933, when it too became non-resistant. In the first part of 1911, my youngest sister Catherine was married to Anton Pfeifer on February 2nd. My sister and her husband have long gone. We had a wet spring and a lot of grain in low-lying fields was drowned out, but the yield of grain was very good and even though some was drowned out, it was one of the biggest crops in that district.

1912 started with a mild winter and very little snow. However, as soon as the snow melted, it started to rain and all through the month of April and until the early part of May we had rain every second day. Our land was not ploughed the fall before as it was too wet, and it was getting late for seeding. We got on the field around the 15th of May, and we had to plough all of the land that was to be planted, so we did not plant very many acres. The grain was late and also hampered with excessive moisture. It was late in fall before we started cutting. We had just cut about one day when we got a very heavy rainstorm during the night. Every ditch was full and there was water standing in the grain. We did not use a binder that year anymore. My dad knew how to operate a scythe and a cradle, so he made a cradle, attached it to the scythe, and that's how he cut 80 acres of grain. He would start at seven o'clock in the morning and start cutting, take a five-minute rest every hour and come in for dinner at 15 minutes to noon, have his dinner, rest one hour, then go back to cut until six o'clock and sometime till seven. His effort that year more than made up for the fact that, in most years, he kept his physical labour to a minimum.

I tried to cut some grain with the mower, but it was too muddy. My job was to rake the grain and sheave lots and bind them with straw. The best way to do that was to follow right after the cutter. When the straw was fresh cut, it was easier to use the straw binder. It was late in fall and quite cold to work with bare hands, but that was the only way it could be done. We worked at the cutting and binding until the snow covered the grain. We did not leave the sheaves out; as soon as we had enough, we hauled them out and stacked them so as to keep the snow from falling on them. That year we started threshing in December. We purchased the threshing machine the year before, so had our own threshing outfit; it being a small separator and a horse-drawn steam engine. We still could not move the threshing machinery as the ground did not freeze enough to carry the machinery – it was so wet that it couldn't be moved onto the field – so we brought the sheaves out of the field and threshed them in the farmyard.

Another event was that there was another school built, four miles east of the school I attended. It was called the Greenoak School. Some children had to walk four and five miles before the school was built. Also this year, the town of Beausejour was incorporated. Even with the weather being so wet and the hard work to harvest the grain, the price of wheat was about 10 cents lower than 1911, being 45 cents per bushel.

1913 started with a cold winter and lots of snow. Oxen teams had disappeared; the farmers had traded them for horses. The horse dealers would bring out a car lot of wild horses, or broncos. They were no bigger than drivers or trotters; about 800 to 900 pounds. The dealer would take the team of oxen in trade and still made out a note in favour of himself to the amount of $150 for one small horse. And if the farmer paid about $100 and couldn't pay the rest on time, he took the horse away so he had the oxen, $100, and a horse.

The summer was dry. The crop was the poorest of all years. It was spring ploughed and held no moisture. The only plants that grew were weeds, and they robbed the soil of the last bit of moisture. The fall of 1913 was dry, too. We got for the first time a new gang plough and it ploughed very good. The land was in shape for 1914. The crop was poor but the price was about 15 cents higher per bushel. Another event was that my older brother was married that year on the 20th of May to Caroline Door.

— John James Schreyer

EMELYN AND I PACK up the car and the girls, and head to the farm to stay. It's another cloudy, drizzly day, and I have reservations about going out there today. We stop in Beausejour on the way to the farm, first heading to the local Co-op supermarket to get provisions and to thank Cousin Greg once again for moving out for us; he will be staying with one of his Baker cousins from today.

Then I buy tickets for the circus that has come to Beausejour for one night only. I want the girls to have something to keep them entertained, in case life on the farm is not as much fun as they had imagined based on my repeated recitations about all the things we would do. Planting the garden, climbing the gnarly fruit trees, playing hide-and-seek in the wheat, picking flowers (wild offspring of the glorious flower garden my grandmother had once kept); it occurs to me that none of these things can be easily done in the rain.

We also go for a drive around town, and I scout out places where I can take my girls on a nicer day. We drive to the Beausejour Cemetery at the edge of town, where I know my grandfather John James, and my grandmother Elizabeth, are both buried, although I do not remember exactly where. I scan the rows from the car but cannot find their grave markers, and with the weather the way it is, today is not the day to look for them. Next to the cemetery is the glass factory my grandfather had written of, now not much more than a stone foundation and a commemorative plaque — not fun viewing for two little girls. But a nature trail is also next to the cemetery, and we will come back soon to explore, and then I will have my chance to introduce my grandparents to their great-granddaughters Emi and Blaise.

On the way out of town, I swing by the local high school, named after my father. I cannot resist telling Emi, "That's Grandpa's School". I am interested to see what her reaction will be. I realize Emi may understand this to mean that her Grandpa went there as a child, so I point out the words *Edward Schreyer School* written above the entrance to the building.

From the rear-view mirror I see Emi nodding, and then I remember again that she can't read. Oddly enough, she is silent, not questioning why the school should have her grandfather's name written on it. I suppose she has gotten used to such things where her grandparents are concerned. After all, Grandpa gets to dress up in big blue and gold robes and go on a stage, and then sit in a great big chair — right next to the left-handed governor (whose chair is bigger, but not by much). Emelyn looks at the school, and acts impressed, but she has also gotten used to such things.

Just a few days earlier, Emelyn had asked if we could go to the post office so she could mail some letters, and my mother was giving her some stamps from her desk drawer. As she did so, I glimpsed something that seemed vaguely familiar on all of them; a coat of arms on royal blue background. It was the coat of arms of the governors general of Canada. I took a closer look and saw that these 48-cent stamps were commemorating 50 years of Canadian governors general, and that the name *Schreyer* was on the stamp, halfway down the list.

"Mom, are you sure you want to *use* these stamps?" I had asked my mother under my breath, as Emelyn placed began licking them and placing them on her letters.

"Why not?" was my mother's reply.

"Well . . . aren't those stamps — special? You, know . . . *souvenirs?*"

I was whispering, but by then Emelyn sensed something was up and she heard me. I watched her as she took a close look at the stamps, now affixed to the envelopes, and saw her eyes grow wide. "What do I do?" Emelyn asked gravely.

My mother and I started to laugh. My mother assured Emelyn that there were plenty more where those stamps came from. Later on, I took two sheets of those stamps and squirrelled them away — one for each of my daughters. They would not be used on any letter — at least not for now. They would be going into their memory boxes. . . .

Finally, we arrive at the farm. The moment has come. We are officially settling in, and even the inclement weather isn't going to put a damper on our excitement now, it appears. My daughters and Emelyn and I first rush to the garden, oblivious to the rain, and note with glee that most of Uncle Leonard's chives have sprouted their little purple blossoms. There's not much else we can see — except some more weeds and a lot of quack grass — but never mind. We are buoyant. My girls are sensing my excitement — or perhaps they are just anticipating the circus tonight. We head into the house, up past the rickety second step that Cousin Greg had warned me about, and into the kitchen. We unpack the food and the toys first. While Emelyn makes the beds, I gather Emi and Blaise to me and amuse them with a stack of old photos from my backpack. Most are reproductions that my mother had ordered a few years ago, but some are originals, and very delicate. Blaise, of course, wants to get her hot little hands on them, and balks when I resist. Emi, I am pleased to see, really is interested in the *who's who* of it all; she understands, by now, that all of us grown-ups used to be children once, with parents and grandparents of our own.

I show Emi and Blaise photos of my grandparents when they were my age. Their children standing with them are considerably older than my own are now. I am not a young mother, but I am a new one — and I wouldn't change it if I could. I pick up one family photo, taken in 1941, and it shows a little tousle-haired boy standing between an elderly stern-faced couple. Emi has seen it before.

"That's Grandpa Schreyer, remember?" I say to Emi. "Mummy's daddy . . . when he was a boy."

She giggles and nods. She remembers this photo from the day of her great-grandpa's birthday. Blaise "OOOOOOHs" and reaches for it with her fat fingers.

I hide it behind my back and divert her attention with another photo. "Here's one of your grandpa standing by a cow. He's pumping water from the well."

"What's that?"

"It's a pump."

"What's a pump?"

Hmmmm.

"Like at Spirit Sands?" Emi then asks. There was a pump next to the car park at Spirit Sands. I remember showing Emi how to use it, thinking it would be her only chance, and how quaint it seemed that it was there in the first place.

Later, when the girls are napping, I place an assortment of these photos on a shelf in the living room. It is a shrine to the generations. There are photos of both sides of my family: my mother's mother and her eldest brother Herb standing in a field of wheat that reaches up to their waists; a picture of my father's maternal grandparents on the front steps of this house, in front of two young men, whom I recognize to be Uncle Leonard and Uncle Tony; the picture from 1941; and several others. I add one colour photo; my own grade-one class picture, that I came across back in my parents' storage shed in Winnipeg. Emi and Blaise are sure to get a kick out of that one.

I notice that no one smiles in the black-and-white photos. No one, that is, except for my father — who was too young to know better, I suppose.

Why did they all have such stern faces? I noticed a similar custom when having school photos taken with my colleagues as an English teacher in Japan. While going through my boxes just earlier in the week, I had come across the yearbook from the primary school where I had taught. There I am, the only blonde in the group of solemn black-haired Japanese fellow-teachers. I am not smiling in the photo either, determined, I suppose, to do as the Romans do. I smile in every photo these days.

*   *   *

We are alarmingly chilly in our new home on this rainy first day at the farm. By dinnertime, we find ourselves huddled together under a blanket on the sofa watching fuzzy TV. "Farmer vision," Cousin Greg had called it: the cable was on the fritz, and there were only three channels, compared to the 150 or so in Winnipeg. But living in Hong Kong, we are used to the small English-language selection, and soon we are engaged in my daughters' favourite rainy-day pastime; dancing around to their eclectic assortment of favourite CDS: ABBA, the Bee Gees (introduced to them by Aunty Emelyn), and a Hong Kong children's duo named Scotty and Lulu. Before we know it, it's time to head to the circus, which turns out to be, quite literally, a dog-and-pony show — but with six tigers and a snake included! The anachronism of dancing animals, so politically incorrect in this day and age, appeals to me. It makes me think that I have come to the kind of circus that my grandfather may have seen when he was a boy — or at least maybe my father. I'll bet he saw a dog-and-pony show, too.

When the circus under the soggy Big Top is finished, everyone makes their way slowly across the slippery mud to their cars. Our sandals are weighed down in inches of muck, cold drizzle is chilling us to the bone. It's June, but the house we come back to is freezing. Emelyn and I bundle the girls for bed in multiple layers, and I put my running tights on under my own pyjamas, along with two pairs of socks on my feet. Emelyn is bewildered by the cold. "This is nothing compared to a Winnipeg winter — you'll see for yourself someday," I tell her. But *that* cold will be mitigated by the magic of a Manitoba Christmas. At least, I hope it will be; I haven't been home for Christmas in ten years.

My daughters are exhausted, and so am I. We go to bed together, three in a bed, giggling and cozy and toasty warm, enjoying the special closeness (Daddy has rules about having kids in the parents' bed, and besides; it's far too hot in Hong Kong to snuggle like this most of the year).

Soon Blaise — looking like a Teletubby all bundled up — falls asleep, and I gently lay her in her travel cot beside the bed, returning quickly to the warm sanctuary that I share with Emi. At four o'clock in the morning Blaise wakes again, which causes Emi to stir next to me. The air is cold on my face — the only part of me exposed — and I know little Blaise must be feeling it too, sleeping all alone when the air around us is so chill. Her arms are already stretching out to me as I reach down for her, and I am glad for the chance to bring her to bed with her sister and me. The three of us snuggle down together, getting warm again. So here I lay, in the room where my grandparents and great-grandparents used to sleep, one daughter on each arm. And as the sounds of their breathing slow down once again, I find my head filling with my childhood memories of this place; the land, the house — this room.

So I can't sleep. I look at the blind covering the small square window, and imagine that it is becoming ever-so-slightly light outside. I close my eyes for five minutes, and when I open them I see that it is indeed true; the day is starting to break already. I look at my watch: 4:30 in the morning. This is one of the wonders of the Manitoba summer and being a morning person I don't mind, but my kids' bedtime has suddenly shifted to 10 p.m. due to the endless summer evenings — about two hours later than normal — and I am not sure how well I will cope without any evening downtime to myself. I snuggle down in the covers with my sleeping girls, hoping for just a few more winks before they wake up and make me start the day. And then, before I know it, bright morning light is shining through the cracks in the blind, my two daughters are still asleep in my arms, Emelyn's got the coffee on (her fix as much as mine) — and I am thanking God for making me, at this moment, the luckiest woman in the world.

And so ended our first day on the farm.

CHAPTER 9

Politics

1914 STARTED WITH A COLD WINTER and a very early spring. We were on the field on the 10th of April. The fields were all fall ploughed, and by May 15th seeding was completed. There was a provincial election that year. The Conservatives were in power and in order to get the farmers' vote, they gave them jobs digging ditches and cleaning out ditches and hauling gravel to fill up holes in the highway. There were about 50 teams working at one place, and there were others about two miles away. The Conservatives knew that they would not be re-elected on account of the fraud they pulled off building the Manitoba Legislative Building, where the contractor did not do his job. But they tried hard enough to fool the people as they always did.

I was one of a number of young men ditching during the day, and in the evening after work, we would drive to Winnipeg, to the Liberal headquarters, and bring back all kinds of campaign literature. We brought back hundreds of stickers, which were the size of a dollar, and we pasted them on the horses' bridles and harnesses on every team who worked with us, and during dinner hour we would go to the other hands and give them the business. If there were farmers driving we would stop them and give them the same treatment. Our teams looked dressed up like Christmas trees. The theme was 'It's time for a change. Vote for it!' We kept this up until the last day before the election. We did not finish the day. We were laid off at four o'clock, but we were glad we could go to town in the evening and be prepared for the election the next day.

Election morning started out as usual. When we arrived, the deputy returning officer and the clerk were already there.

The scrutineers handed in their credentials and all was ready for voting. The Liberal candidate appointed two farmers to police the voting procedure. It did not take long for the Conservatives to come into the place of voting with cards and pictures to show the people how to vote and who to vote for, and when we objected they started calling the farmers names. When the two farmers that were appointed as police came to restore order, the fighting broke out. The police were badly beaten up and some Conservatives, the town businessmen, were still in the room where the vote was taken. There were five of them. On election day there were always a lot of farmers in town, so we had to get help. We got about six men that were at the store and brought them in. It ended with the town businessmen getting the beating of their life. These men were always tough, but for once they got a beating they never forgot and were later even better to do business with. They laid charges of assault against the farmers. The farmers were fined ten dollars each, but claimed it was worth ten dollars any time to teach them 'main-streeters' a lesson. And with the defeat of the Conservative government and the election of a Liberal government, the farmers were more than happy. We had a fair crop that year and the harvest was over by the 1st of September.

The other event was that the First World War started on August 4th. Everything changed for unemployed young men that were looking for a job. They were asked to join the army, and a lot of them did. The following year we did have the best year since the beginning of the century. We had a very heavy crop and grain and cattle, hogs, cream, and eggs were higher in price. Most of the increase was due to the war, not government policy. Not much was done in building roads, except the most necessary things, because we had to do everything possible to help the war effort. Farmers raised more cattle and hogs and the price went higher by the month.

1916 was uneventful except for the war. The crop was poor, but cattle and hogs and other produce were paying better. This was the first time, too, that we were building a barn with boards, the other buildings were made from logs. Other events were that our Prime Minister was summoned to London to meet with the British Cabinet. It was to elect a Union government and to conscript the young men of Canada. This was also the year that the people voted on the referendum and that prohibition won. People were prohibited from buying their liquor in the province of Manitoba but could import it from neighbouring provinces. A short time later, prohibition was enacted in all provinces except Quebec.

The four years of the war started as usual: higher prices for grain and produce. On the 21st of June there was a general registration, and every man, woman, and child had to register. The authorities wanted to know how many people there were available for work, and also how many they could conscript for army service. In the fall of that year, the Borden government, which was Conservative, formed a coalition with some Liberals, and called an election against the true Liberals, which were led by Sir Wilfred Laurier. The Union government was elected, but by foul means; there were hundreds of people who had voted since 1902 disenfranchised under the War Measures Act. The government later wanted the sons of those fathers to enlist and tried to force them into the army. They were told to report for duty, but not many did. The result was that they sent out military police to bring them in. A lot of them kept hiding in old barns and bushes. And the police kept hounding them.

Other events were that I bought my first automobile, 1917 Ford. It was different from any other Ford; it had wire wheels and a battery starter and a foot accelerator. The sad part was that I had just got my car when I was called to report to military training the following spring. When spring 1918 came around I asked for farm leave and got leave until after harvest. My leave was good until November 20th, 1918, and by that time the war was over.

— John James Schreyer

OUR FIRST MORNING at the farm begins full of sunshine and warmth and promise. After toast and juice for the girls, toast and coffee for myself, we skip out to the vegetable patch to see what the day has brought us. The garden needs work, it's true: the stones and grasses and weeds are plentiful, but I am excited when I wave my girls over to the row of onions just popping through the soil.

"Look, Emi and Blaise, can you see it? An *onion!*" I say triumphantly.
"Where?"

"Right *there*," I say. I am pointing to a speck of bright emerald green among black earth, brown dead grasses, and weeds of various lesser shades of green.

"Where?"

I take Emi's finger and touch it to the sprout. She giggles. She is excited, I can tell, which causes me to feel joy — and relief. I haul Blaise into position and snap a photo of both girls pointing to the onion sprout. I will email it to Emi's school back in Discovery Bay, and to her father of course. The beans are just poking through, too, I see. Emelyn comes out and we explore the barn, empty of farming gear, but with a smell that seems familiar to me somehow. It is a certain musty smell that has lingered from the days when I was a girl visiting here on weekends or for longer stays in the summer. I think it's the smell of grain, slowly absorbed by the old wooden pillars and floorboards over a hundred years. I spy a big canoe in the barn and I wonder whose it is; maybe I can borrow it for a solo paddle down the Brokenhead River. And then — what a lovely surprise — Blaise and Emi and Emelyn find some toys, and we haul them out onto the front lawn: a plastic desk set, and a complete bowling set. Later, when I call my mother on the phone, she tells that those toys must be the things that some relatives and other folk have put there for storage. I hope they don't mind if their toys are getting a little extra use.

Three times during the day locals come knocking, introducing themselves and telling us that they had heard that my daughters and I are living at the farm, and to let me know that they are going into the barn to retrieve some of their things. I am surprised that word has gotten around so quickly — we have only just arrived the day before — but I remind myself that this is the way things are in a small community, where everyone knows everyone (or, when I put the question to Cousin Greg, he said, "Seventy-five percent of everyone in the R.M. [rural municipality] knows 75 percent of everyone else"). It makes me feel like we are fast becoming a part of the community. Our first visitor introduced himself as the person living in the house 'where Cromwell School used to be, on the corner of Highway 44 and Mile 74 Road', just two miles south of us, and I discover he is also the father-in-law of the young woman (a Baker, in fact) who lived here on the farm with her husband and young children before Cousin Greg moved in.

I am rolling in the grass by the flagpole when our second visitor drives up. She is none other than the owner of the toys; they are in the process of moving house. I apologize for appropriating the desk set and bowling gear, but she waves it off. She is, in fact, related to our first caller through a marriage. She is a mother my age, and as we talk, she offers some good advice about what to do with kids in these parts. She suggests going to the town of Lac du Bonnet for Canada Day, instead of Winnipeg, saying that the fireworks over the Winnipeg River — which is almost as wide as a lake when it gets to the town of Lac du Bonnet — are better, and that the town knows how to put on a good celebration. I help her put a large shoe rack into the trunk of her car, and Emi, Blaise and I wave goodbye to her down the highway.

Later, when my daughters and I continue our explorations, we take a peek into the chicken coops and find a jumble of old furniture and farm equipment, including ancient, rusty bedsprings. There are a few old bridles, too, still pegged to the wall. Would I find old campaign stickers on them if I took a closer peek? As old as they look, I think probably not. I try to picture my grandfather on a horse and I can't. I don't recall horses ever being on this farm; I'm sure of it — not in my life. Both of my parents can handle horses well, and on more than one occasion have had to ride horses as part of their official duties. Even I found myself riding a horse one summer, during the opening parade of the Calgary Stampede. My parents loved it. As for me, I'm not sure I could get into the moment; I was just praying that the horse would do what it was supposed to do — willing it to just stay in line and not kick me off.

There are two rows of trees that line up in front of the house, framing each side of the front yard. Most of these small fruit trees fork at an ideal place; low enough for me to place my girls safely, yet high enough that they feel like they are actually climbing trees, free of the bonds of earth. I lift Emi up in one and she sits contentedly, a sweet smile on her face, while I put her little sister in the tree next door, not daring to let go of her. Emi and I christen these trees 'The Thinking Trees'. We circle the lot that surrounds the house, and find more of the lovely purple wildflowers that are descended from the ones my grandmother planted.

Later, in the vegetable patch, Emelyn and I don our hats and start pulling up weeds while Emi and Blaise amuse themselves with the toys from the barn in the shade of the trees. We have forgotten to bring a hoe with us, but never mind, my mother and father are coming to visit tomorrow and they will bring one. There is so much grass growing in this garden. And stones. Of course there are more weeds today than the last time I was in the garden, but I swear there are more rocks, too. I remember an aunt telling me that, as a child, one of her jobs was to pick the stones out of fields before planting, and how it seemed to her to be a never-ending task. For many years my aunt believed that stones were things that grew and needed to be plucked out, the same as weeds. Based on the surprising number of stones I find myself removing, I cannot help but think she may have been right. After the day's gardening is over, I take my girls into town for an ice-cream cone and a romp in the playground. We buy some more provisions and I cannot resist buying the *Winnipeg Free Press* to see what's up in the wider world

SARS, Iraq, BSE, NDP. There's always politics, it seems. I flip through the newspaper back at the farm, seated on a blanket under the trees next to my kids and their treasure trove of borrowed toys. I skim a piece about Prime Minister Jean Chrétien being back in President Bush's good books. When I was still in Hong Kong, I had read about how Bush had snubbed Chrétien, cancelling an appointment with him to meet with the Australian prime minister instead. Australia had joined the war effort but Canada hadn't, and our leader paid with a very public humiliation. It seems to be not much different from your average neighbourhood politics: who got invited to the wedding, who stayed away. That sort of thing.

I also come across another article lamenting the low voter turnout in the provincial election last week, and conjecturing where the source of the apathy lay. Well, here's something good: at least there were no election shenanigans of the sort that my grandfather wrote of — not in the election last week, anyway. I am awed to read how my grandfather was so passionate about the politics of his day. How did he even find the physical energy to get involved in politics at the end of a long hard day of farming and cutting and hauling — and now, ditching? But that was all he had known. My grandfather had been active since his earliest years — mentally and physically. That was the way of life for a pioneer. One of my biggest fears for myself and my children is physical inertia — couch-potatoism and its mental counterpart, intellectual entropy — which is the result of the worst of today's pop-culture. So, like many parents are wont to do for their children today, my husband and I fill Emi's life in Hong Kong with dance lessons and art class and gymbaroo and playdates. Work made my grandfather and his wife — and everyone else who lived a life like theirs — who they are.

I will remember this entry in my grandfather's journal as an example to pass on to my children: they are going to be *involved*. It may not be politics, though; given our transient circumstances. Human rights lawyer, pastry chef, dancer, scuba diver, astrophysicist — I'm sure *anything* will please me fine. My daughters will be lucky indeed if they can find the same kind of passion and determination that their ancestors knew.

CHAPTER 10

Death and life

IN 1918, WE HAD ONE of the best crops of all time. We had planted 50 acres of wheat, and we threshed 2200 bushels, which averaged 44 bushels to the acre. For 50 acres of barley we threshed 3000 bushels. Thirty acres of oats yielded 2100 bushels. The price per bushel of wheat was $2.10 to $3.25, barley was sold for $1.20, and oats at 75 cents.

The war was over in November, and it was a good year; good prices and prosperous for a time. The farmers wanted more land, and were willing to pay a high price for land that was close to their farm and cleared of scrub. The farmers that sold the land made good, and there was quite a lot of farms sold at high prices: from $60 to $75 per acre. But this caused trouble later. Many lost that land to the mortgage company and a lot had been paying for over 40 years. A drop of $1.00 a bushel in one year and another drop in the next was a real disaster for the farmer.

The war was over and the soldiers returned. Everybody was happy. The price of grain and hogs were still at a fair price. But there were signs of trouble. People that worked before, or in the war time, were laid off, and the jobs given to the soldiers. There were so many people out of work that they began to riot in Winnipeg. I had been an observer, and the people had meetings every evening. They had such men as Dixon, Ivens, Queen, Armstrong, and the trade unionist Russell leading them. In the night of the riot, the rioters burned streetcars. When that happened, martial law was proclaimed by Mayor Gray. The Mounted Police were called in, with their horses. They were ordered not to fire on the people, but a few of the people did get killed. As to the riot, every means was used. A lot of them were fighting the police on the streets and on top of buildings and had bricks, stones, iron – anything that they could hurl down on the police. It all lasted about two months, when the police rounded up the leaders and jailed them. It was not easy to sort out right from wrong. In fact, they did not do so: J.S. Woodsworth was jailed, simply for supporting the cause of the desperate and the deprived.

The government promised to return men to the farms when they got back home from the war. Some of the men were not farm-bred but wanted farms. The government should have interviewed such men to find out what they knew about working a farm, and also breeding and feeding livestock. The farm was bought for these men and they were given 25 years to pay. They were given two cows and two horses and one sow and 25 poultry. Some of these men did not know how to plough, nor seed, nor feed. One man I knew got tired of the farm in six months. He did not know how to harness a horse, so he asked a neighbour to harness them for him. He later left the harness on the horses all the time, day and night. The horses died with their harnesses still on. He sold the sow; said he did not like pork. He butchered both cows and traded some meat for potatoes and flour, and sold the poultry to some of his neighbours for a few cents. And that was the end of his farm operation.

Another tragedy was the 1918 flu. Some said the flu was brought in when the soldiers returned from Europe. It was the epidemic of the century. The flu missed no district. Ladywood was especially hit hard; 10 to 20 percent mortality. There were some that worked in the bush camp that did not leave soon enough. They did not survive. A lot of women died. Of those that were pregnant only about three in ten survived. My sister Catherine died in the 1918 flu, 26 years old. The flu was over by the spring of 1919. It took about six months for some to recuperate. A lot of people got well when the sun was warm in June.

– John James Schreyer

IT'S A JUNE DAY; the sun is warm. Emi and Blaise are playing in the front yard with Emelyn. I watch them from the dining room window, wiping away the tears that are blurring my vision. No one had ever told me one of my great-aunts died in this infamous pandemic. I never though that it had touched my own family, or that it had decimated the village that this farm had once been a part of. I remember how I felt back in Hong Kong, when the newsreader would tell us each evening that five, or ten — or more — people had died that day. I had felt powerless — we all did.

When the SARS epidemic began in Hong Kong in March 2003, it was dubbed the first worldwide outbreak of the 21st century; AIDS having been the last one of the 20th century. In a way, I feel that my grandfather and I have something in common; almost 100 years later, and the issues of the day are remarkable in their similarity: party politics and election behaviour (shenanigans notwithstanding), war and its aftermath, the price of beef, mosquitoes, drugs, alcohol and disease. I do a quick browse through the Internet looking for facts about flu epidemics, and am shocked to discover that the last great flu epidemic was not the tragic 1918 flu but one that had occurred in my own lifetime, although I have no recollection of it. It was in 1968, and its name sends a chill through me: Hong Kong Flu.

I turn off my computer, I'm done my work for today; now I get to go out and play with my girls. As I start to organize the piles of paper scattered all over the dining table, I hear that sound again: the call of wild geese. I walk to the dining room window, with its westward view, and see a large flock of Canada geese, so low to the ground that they appear to be flying only a few feet above the telephone lines. I imagine that my ancestors looked out this window, and marvelled at the same sight and sound. Or maybe they didn't have time to. No that can't be true! I want to believe that even the nation-builders had time to hear the call of geese; to smell the flowers, so to speak. To smell the coffee. It is a cliché, but like any cliché it is founded in truth; in this case, living on the prairies means that geese are a part of your world. It's as simple as that. It's a Canadian thing; a Manitoba thing. Like the Monarch butterflies that blanket forests in California on their annual southward migration, or the swallows of Capistrano, the northward movement of the Canada geese tell us that a new season is upon us — and for frozen Canadians, it is especially welcome news.

I continue to watch the geese until they are out of sight. They seem to me to be following the highway, north to Grand Beach. What a great idea: company's coming for dinner tonight, but we have all afternoon to play. It is still early in June, I know, and probably too cold for a swim in Lake Winnipeg, but it'll be fun to explore. The cemetery is on the way; the one Darrel thinks my great-grandfather Anton and my great-grandmother Caroline are buried in, and we can check that out as well. I might even find some more family there. So after lunch, Emelyn and I put the girls in the car, along with what seems an inordinate amount of gear, and away we go. Within minutes we are parked inside the gate at Saints Peter and Paul's Roman Catholic Cemetery just off the highway beyond Ladywood.

"Where are we? Where's Grand Beach?" Emi asks, full of questions as always, as I take the key from the ignition, and turn to her in the back seat.

"You're right Emi. We're not at Grand Beach yet. But I just want to stop here for a bit because I am looking for your great-great-grandparents," I tell her mysteriously.

"I'll go with you." Emi says in an instant, and is tugging impatiently at the door handle.

I take Emi by the hand, and we head straight to the small worn grave markers at the back of the cemetery along the perimeter of a wheat field. I assume that, if my great-grandparents *are* buried in this cemetery, this is where they will be, since they died such a long time ago — years before I was born. But as we walk along the back boundary, I can see some of these grave markers have been placed here late in the 19th century. Old Anton died in 1950; his wife 10 years before him. It is a shock for me to see the year of death on these grave markers starting with the number 18 instead of 19. Several stones are so old that the words engraved on them have been worn smooth by more than a hundred years of wind and rain. There are many plain wooden crosses, marking graves but offering no other information, and I wonder how many people here were buried quickly, perhaps in groups; their final, gentle laying to rest done hastily, from fear of contagion.

At one side of the graveyard, the name Schreyer catches my eye: Caroline Schreyer; died in 1930. That's not my great-grandmother, although they share the same name. Could it be my grandfather's second-oldest sister? (His oldest sibling, Anna, had stayed behind in the old country.) There were several families of Schreyers that emigrated from the village of Beckersdorf back in the late 1890s, I have been told. Maybe my great-grandparents are not in this cemetery after all, I start to think.

"Over here!" Emelyn calls.

I turn to see Emelyn and Blaise standing right in the middle of the graveyard, by a gravestone that looks like it could be the biggest one in the place. Emi and I walk carefully past a row of uneven gravestones towards them. And there they rest, my great-grandparents Caroline and Anton Schreyer. I am thrilled to finally make their acquaintance; the emotion surprises me. I have seen their pictures in ancient photographs, heard tell of them over the years — and now I am as close to them as I may ever be. At this moment, I don't think the opportunity to sit with them and talk with them in real life would have made me feel any differently, I feel so close to them right now. I gaze at their gravestones and like the way they are defined: beneath the name Caroline Schreyer it reads 'mother', and 'father' is written beneath my great-grandfather's name. Those words really do sum it up, I think; this is how I define myself first as well.

Hello there Great-grandma and Great-grandpa. I am Karmel, your great-granddaughter, also a mother. Here are your great-great-granddaughters Emi and Blaise, and our friend Aunty Emelyn. My husband can't be here today —

I am distracted by some movement I see from the corner of my eye, and I look up. Blaise is off and running across the graves to the far corner of the cemetery. I watch her with my breath held; I know what is going to happen. Blaise has been walking since she was nine months old, as I am always quick to tell anyone who cares to hear it, but the ground in this cemetery is lumpy, and sure enough, my 16-month-old takes a tumble. She is sprawled face down for a few seconds. I squint and can just make out the name on the gravestone. It appears that Blaise has tripped over a Rattai. Well, at least we're related. Rattai is the maiden name of my Aunt Lillian; Uncle Tony's wife. I watch Blaise look up at me and smile, as if to say 'I'm all right, don't worry!' and a giggle escapes my lips. Emi, holding my hand beside me, responds with her delightfully luxurious belly laughter, and I am once again reminded of the joy of watching my two girls make each other happy. Aunty Emelyn, however, perhaps because she is a devout Catholic, is not amused. "No, no, no," she says, as sternly as I have ever heard her speak. She marches over to Blaise and returns with the 12-kilogram bundle in a football grip.

I plunk Blaise down next to her great-great-grandmother, and tell Emi to stand next to her great-great-grandfather, then snap a quick digital photo (which is later transformed into a screen saver on their grandfather's computer). There is a line of German written across the bottom of the gravestone, and I take a moment to write it down: *Ich Weiss Dass Mein Erloser Lebt.* Looking around me, I note that I am familiar with many of the names I see: Weselak, Door, Modjewski, Greshchuk — and Rattai, to name a few. I want to linger, but Emi and Blaise are getting antsy, and Aunty Emelyn and I retreat to the car with them in tow. As I am driving out, I regret that I haven't had a moment to sit quietly with my great-grandparents. It had been first introductions today; I wanted to talk to them, to tell them that, although I had never met them before, I — and my daughters, too — were glad to be making their acquaintance now, and that they weren't forgotten. There is so much to tell them. *I'll come back,* I tell myself, and them.

It's my girls' turn next; we're off to Grand Beach now. We turn out of the cemetery and head north on the highway, with the Brokenhead River on our right. We pass a blue road sign that says 'Dencross', and I notice a large boulder at the corner of this highway and the one heading in an east-west direction; to Libau and to Lac du Bonnet. The boulder has a plaque on it, but with my girls eager for the beach I can't stop now, as much as I'd like to. A kilometre or so farther north we come to a sign that says 'Greenwald'. But just like Ladywood, Cromwell, and Brokenhead, the Greenwald my grandfather wrote of now exists as little more than a farm, a church — and two blue road signs. But this place has something else; Greenwald has a bridge.

"Emi!" I shout into the back seat of the car. "We are going over a river in a second. A very important river. Take a look," Emi sits up in her seat to get a good view. We pass the river, and its banks look so lovely and inviting, I make a promise to myself that I *will* get out in a canoe before the summer is over. "Do you know what river that is, Emi?"

"No."

"It's the Brokenhead River, Emi. *The Mighty Brokenhead,*" I tell her. I say the words reverently, as I had heard them uttered when I was Emi's age by my father. "Say it."

A pause, and then, "The Mightyhead."

I guffaw, and then collect myself. "No — *The Mighty Brokenhead,*" I reverently repeat.

"The *Mighty Brokenhead,*" Emi repeats. I detect a note of awe in her voice, too. Perfect.

We pass the village of Thalberg, too, which my grandfather also wrote of, with its lovely onion-dome church. Then, before I realize we have arrived, we are passing through the gates of Grand Beach Provincial Park. This would have been an all-day trip in my grandfather's day. The park is quite a bit farther from my parent's home north of Winnipeg: the trip from the farm has taken us only about 30 minutes. The sun is hot, but the breeze is cool, and the water — Lake Winnipeg in early June — is frigid. Nonetheless, I am surprised by the number of people out on the beach this day, tanning and swimming. Manitobans waste no time getting out in the summer, and I am painfully reminded of how much time Hong Kong residents spend indoors in the summer months, not so much because of the heat, which is no greater than Manitoba's, but because of the morbid humidity, which will cause your entire body to break out in a sweat within a minute.

While the girls amuse themselves in the sand with Emelyn, I walk along the boardwalk to read up on the history of Grand Beach: how it was a renowned resort back in the early part of the 20th century, accessible by train, with an enormous wooden dance pavilion where famous bands would come and entertain. Photos of the era showed the beach jam-packed with revellers. On another sign, I read that fire in the 1950s burned down the pavilion, which was never rebuilt. The large-scale commercialism of the beach fell away, and I see that the place where the pavilion once stood is now some volleyball nets among sand dunes. Well, there's something good.

After a couple of hours of splashing in the shallow water of that magnificent lake, we head back to the farm. On the way, however, I notice a sign in front of the Ladywood Church: *Pews 4 Sale.* I step on the brake and park the car in front of the church, whispering apologies to Emelyn as I open the car door and leave with the motor still running. I pass the lawn ornaments I noticed before, and walk slowly up the stairs of the church. There are two people sitting in lawnchairs at the top of them.

"Are you wanting some pews?" the man asks.

"I'm interested," I say, not having a clue how I'd get one back to Hong Kong. I follow the man into the church, take one look at the pews, and realize that I would have to cut one in half for it to even fit in my apartment in Hong Kong. I tell him I was confirmed in this church (which, I later am told, by my neighbour's mother, Mrs. Baker, is incorrect; I was confirmed at the church in Beausejour) and he offers me a discount. He says the lot will be heading for auction in Winnipeg — and the Internet, too — next week. My eye spies a name tag, handwritten, on the back of the pew right in front of me, marking the seat: *Schreyer.* And beside that seat; *Anton Pfeifer,* my great-uncle. I am fascinated by what the man has to tell me about the church, and about how it came into his possession. He takes me to the altar area to show me the various Bibles, written in Latin, and the sermon books, written in Polish, that the church administrators had just left behind when they closed down the church in 1998. In the vestment room, the man opens a cabinet and I can see a large brass candle-snuffer hanging inside. Tomorrow, this man tells me, three feet of water are going to be pumped out of the basement. He and his sister are restoring the place, for what reason I am not sure. He is not a former parishioner, but he says that many of them have stopped by since they bought the place and he has given many items away.

As we head back out the door and down the stairs, I notice that Emi, who had been asleep when I snuck out of the car, is now looking at me through the front window, her eyes full of reproach. I will pay for this. I say goodbye to the couple, then grab Emi and head across the street to the yellow store. I am trying to make amends. If I tell her I will take her in the store for an ice cream, she will be placated, but of course I know this shop is abandoned. I carry her up the stairs and we peek in the window.

"I'm sorry," I tell her at the window, "This store is not used anymore." Emi does not have time to react before we are both startled by the appearance of a bearded man at the door. There is no smile on his face, a contrast from the genial couple across the street. He unlocks the door and steps onto the porch, and I feel compelled to apologize for looking through his window.

"Come in and take a look," he says matter-of-factly. Emi and I follow him in and our eyes scan the dimly-lit room. The place is a home-made museum. The large interior reminds me of an old-time general store — perhaps I am thinking of what I saw on the old television series *Little House on the Prairie*. But the shelves are bare here, except for some antique household implements and photos on display. I realize that my hunch about this place was correct; this was indeed the Gable General Store that my grandfather wrote about.

*   *   *

Later that evening, at the dinner table with my parents and Cousin Greg, I pepper them with questions from our day of exploration. "Did Grandpa and Grandma ever go to Grand Beach?" I ask. "I saw old photos of it — all the people coming by train from Winnipeg, dressed up in their Sunday best." I am hoping that my father will say they had. I want to believe my grandparents had some time for rest and recreation in their lives.

My father shakes his head, "I am sure, Karmel, that *that* is one thing they *never* did." To be honest, I couldn't picture it anyway: the form of recreation I saw pictured in those sepia photos on the boardwalk at Grand Beach was not a part of the lives of my pioneer family.

"And what does *Ich Weiss Dass Mein Erloser Lebt* mean?"

My parents, both German-speakers, ponder this. I don't get a satisfactory reply. For some reason, the translation is tricky — that, or neither of my parents want to admit they don't know what *Erloser* means. Since there is no English-German dictionary at the farm, I make a mental note to call my friend Iris, from Dusseldorf, now living in Hong Kong — and the mother of Johann Wong — to find out.

Over coffee, strawberries and coconut macaroons, I ask my parents when they last ate in this room. "1978," my father replies after a moment. That's the year after his father died. I am proud to be the one to give him this chance again, and we enjoy hearing his stories of life on the farm. My father is animated, laughing, as he recalls his memories of growing up here. My ears prick up when, in the midst of an anecdote, he mentions Barski's team: the ox and the horse. So people are still talking about Barski's team. Cousin Greg mentions a history book of the Beausejour-Brokenhead region that was compiled in 1981 by the residents of the area. His father, my Uncle George and my father's eldest sibling, had contributed the chapter about the Schreyer family.

"It's in the local library," Cousin Greg says off-handedly, and I start calculating when I can find the time to go there and check it out.

"That book is 600 pages," my father adds, laughing. "When the book was launched, I told them, 'Toronto published a similar book, but it is only half the length.'" I am not surprised by this. If my grandfather's chronicle of a pioneer life is anything to judge by, I'll bet it is a lot more interesting, too.

It is late, although the sun is still in the sky, by the time our first-ever dinner guests take their leave. Emi and Blaise and I stand on the front lawn to wave goodbye, and watch the two cars head south down the highway as far as the Baker farm. It has been a good, full day, and I am feeling contented and comfortable, like I belong here — and I can tell my girls are feeling the same way. We have begun something altogether new. We are a world away from our life in Discovery Bay, Hong Kong — and pioneers in our own right.

CHAPTER 11

Marriage

THE MOST IMPORTANT EVENT in my life happened in 1919. I got married on May the 18th of this year to a very lovely girl, Elizabeth Gottfried, who still is a good wife and mother. We had a family of six children, five sons and one daughter. She is very good with the sewing machine. She made all the clothing for the boys and daughter and for herself and still helped to put up shucks while I was cutting with the binder. Our sons and daughter have left us a long time ago and are on their own. We are now 54 years married and still living on the old place where I was born.

As there were only two automobiles at our wedding, one of them was supposed to take the bride and best man to church while the other had to take the groom. It so happened that the Model-T Ford that took the bride was new, while the other was old. The new auto left a few minutes ahead of us. There was a 14-mile drive to church. There were no roads, only trails – and muddy ones too. The first car got there about an hour ahead of us. We got stuck in the mud and we had to get the bridesmaids and myself to push the car out of the mud. We did not look like groom and bridesmaids, as we were pretty well covered in mud. Although I got there late, I got there in time to get married.

Another event was that we bought a farm tractor from the International Harvester. It was called the Titan and ran on coal oil.

– John James Schreyer

I FLIP THROUGH my grandfather's journal and find the pages I am looking for; the passage he wrote about his wedding day. I reread the first line several times: *the most important event in my life.* He wrote the sentiment when he was 54 years married; his pride in his spouse still so obvious after a lifetime together. More important than being a parent? I wonder. Maybe so. Maybe — if you want to have a marriage that lasts forever. Perhaps I have just come across the secret — in one sentence — to that rare thing: a long and happy marriage. I am reminded that my parents' wedding anniversary is coming up. They were happily married in 1960 and still are. Having been married only five years myself, and having spent so little of that time with my mother and father, I've not had the opportunity to take advantage of their experiences in the marriage department. I've never had the conversations — the ones in which, I assume, happily-married mothers will try to impart their wisdom to their daughters on how to keep a marriage going.

Rereading my grandfather's journal makes me think of my own wedding, and how different it was from his. In fact, I can't imagine anything more different, unless we had chosen someplace extreme to say our vows; underwater perhaps, or from a hot-air balloon. My wedding to Darrel was a civil ceremony at the Hong Kong Marriage Registry located in a lovely park surrounded by towers of glass and steel, in Hong Kong Island's busy Central District. I walked with my parents to the registry, where my husband, his entire family, and some friends of ours were waiting; we sat down by the cash register to fill out forms and write a cheque to the Government of the Hong Kong Special Administrative Region, then went into another room to be sworn in by a jolly Chinese civil servant, who asked us to read out our vows from little pink cards (I didn't insert my husband's name in the correct place and had to do it over). We had a lunch afterwards at a restaurant on The Peak, with breathtaking views overlooking all of Hong Kong and the harbour. The photographer we hired took the usual set of wedding photos — and the unusual; he ran off at one point, which surprised us, returning a few minutes later with a man pulling a rickshaw! In the evening we held a reception aboard one of the famed — and ancient — Star Ferries for a three-hour cruise of the harbour, which included watching the planes land at the old Kai Tak Airport. My husband and I then took our visiting families to the neighbouring Portuguese enclave of Macau for the week-end, for the 'church' wedding, performed by a 90-year-old Portuguese Jesuit Priest in the chapel of an old fortress that had been converted into a hotel. The hotel supplied the wedding certificate.

Then, several days after that, I accompanied my parents on a cruise down China's largest river, from Chongqing to Yi Chang, to see the famous Three Gorges before the dam would begin to fill them up with water. My father is drawn to any big construction activity as well as being an expert on hydroelectricity, so he couldn't resist the chance to see the mother of all dams. I had been thrilled when my father surprised my husband and I with the offer to take us. It turned out my father got a bit of a bargain though, because with no more holidays to spare, my husband had to regretfully decline. So it was I spent my 'honeymoon' on a cruise down the Yangtze River in the company of my parents.

This was all unconventional enough, but the lead-up to these wedding plans was just as bizarre. The process for getting married in Hong Kong required registering for an appointment three months prior to the event. In Chinese culture, some days are more auspicious than others to get married. I had often seen long lines of dishevelled young men sleeping against the wall outside a large office building located next to a popular shopping mall. Eventually, I learned that the central marriage registry was housed in that particular office building, and that the lines along the wall meant that an especially auspicious day to get married was exactly three months away.

Three months before I was to get married, I told my friend Tak Hung what day my husband and I had chosen. My friend checked the *feng shui* chart and told me the grave news: November 15th was a somewhat auspicious day — at least that year. How auspicious he couldn't exactly say, but as a busy freelance illustrator he was always moving about town and would swing by the central registry offices to find out. He called me at work later with the news I had dreaded. It was only mid-afternoon, and future husbands were already lining up, with pillow and dinner in a bag, preparing to spend the night. I called my husband at his office and told him the bad news. His parents had already booked their flights and we had to stick with the date, so around four in the morning I watched from my apartment window as a ferry moved away from the pier towards the lights of Hong Kong Island, 12 kilometres away. My future husband was on that ferry. Perhaps it was at that moment that I realized how much I was loved.

I joined my fiancé around 8:30 that morning with hot ham-and-cheese croissants and cups of tea. As the doors to the office building opened, and what was now a long queue of tired men and nervous young women filed through to sit in assigned seats, a scuffle broke out between the two couples immediately behind us. I could tell that the staff was used to such things; they defused the situation admirably. But I was shocked to see that, despite my future husband's gallant effort, we were couple number 50 in line. Fortunately for us, however, the Cotton Tree Drive marriage registry office wasn't a popular venue and we were granted our desired time slot in the park. We were given a small card with the time written on it, to confirm the good news: we would be married from 10:45 to 11:00 on the morning of November 16th.

When I swap wedding-day stories with friends, I know that my story seems too weird, and unromantic, to some. But it is very romantic to us, just as I know arriving muddy and late could not take the romance and excitement — that sense of promise — out of my grandparents' wedding day. Who doesn't feel this way about their own wedding? The funniest thing about my wedding, I think, is that in spite of it all I ended up doing something once considered so 'normal' that it is considered cliché: I married the boy next door, or more precisely, the boy across the hall. We had met at the bus stop (actually, my husband insists that we first met in our elevator — but I don't remember it). After we got married, he told me that I had played my music rather loud, but since he never complained about it, I never knew — and it took six months for us to finally say hello to each other. Yes — as odd as it may sound in this day and age, I married the boy next door. But I had to go to the other side of the planet to do it.

My grandfather John James, however, didn't marry the girl next door. My grandmother, Elizabeth Gottfried, came from Camp Morton — clear on the other side of Lake Winnipeg — and I think it is a miracle that they ever got together, at a time when a trip to Beausejour from the farm was an all-day affair. But I'm not the only one who dared to do the ordinary; at a pre-nuptial party in Manitoba the summer before I got married, I learned that my Uncle George — my godfather — did the exact same thing. I never knew my Aunt Lil, the matriarch of the family — and my godmother to boot — was a Baker. I remember being impressed and full of pride upon learning this fact. I could count the Baker clan as part of my own family. I make no distinction for marriage; the bigger the better.

And who doesn't dream about their children's weddings? I've pictured my girls walking down the aisle while I've changed their diapers. Emi is showing a keen interest in wedding dresses at the moment; ever since she put two and two together after seeing so many photos of so many mothers wearing fancy white 'princess dresses'. Just the other day, my mother showed Emi her own wedding photo and wedding dress. At the age of three-and-a-half, Emi thinks she knows what it means to be married. She asked me to marry her last week.

Who will my children marry? Where on earth will they end up? Well, one thing I know is that I will tell my girls that marriage is not a fairy tale. And I'll say they may travel across the world to find their love; they'll have to look long and hard, and they will be lonely at times. Maybe they will never find their true love, or will choose not to marry even if they do. But, I will also tell them they may end up marrying the boy next door. It does happen, still. I am reminded of this every time I stand in the front yard of the farm and look across the field to the Baker farmstead. What's more, there is another house of Bakers just one road over; a house which has been more recently built and is, I have been told, full of a new generation of young Baker boys — three of them.

It's a reassuring thought.

CHAPTER 12

Opportunity

In 1920, we sold some of our possessions and moved to the city of Winnipeg. We rented a small house in the city, and I worked at odd jobs, then got a job at Gallagher's Abattoir. I worked a month then was laid off for the winter. Later, I found a job hauling wood and coal for a small wood yard for $18 a week. When there was warmer weather, I worked till lunch and was laid off and deducted if not a full day. If there was cold and stormy weather, I worked 16 hours a day with no more pay, but there was nothing that could be done.

As I did drive a team of horses, I had to go to the Canadian National Railway freight yards to pick up the wood. I drove down Princess, and saw that there were hundreds of men standing on the street for about three blocks long waiting, and the line was three abreast as they moved forward to get a bowl of soup and a piece of bread. This menu was given to them twice a day, from ten o'clock to noon in the morning and four to six o'clock in the afternoon. The people with family got their food delivered and that was going on every day until late spring. There was another such place on Portage West. Another very important event was that my first son George was born on May 8th of this year.

In 1921, I was again with the wood yard and stayed until February 20th. Then I quit my job and started looking for a new job. I walked every morning for two months till at last, on June 2nd, I got a job with Sherwin Williams Oil and Paint Company, and I started working in the evening, 12 hours a day six days a week, and some weeks even on Sunday. I was doing a little better as I was getting 41 cents an hour. We were working on the oil presses and producing linseed oil. The temperature was about 100 degrees as we worked near where the steam vented. I worked there from 1921 until 1928 in the spring, and in the seven years I was employed, every year in their financial report they would remind workers with a card that they would put in your pay envelope. The theme was: *Come a little earlier, work a little harder, think a little deeper, so that we can make a million over last year.* But for the seven years I worked for them, they raised us one cent.

On the farm scene, the price of grain was by now about $1.00 lower per bushel, and beef and pork were down, too. Other events were that J.S. Woodsworth was elected to the House of Commons, and I was happy to have been one of those who helped to make it possible by distributing pamphlets and literature. My brother George got married on January 21st to Mary Weselak, the last marriage in the family. The crop this year was average, but the price of grain was lower. The most important event was that the Conservatives under Meighen were defeated, and the Liberal government of the Right Honourable Mackenzie King came into power.

In the provincial election of 1922, the United Farmers won. But they had no leader. They got the Honourable John Bracken of the University of Manitoba as leader. Also there was prohibition since 1915, which had to be resolved. Most of the people were against bars, they wanted only beer by the glass and small tables so they could sit; no wine and no whisky. They had a referendum, and the anti-prohibitionists won. Since then it always went a little deeper and now they have wine in the beer parlour. There was no difference as to employment, there still being a soup kitchen in winter. In summer it was a bit better. The price of grain was about the same; 95 cents to $1.00 for wheat and 75 cents for barley and 50 cents for oats. Beef and pork were lower than in the previous year.

In 1923 my second son, Henry, was born on August 29th, and I moved to another place. On the farm scene, prices were about the same as last year for wheat, with barley about 25 cents lower and oats 25 cents lower than barley. By now the farmers had a referendum and pledged to sell all of their wheat to the Pool and that kept the price up until 1929. The barley and oats were still sold by the grain exchange. Prices for beef and pork were beginning to slip.

— John James Schreyer

IT MUST HAVE BEEN very difficult for my grandfather to take a job in Winnipeg. He had just gotten married and, since he was not the eldest son, it was expected that he and his new wife would not stay in the family home, even though I have a hunch he may have wanted to. Once again, my grandfather's journal reminds me of what life was like back then: a life where workers pound the pavement for two months before finding a job, then 12-hour days in the sweltering heat of a paint factory. And these people considered themselves lucky. But there were always the milestones to celebrate: marriages and births. And elections.

I am going to take the girls back to Winnipeg for the weekend. Emi and Blaise are missing their grandparents — not to mention their father in Hong Kong. Father's Day is coming up and we are going to celebrate it all weekend long. Emi and Blaise will not be able to be with their own father this year, but *I* am lucky to have this chance. Saturday dawns bright and warm; another lovely day for the beach, so my parents and I decide to head out, convoy style, to the other side of Lake Winnipeg — the west side, near where my grandmother was born. On the way, we cross the Red River at Lockport, with its giant water slide and hotdog restaurants that have been around for ages. We drive by Little Britain United Church, the oldest stone church in western Canada still in use, where Blaise was christened last summer; Lower Fort Garry historic site, where I lived for a time as a teenager one summer; and the town of Selkirk, where my cousin Christy will get married later this summer. There is personal significance in everything I see.

We have parked the cars and are camped out in the sand at Winnipeg Beach within an hour. I like the fact that I can walk with my infant into the water, and yet, about 50 metres in, she is still only up to her waist. We turn and wave back to her grandparents sitting on the sand, and watch them wave back to us. The girls and I are enjoying this beach: the tepid shallow water and the gentle waves. It is funny how this side of the lake seems not as rugged as the other side. I turn to look across the lake and can see land on the horizon, but just barely, and I assume it is Grand Beach, or Victoria Beach. I don't recall ever being able to do that before. I had always thought, and bragged to my foreign friends, that there is a place in the middle of Canada that makes you feel like you are standing by the sea. I don't think any of them believed me.

Later, when I am seated in a lawn chair next to my dad, watching Emi and Blaise build a sandcastle, I comment that the lake seems a little low this year.

"Yes," my father replies. He launches into a lengthy explanation about how water levels were relatively unstable on Lake Winnipeg, and could become even lower, until a control gate was built at the northern extremity, where the Nelson River starts. I await the words which usually follow pronouncements and explanations such as this: "I was very much involved in the decision to build it, you know."

No, I didn't. I didn't know there was a control gate at the northern extremity of Lake Winnipeg. I didn't know your father and mother ever lived away from the farm, or that your dad worked in a paint factory. I didn't know that Uncle Henry was born in Winnipeg. I didn't know Grandpa was a witness to the Winnipeg General Strike. I didn't know he was so involved in politics. *There's so much I don't know about you, Dad — and you, too, Mom. But I want to know. I really need to know. That's why I'm here. That's why my girls and I are living in your old home. I'll start at the beginning, as far back as I can go. I'll retrace your footsteps, if I can. I'll bring my girls with me on this journey. I want to know more.* This is what I want to say to him.

"No, I didn't know that. How interesting," I reply.

*   *   *

When it is time to head back home, Emi goes off with her grandparents in their car, while Blaise, Emelyn and I follow. But as we pass Lower Fort Garry, I decide to swing by Uncle Leonard's place, to see how his garden is growing. I don't admit to myself that I am checking out the competition.

Uncle Leonard meets me at the door before I have had a chance to knock. "We're just eating dinner. Can you join us?"

"We're just here to see your garden," I tell him. I am sorry to decline an invitation for dinner, but Emi and my parents are expecting us back at the house.

Uncle Leonard nods. "It's looking good," he says matter-of-factly, before heading back inside.

Emelyn and Blaise and I hike over to my uncle's enormous vegetable patch, and, as we approach, I am awestruck. Uncle Leonard's garden is an amazing sight: onions two feet tall, heavenly thick rows of lettuce and spinach. My mouth waters at the thought of the unlimited supply of salads, and I think of our little garden, which I thought had been coming along quite nicely — with its teeny row of sprouting onions, thank you very much — until that moment. As I survey Uncle Leonard's bounty, I start feeling sorry for myself — and more than a little jealous. I pick up Blaise and stomp back to the car, but not before stealing the biggest onion

I can find and dropping it down the front of my overalls. I can hear Emelyn's laughter behind me.

As we near the drive, with my big little girl in my arms, I am thinking about how I can extricate the onion before I sit down in the car, without my aunt and uncle seeing, just in case they are watching us from their dining room window. With each step, the onion has been sliding down the pant leg of my baggy overalls, and I squash my baby harder to me, in an effort to keep that onion from falling out the bottom onto the grass, and to avoid being caught red-handed with stolen property. But as I turn the corner of the house, I am taken aback to see my aunt standing at the car with some plastic shopping bags. I am holding Blaise so tightly she can hardly breathe.

"Go ahead and pick some spinach, lettuce, and onions," Aunty Elsie says. "There's rhubarb, too."

Emelyn takes the bags while I thank Aunty Elsie profusely and guiltily, then insist that she head back inside before her dinner gets cold. I watch the door shut behind my aunt and then, with a shake of my leg, the onion falls to the ground by my foot. I snatch the stolen onion and throw it onto the front seat of the car. We are both laughing now, Emelyn and I, as we return to the garden; Blaise and I to the rhubarb patch, Emelyn to the lettuce and onions. We pick until the bags are full, and can't wait to get back and show what we've got to *Lolo* and *Lola* (Emelyn's terms for my mother and father, meaning 'grandpa' and 'grandma' in Tagalog). At dinner that evening, the salad tastes so wonderfully fresh that even Emi, not one to enjoy her greens, says it's delicious, and her grandfather swears he can taste the land, and the chlorophyll. I am a little sorry Emi wasn't with us to make the connection from pulling something out of the ground and eating it, but this will come later; in our own garden at the farm. And as clever as she is, she won't be able to make any unflattering comparisons between her award-winning Great-uncle Leonard's garden, and our own. I'm glad about that, at least.

*   *   *

The next day, after a big Father's Day breakfast fry-up (my girls both love bacon, a predilection they've inherited from their grandfather), I take my girls to a kite festival at Assiniboine Park, and a ride on a toy train, where we find ourselves deer-watching, including, as Emi says, a 'Bambi': a baby deer, with its little white spots. She is thrilled and we wait for a second go on the train. I am reminded of one evening my mother and father wrapped us kids up in blankets (we were already dressed in our pyjamas) and bundled us into the car off to see the Disney movie. I remember being bewildered that my parents thought of doing such a thing — but grateful that they had. And it was with similar excitement that I put the *Bambi* DVD into our player back in Hong Kong, just a few months ago, to watch the movie with my girls. I must admit I was a little disappointed: perhaps the magic that movie held was not due to the story itself, but because it was the night my parents wrapped me up in blankets and sat with me in a drive-in movie theatre, snuggled together in the front seat of the car — and quite possibly the only time my entire family watched a movie together.

In the evening I go out with my parents to a political fund-raiser: a 'Greek night' for Steve Ashton, the newly re-elected MLA for the riding of Thompson. Mr. Ashton is of British descent, but his wife is Greek, and in the course of the evening, I discover that he has become very Greek himself. He speaks the language fluently, and has championed the cause of the Greek community, most notably in his efforts in speaking out for the return what he refers to as 'the Parthenon Marbles'.

Mr. Ashton begins his speech that evening by saying it was because of my father that he got involved in politics, and I look across the table to my father to see his reaction. He is smiling, blushing a little, pleased. Many people say the same thing over the course of the evening, and come up to my father to shake his hand, and to say he was the best premier this province ever had. Living abroad as I do, I find it surprising that it still goes on. My brother says it happens all the time.

Between speeches, I bring up what has become, for me, a perennial plea to my father: *Write your memoirs — please! Don't wait any longer.* I tell him that it is his obligation, part of the duty of a former civil servant, member of parliament, member of the legislative assembly, premier, governor general, and high commissioner. In previous years, he would wave off the idea. But this year, I can tell he has become more receptive.

My father then tells us a story about how, many years ago, he had been offered a large sum to write his memoirs but had refused, not wanting to be tied down to a schedule, nor to a particular publisher and their expectations. "Writing memoirs is what one does when they're retired," he adds. "And I haven't retired."

"Too bad," I say selfishly. "The royalties from that best-seller could have been my daughters' assurance in an increasingly unsure world." I was launching into a thought that I had never admitted to my parents before, although I assume it is something everyone considers when they decide to have children. *What will become of them? Have we done the right thing?*

Whenever I allow myself to ponder these questions, I can become quite concerned and almost frightened. So, when the truth of the matter makes me nervous, I try to deflect my feelings with humour: "When you give birth to a child in 2002," I say to my father, "you wonder if they'll be eating Soylent Green by the time they're 65."

My brother and I are laughing, but I can tell my father doesn't know what on earth I am referring to. My father has obviously not seen the movie *Soylent Green,* and so I launch into a brief synopsis of the 1973-version-of-the-future science-fiction movie starring Charlton Heston and Edward G. Robinson. But just as I am getting to the part where Thorn (Heston) discovers the hideous secret behind the government-issue food product, shouting a final — though predictable — anguished cry: 'Soylent Green is *people!',* my father interrupts. I think he knows what's coming and — not a big fan of movies, and definitely with a low grossness threshold — he doesn't want to hear it. He looks at me seriously. I am still giggling, but inside I am getting embarrassed.

"Well, I don't know that what you're talking about was so different from your great-grandfather, Old Anton, leaving everything behind in Europe to bring his family to a new country. . . ."

I stop laughing. I had never though about my family's arrival like that before. But what my father is saying now sounds so true. It was never any different for those people; my great-grandfather and everyone like him. I had assumed they had thought of Canada as a land of hope and promise — I know they did — but with that came fear and uncertainty. The future was an empty space in front of them, waiting to be lived. It is the same for us all, I realize. *Oh, for a chance to see the future; my own, a daughters'. I don't care which. For just one opportunity to know that everything will be all right —*

Some more people are starting to come by our table to talk to my parents, so I take the moment to collect my courage and introduce myself to a couple sitting at a table nearby. I cannot resist having a conversation with the parents of Winnipeg's Greek Goddess, Nia Vardalos, who wrote and starred in the hit movie *My Big Fat Greek Wedding.* I saw it when it finally made its way to Hong Kong, and it affirmed what I had been thinking since my own daughters were born: if you're smart, you will *embrace* your family roots. I mention that my father's secretary had faxed me a lovely photo of their daughter sitting with Queen Elizabeth and my father, when the Queen visited Winnipeg a few months earlier, and Mrs. Vardalos tells me that having dinner with Queen Elizabeth was more important to her daughter than being nominated for an Academy Award. I smile when I think that Mr. Ashton might be a little annoyed to hear how much Manitoba's Greek Goddess enjoyed meeting the living embodiment of the government that pilfered, and still refuses to return, his beloved Parthenon Marbles.

On the way home, I find my thoughts flitting from Greek Orthodox priests, to Old Anton, to Charlton Heston, and then to an image of the Parthenon — a.k.a. The Elgin — Marbles, whatever they look like. Despite the incongruity of an MLA in Manitoba vowing not to rest until the Parthenon Marbles are returned to Greece, I was greatly moved by Mr. Ashton's passion. In the car, I ask my dad why he doesn't try to help Mr. Ashton in his quest. My father has no reply, and I don't pursue it. I think I understand: it's just not something he ever thought of doing. Energy resource management and sustainable development — those are my father's passions. Those things — and hanging out in the R.M. of Broken-head. One can't do everything.

"Well, Karmel, you might recall that you have met the present-day Lord Elgin. Why don't you ask him yourself?" my father finally says. I can see his eyes in the rear-view mirror, and I know he is smiling. I laugh at the ridiculousness of the idea, but my father is warming up to it. "And don't forget, you also met the president and the prime minister of Greece. And the Greek culture minister."

It is my turn to be nonplussed. I do indeed remember our lovely holiday in Scotland when I was a teenager. Lord Elgin — the descendant of the Lord Elgin responsible for having the marbles in question removed from the Parthenon in 1801, while he was the British ambassador to the Ottoman Empire (and whose son was governor general of Canada from 1847 to 1854) — and his wife invited our family to holiday with them at their country estate in northern Scotland. And how could I forget our state visit to Greece; meeting President Karamanlis of Greece, and the Prime Minister Andreas Papandreou (whom my parents knew well; he had become a family friend while living in exile in Canada in the early 1970s). I remember being greeted at the airport upon our arrival by rows of skirted Greek soldiers, and the minister of culture (a heavily made-up Melina Mercouri, who had been a famous movie star before she ventured into politics) had given us a personal tour of the Acropolis. . . .

"— and you know the Queen rather well, too," my father adds. He chuckles. "The more I think about it, the more I think you are infinitely suited for the job, Karmel."

We all laugh, but for the rest of the ride home, I start to wonder how to best go about getting England to return the Parthenon Marbles to Greece (and, while I'm at it, the Sphinx's beard to Egypt).

CHAPTER 13

Duty

IN 1924 I PURCHASED A DWELLING for my family on College
Avenue, No. 704. We have lived south of the tracks or in the
centre of the City. I had to live close to my place of work, as I
had to walk every morning to be at work at 5:30 and the buses
did not run at that early hour. The place I now owned was
about two miles away or about 25 minutes fast walking, but
we liked it. My wife was very happy to live in our own home.

My younger brother lived with my parents when he got
married, but after two years they could not get along with one
another so he packed up and bought a place in Dugald, and
left our parents by themselves. They were too old to farm or
even to look after themselves, so they asked me to come back
and farm and look after them. I was willing to go back as I
knew I would do a lot better there than working in the City.
But I left the decision to my wife and waited to see what she
wanted to do. I told her not to act too fast and to take her time.
She had her answer in a few hours. She thought it was the right
thing to do since it was better for the children, cheaper to live
and better too, so we told our parents that we would come in
about two years' time, as the land was already rented out for
three years. The other event was that the City of Winnipeg
celebrated its Golden Anniversary.

A daughter was born to us on June 16th, 1925. We were
both very happy as we now had two sons and we wanted a
daughter. The saying is that 'there is no home without a
daughter'. Now that we promised our parents that we would
come back to the farm, we tried to buy articles which would
be useful there. We could not sell our home yet, furthermore,
we had to look for buyers who would pay cash as we would

need the money for farm wagons, machinery, and horses. I was also looking for articles in the advertisement column. I noticed that there was a tractor, a three-furrow plough, and a nine-foot cultivator and a grain grinder. The mortgage company that had loaned that farmer the money to buy this equipment had to take it, as the farmer left the farm and the equipment.

It was on a farm about 25 miles southeast of the City. I looked it over and started the tractor. It seemed to have been in fair shape so about two weeks later I took two weeks from my job and tried to bring it home. I took it up the road about five miles. It got dark and had no lights so I left it beside a fence and went to look for a place to rest for the night. When I came back in the morning the pulley of the tractor was gone. I began to inquire as to who might have taken it. I was sent along from one to another, and I could not get no place with these people. I went back to Winnipeg to Dominion Motors and traded the tractor for a new one and was allowed $150.00 on the deal. They brought the new one with the truck, and we loaded the old tractor by pulling it on with the new one and in about one hour I was on my way with all the equipment.

After the federal election of 1926 no party had a majority. Both old parties had the same number of members. But we now had two socialist members: J.S. Woodsworth representing Winnipeg North Centre; and A.A. Heaps representing Winnipeg North. J.S. Woodsworth said he would vote for the party that favoured old-age pensions. The Conservatives were too reactionary to even think to help old people. Mackenzie King promised that if he got the two socialist votes he would bring in the old-age pension. J.S. Woodsworth wanted $25 per month, while Mr. King would only go as high as $15. They later compromised on $20. But that was not made a fact until 1928. And so it was that in the City the board paid the pensioner $20 and on a farm, $15. And if he had about $200 saved, no matter how old the pensioner was, the board would pay them $5 a month. But it was a little better than nothing. I knew a case where the board paid a pensioner $1.98. And so the King government was in power until 1930. But prices of grain always went lower, although the wheat price stayed up because all wheat was sold to the Pool.

– John James Schreyer

I AM RELIEVED TO LEARN that my grandfather wasn't going to have to spend too much of his life away from the farm, although two more years must have seemed like a long time. After spending the weekend in the city, we head back to the farm early on Monday morning. As I get behind the wheel of the car, I realize just how eager I am to get back there. We all are. I am trying to figure out what it is exactly that compels me. The sound of the wind? That awesome big sky? There's that, but also our neglected garden. When we drive onto the farm, all our heads swivel to the left to get a good look at it, and my heart sinks a little. I see so much quack grass that the rows of vegetables are hardly distinguishable. But never mind, we have a hoe — and Grandpa's borrowed garden hose. At least there won't be any more filling of watering cans in the bathtub.

But I am also in love with the idea of having my own place with my daughters: we live in rented accommodation in Hong Kong, and previously here in Canada, we have spent our time in hotels and motels, and Grandma and Grandpa's house. When my daughters and I walk about the farm, and look across at the fields of wheat and sunflowers that are being grown this year all around us, we pretend that all of it is ours. The grass and the trees, too, are a big deal to people who live in an apartment without so much as a balcony. I know we are just playing farmer, but already Emi can tell the difference between a potato plant and the beans, onions, and chives. I haven't been able to teach her about growing carrots because they haven't come through yet. But some things about farm life Emi already knows, undoubtedly from years of singing songs like *Old MacDonald.* When we first arrived on the farm, I asked Emi what the big red building was called. She knew it is called a barn, and I am sure I never told her. I am glad to be able to show Emi that farms really do exist — not just in nursery rhymes — and that she and her sister now have a barn to call their own for now.

It doesn't take long for all of us to get into the garden, pulling up mounds of weeds and quack grass, and then giving the rows of newly-sprouting greens a good watering. Emi insists on using the hoe, and I send her to a 'safe' area, the onion rows, where it is quite clear which are the wicked weeds to smash and which are the good baby vegetables to be avoided. The Chinese cabbage and carrots have Emelyn and I perplexed; are they ever going to show themselves? Or have they already, and we just don't recognize them among the surprising assortment of unwanted greenery. By the time we call it a day when the noon suns beats down, we are still not sure.

*   *   *

After lunch, I have a special treat in store for Emi: a trip to the Brokenhead Public Library. She claps her hands with glee when I tell her, and when we pass the row of computers and walk through to the back of the building, Emi is walking smartly ahead of me, and I hear a gasp as she runs off to the children's corner, which is well-stocked and inviting with its kid-size tables and chairs and stuffed animals to read to. Emi quickly spies some children's books that I assume she knows from school, takes them off the shelf, sits herself down and starts to 'read'. Perfect. I head over to the nearby reference section to find the history of the Rural Municipality of Brokenhead that Cousin Greg had mentioned. But first I skim the library's young-adult section, which is also surprisingly large. They don't have what I am looking for: my own two novels. I'll have to fix that.

I sit myself next to Emi in the children's section with my big blue book, and scan the cover: *They Stopped at a Good Place: A History of the Beausejour, Brokenhead, Garson and Tyndall Area of Manitoba, 1875–1981. M. Czuboka, Editor and Bill Horodyski, Chairman.* Just as my father had said, the book is massive. But by now I am not surprised; I am beginning to understand just how much can be said about living by the Brokenhead — and how much it needs to be told. I am grateful that it got done. Just as I begin to flip through the book, something familiar catches my eye, and I flip back; there is my father in one of his earlier official portraits as governor general. My father has written the foreword, it appears. He hadn't mentioned that.

As I have done countless times over the last couple of years, I have shown a book to Emi, pointed to a picture, and asked, *Who's that, Emi?* Answers were always in the range of Little Red Riding Hood to Snow White to Franklin the turtle to Jesus, and I wonder how she will respond this time. I push the big blue book over to Emi's side of the table.

"Who's this, Emi?"

My daughter studies the photo for a second. "Grandpa," she replies matter-of-factly, then returns to the adventures of Franklin (the turtle).

Her response surprises me; I expected a little more surprise, perhaps even an indication that she is impressed by the fact that her own grandfather can be found within the pages of a book — especially one as mighty as this. I watch her for a few moments, thinking about a story my father still tells; about the time he took my sister and I on our first airplane trip. He was holding my sister in his lap, and they were looking out the window. He pointed to the billowy clouds beneath the plane. 'What are those?' he asked my sister, his voice filled with excitement. 'Clouds' replied my sister in a bored tone of voice, as if to say, *Don't you know that?* I think my father lost a part of his innocence that day.

With Emi engrossed in the adventures of Franklin, I start in on my chosen book, reading a brief outline of the physical geography of the Brokenhead-Beausejour area, by Ron Jackson. He writes: *A complete understanding of the history of an area involves not only a study of human settlement but also a study of the natural history in order that settlement patterns and the evolution of present land use can be more readily understood.* How true that is! Soon I am being immersed in fascinating factoids about the land: its bedrock geology, for example: *The bedrock geology within the Beausejour-Brokenhead area consists of rock originally formed between four billion and 230 million years ago*; and its surficial geology: *The event which perhaps had the greatest effect on the Beausejour-Brokenhead area was the Pleistocene glaciation and associated with that, glacial Lake Agassiz. . . .*

I wish I could take the book home with me, but it is a reference book, so I start flipping through the pages for things I can photocopy, and come across other surprises. Here's a report, with photos, of the opening of Edward Schreyer School, complete with an Air Cadet Honour Guard. My mother and sister were there, but I wasn't, and I can't remember where I may have been, or why I didn't go along. I find photos of old Cromwell School. In Cromwell School's class of 1943 there's my father, in the second row, between Virginia Ilchena and Leonard Ottenbreit (who would one day be the uncle of my own classmate). I see a photo of what looks like the farmhouse, and do a double-take. It is indeed the farm, and there are four young people standing in front of it. The caption reads: *Four exchange students from eastern Canada standing in front of Governor General Edward Schreyer's home.*

The book contains family histories of most of the old-guard settlers to the Brokenhead district, and I come across a rendering of the Schreyer family tree, compiled by the book's editor. I photocopied that page. It was precious information to me, as it included clues to my great-grandfather Anton Schreyer's parents, as well as my great-grandmother Caroline's parents. My great-great-grandparents, of course, never made it to Canada. From this chart, I learn that my grandfather's maternal grandfather, Jacob Hepp, was Alsatian. Does this make me part French, I wonder? It is interesting news. But what I also learn is that my grandfather's maternal grandmother, Margaret Martini, was Polish-Ukrainian. So we are a little bit Ukrainian after all! I feel I need to remind my father of this, as he had often told me we were pretty much German — and one of the few German families in an area that was predominantly populated by Poles and Ukrainians. I had always felt a little disappointed to be reminded of this, as I knew my father had always secretly (or perhaps not-so-secretly) wished he were Polish and Ukrainian, just as Steve Ashton probably wishes he were Greek.

Time is flying at the library but Emi is starting to get antsy. I flip through the book one last time, and come across an article entitled: *Beausejour-Brokenhead Home Brew,* by Michael Czuboka.

Apparently the Beausejour-Brokenhead area had become a major producer of 'white lightning' early in the 20th century. *The Ukrainians, Poles and Germans became particularly enthusiastic distillers of home-made alcohol mainly because the official variety was expensive and difficult to obtain,* Czuboka adds. There is even a recipe included. Funny how my grandfather never mentioned *that* in his memoirs. I know that Nellie McClung had a lot to do with prohibition, and I wonder what my grandfather thought about it. When my grandfather wrote about prohibition in his memoirs, he seemed rather off-hand and emotionless about the issue. Although I am not sure why I am compelled to photocopy this page, I am chuckling as I do. The memories are coming back. . . .

One of the first German words I ever learned was the deliciously German-sounding *schnapps,* courtesy of Grandpa. I know he liked his *schnapps* at the end of the day, and I remember quite clearly the day I first heard that strange word, when I couldn't have been more than seven years old, and he and my grandmother were baby-sitting us while my parents were off on one of their lengthy trips. On that day, I found him sitting at the dining table before I was off to bed, as usual, but this time there was a glass of clear liquid in front of him.

"What's that?" I asked, pointing to the glass.

"It's *schnapps,*" my grandfather replied.

I giggled at the sound. "What's *schnapps?*"

He smiled at me, and looked over at his wife, who returned his look with a warning glance. How to explain? "It's — spirits."

"Oh." *That* word was familiar to my ear — but the context was different. Just the same, I nodded in understanding. Grandpa wasn't offering me a taste.

"Can I try some?"

Grandpa smiled again, and looked over at Grandma standing in the kitchen. She shook her head at him. He turned back to me, "No, it's not for little girls." Still smiling.

I didn't press the issue. I had a better idea about what *schnapps* was, anyway, if it wasn't for little girls. I knew all about prohibition. . . .

By now Emi is pulling on my arm, and I am barely able to get the book back on the shelf. I reward her for her good behaviour with an ice-cream cone at the Dairy Bar, then off we go to a park on the Brokenhead River, where we spend an hour making sandcastles and chasing tadpoles with a net. I know that, right now, these are the things my daughter will remember: Our Vegetable Garden, Grand Beach, the Thinking Trees, the Big Red Barn — and now, Chasing Tadpoles on the Brokenhead River will be added to that list.

I get down and dirty in the sand for her. I hold slimy tadpoles in my hands for her. I am aware that when I am reading through reference books, I am doing it all for her, and for her sister. All of this is a part of my mission; my motherly duty. But I won't fool myself — I am doing it for me, too. And I am enjoying it very much.

CHAPTER 14

Return

1927 WAS AN EVENTFUL YEAR for myself and my family as it was the year that we moved from the City to the farm, where I was born. We had to move; as I had sold my dwelling, and moved farther away from my work. Now, if I had to walk, it would take me more than one hour. But I was lucky as the night engineer was living my way and I got a ride with him morning and night. It was also the spring that The Strangler was scaring the women. It was not a pleasant idea when some men were working on the night shift. It was quite a relief when he was caught and jailed.

It was also the year that Canada celebrated her Diamond Anniversary. I took my wife and family to see the parade, and it was the last parade we have seen for a long time, because at two o'clock that same day we took the train for Beausejour and home to the place I was born and raised and was very happy to come back to. All our friends came to the station to bid us farewell and good luck. When we left the City some of them wondered how we could be happy and thought that the farm was an awful place to go to. But the children were happy when we got home, as I would describe it. There was a nice black and white dog, which followed the children wherever they would go, and in a few days the dog and children were inseparable. And they liked the horses and the cow we bought, as they could get all the fresh milk they wanted, and the children liked their grandparents and got along with them very well. I did not quit my job yet, as the land was still rented, so still worked till spring of 1928 but took two weeks time to come and plough about half the land which the renter gave up.

I came back every weekend to see how the family was getting along, and see if the horses were not sick and brought in some feed while out. The superintendent at the mill always came to chat with me. When I told him I was quitting my job he thought there was something wrong with my head. He thought, here is a man with a steady job, which was hard to get at that time, and did I not see so many men walking the streets with no prospects? My argument was that if I worked so many hours at the farm as I worked here at the mill, I'm sure I would make better. He said that I would come back begging for work, but if he was still around he would see to it that I would never get another job with the mill, and so we parted not as friends. But on my last day he came around and wished me all the luck, saying that I would need it. I came to see him a year later. He was gone and in the hospital. As I inquired later I found out that he was dead. And so ended the City life to start another way of life – the farm life – which started on April 2nd, 1928.

Another son was born to us, on January 28th, 1928. He was named Anton, the name taken from his grandfather, which made the grandfather very happy. He liked this grandson better than the rest, perhaps because of this name. This spring we planted barley and oats, as the land was not fit for wheat, and the grain was fair. I sold some barley in the fall at 65 cents a bushel, which I thought was not too bad. Beef and pork prices were down, wheat prices held, because most of the wheat was sold to the Pool. But the grain exchange paid about 10 cents a bushel more; it was to try to prove that the open market was better for the farmers. This almost always is nonsense, but we seem to need to realize that same lesson every second generation.

– John James Schreyer

IT IS MORNING AGAIN at the farm, and we are happy to wake up to it. As soon as the girls and I are out of bed, we head out to the garden in our pyjamas to check on our vegetables. There's a cool breeze at eight in the morning, but the sun is warm already and promising to be a scorcher. Emi and I review the names of the different rows of sprouts; the spiky onions, the pale green peas, and the beans. We have been able to clear away all the weeds from these rows and I am gloating at how neat they look. But I don't teach her what the next three rows are — the Chinese cabbage, leeks, and carrots — because I can't recognize them yet myself. In fact, I am still not sure that there is anything there at all, and neither is Emelyn. What we see are three rows, made neat by diligent hoeing, of quack grass and assorted other things, that could be vegetable, but perhaps not. After these are the beets, which are looking awfully sorry, then two rows of potatoes, and finally a row of corn. The potatoes are growing like weeds and the corn is looking good, too, at three inches in height. I snap pictures of Emi and Blaise standing with the hoe and water hose in the middle of all this, and it will fly through cyberspace today to Mrs. Rao and Mrs. Rollinson and Emi's classmates at Discovery Bay International School in Hong Kong.

I do a bit more hoeing while the girls play by the barn, and stop to examine the rows of beans more closely. There are tiny holes appearing on the leaves of my lovely bean plants. Is this normal? I tell myself that's just the way beans are supposed to look; it's been so long, how would I know any differently? I brush my niggling concern aside and continue weeding around the potatoes and corn, but before long Blaise starts to pout, which Emi translates as a need for breakfast, and I guiltily bring the girls back inside. I look outside the kitchen window at the garden as I make the toast, feeling neglectful on both sides, but not for long: the smell of the bacon that Emelyn is frying makes me realize how hungry I am as well. After breakfast, I take some time to work at the computer, while Emelyn takes the girls outside to play. I set up at the dining table as usual, in front of the big picture window that looks out past the highway to a western exposure: big clear sky today, flat green field, a row of tall trees at the far horizon. The sun sets, too, just outside this window; these days, it occurs at about ten o'clock in the evening. I watch some geese as they continue north, to Grand Beach, until I can no longer hear them, and remind myself to ask my father if he ever watched the geese from this window when he was a boy.

The girls are excited because Grandma and Grandpa are coming to the farm for a picnic lunch today, and they arrive just before noon. When my girls and I go out to greet them, I notice the back seat of the car is packed with boxes, which I know are filled with old documents, destined for the Beausejour-Brokenhead Public Library. A special project is in the works; weeks earlier, my father mentioned to me that the library in Beausejour was going to inaugurate an 'Ed Schreyer Reading Room'. I know there are documents in those boxes that are from my grandparents' lives as well, and I am dying to take a peek. As my mother emerges from the car, she gives me a few black-and-white snapshots of the family at the farm, mid-century, and I eagerly pocket them. They will be an excellent addition to my 'shrine'. But I want more. When I see my mother and father at play with the girls on the lawn, I steal a look in an open box and pull out a few items off the top: a farm planner dated 1932, in which my grandmother had kept a record detailing every household expense, right down to a couple of eggs; a government-issue pamphlet about scarlet fever; a ration book with my great-grandfather's name on it — I assume it is from one of the world wars, but I can't tell which. I stash away all these things, too. It seems my grandmother was a 'saver' — a packrat, in other words — and I have inherited the trait.

During lunch by Emi and Blaise's Thinking Trees, I ask my father about the geese; if he had ever watched them from his window, and what he thought about them. *Did the sound make you stop what you were doing? Did it make you stop and think about something — anything?* His answer surprises me. "There weren't that many geese. Conservation efforts over the last couple of decades have done a good job bringing them back. There are far more geese now than there were when I was young." There is hope.

The girls and my parents and I chat about the special project at the library, the reading room, how the garden is progressing, my trip to the library with Emi, and the tadpoles in the Brokenhead. We don't notice that the sky to the northwest is turning dark until it moves directly over us. It has become blue-black and mean. The wind has picked up, sending dust scudding across the highway in front of us, and within minutes the temperature drops a few degrees. I can feel a few raindrops on my arm and we all quickly pitch in, gathering up food and plates and blanket and heading inside the farmhouse for coffee and coconut macaroons bought from the Co-op in town. We sit at the dining room table, look out the big picture window, and wait for the rain to come down — but no rain comes. A few more minutes and the dark clouds have gone. The sun is out, and it is hot once again. I step outside to see where the stormy weather went and notice lightning to the east, over the Brokenhead River.

Later that evening, Cousin Greg stops by for a chat. I tell him about our trip to the river to play with the tadpoles, and what a pity it is that Beausejour doesn't have public access to the Brokenhead River. He tells us that there is somewhere very close where we can go swimming whenever we want; an old gravel pit just north of Ladywood. "The R.M. has even put in a pier to jump off of," he adds. Great! I look forward to taking the girls explore there, perhaps tomorrow.

Cousin Greg asks me if we had had hail here earlier in the day and I tell him no, just a few drops of rain. He informs me that a big hailstorm had cut a swath all around us, from Ladywood all the way to Milner Ridge, about 30 kilometres directly east; where the prairies end and the Canadian

Shield landscape of rocks and trees begins. We are lucky that it missed us, I think; I could imagine my daughters' disappointment if our prize onions were flattened. I am thinking like a farmer, and I am concerned for the crops that are growing in the areas that were hit. I have noticed that some serious farm activity is going on around us already. The wheat growing on our land is still young, but the tractors were out just one mile south of us yesterday, swatting down some crop that I wish I was familiar with. Cousin Greg asks us how we are getting along at the farm and I tell him how it is growing on me, and on the girls. We are slowing down, or at least I feel I am. My heart is slowing down. I love it. My cousin smiles and nods knowingly; happy that I am beginning to understand what he already knows.

"The northern lights were out in all their glory just last night and will probably be out again tonight. Just turn off all the lights, and walk out beyond the barn. You'll see them," he says before heading over to another cousin's place, where he is staying.

I had forgotten all about the northern lights. I wonder if I'll be able to stay up that late; it would have to be after 11:30 at night, I suppose, for the sky to be pitch-black. I am sure that it has been years since I stayed up that late, especially in Hong Kong, with its summer nights hardly any longer than its winter ones. I want to show Emelyn and my girls the magic of Manitoba's aurora borealis. This would be a perfect place to do it if we got lucky — and if we could stay up that long. I tell myself we will give it a try, but I'm not hopeful. Normally, I tell the children it is quiet time in the evening, to get them settled down, physically and mentally, for bed. But now I want to keep them up, and myself, too. What can we do in the meantime?

I decide it's high time to pay a visit to the Bakers next door; neighbours, cousins, life-long family friends. In fact, this visit is overdue, but I am shy about it, and I think the reason is rooted in my childhood. One of my most enduring memories of the Bakers is my mother's remarks about the 'Baker Boys', who are about the same age as my sister and me. When I was a young girl, and not interested in boys, I remember my mother saying how nice and handsome they were; the phrase 'Baker Boys' always accompanied by a bit of a swoon. I know that one of these fabulous Baker Boys now lives in the farmhouse next to ours, the same one in which his own father grew up; in which his Aunt Lil grew up and met my Uncle George and — well — the rest is history. This Baker Boy has his own family now — I think it was his wedding I went to over ten years ago — and now my girls and I are going to go over to say hello, finally. Maybe there will even be a little girl for Emi to play with.

I put Blaise in the stroller, and attach the Buggyboard behind it on which Emi stands. My girls are as excited as I am as we set off down the gravel drive towards the highway, We will not take the car just to go the kilometre or so to the Baker house. I intend to walk along the shoulder of the highway, but the gravel there makes it slow going, and I find myself wheeling two little girls in a stroller south down the middle of Highway 12 on a summer's evening. I am embarrassed when a car comes along, slowing down as it goes by, and I wonder what they must be thinking at the sight of a woman in baggy striped overalls jogging along the highway with a stroller and two kids. Luckily, no other vehicle passes us during the whole 12-minute trip to the Bakers' farm.

We are greeted by a noisy chocolate Labrador, which scares Emi. As I struggle with her struggling to scramble into my arms, I am unable to stop the dog from licking Blaise's face, and when I see there is no reaction from her, I come around to face her and discover she is fast asleep. But it looks like no one is home and just as we are heading back to the highway, the lady of the house, Laurie, comes out from behind a row of trees, and quickly invites us in, where Emi is introduced to the best kind of neighbour imaginable; a girl, aged ten, who dances ballet and has a basement full of Barbie dolls. I apologize for not coming by sooner, and she does likewise; Cousin Greg had told them that they would be having new neighbours for a little while. Her husband Terry, the youngest Baker Boy, is out golfing today, but as we are chatting, the woman's brother-in-law, Andy (the eldest Baker Boy) drops by. I am nervous — and awestruck. He is a real farmer — not a pretend farmer like me — and as I see him come in the door, with his farmer cap on, too, I think this farmer is so good-looking that I won't be able to look at him for very long; a self-respecting, happily-married mother will look away. I focus by quizzing him on things of an agricultural nature, and he happily educates me about the goings on; it was alfalfa I saw being harvested and tied up into big bundles. It will be shipped down to the United States.

Andy's father, Clarence, is a former Mr. Manitoba Farmer — and the sons are carrying on the tradition, one of only a few farming families left in the Brokenhead district. They are big-time farmers, as one has to be these days, working my father's land and others', too. When I ask Andy how many acres he is farming, he tells me in sections, then translates that into acres — about 3200 — and I am sure he must be farming every inch of land between here and Beausejour. He offers to take all of us in his truck to check out the crops on our land, and when I tell him that we will be here for the whole summer, he offers to take us all for a ride in the combine at harvest time, which I eagerly accept.

Blaise wakes up and, shocked by the sight of a stranger seated on the steps right next to her (as handsome as he is), she starts to whimper, so I quickly scoop her up in my arms. I call Emi up from the basement, and she surfaces with Barbie doll in hand, a gift from her new friend Alyssa I tell her that it's time to go and she reluctantly obeys. Blaise is crying disconsolately by now, and we head back to the highway with the stroller. Laurie offers me a ride home but I decline. I want to walk, and I take off at a jog; Blaise strapped in, Emi riding shotgun on the Buggyboard clutching her Barbie, the cool evening wind in our faces. Blaise quickly stops crying. We are all smiling now. This is such a thrill: jogging down the quiet highway with my two girls. It's a thrill-a-minute in the R.M. of Brokenhead. I keep on jogging; I have energy to burn. *Remember this moment* I say silently to myself, and then out loud to my girls, "Remember this moment!" Speeding north on Highway 12 at dusk. In a stroller. *Weeeeeeee!* The sun is low in the sky, it seems suspended; a fiery orb over the distant trees. We are back inside our farmhouse by ten o'clock; Emelyn was starting to worry about us. By 10:30 we are all tucked up in bed — and I have forgotten all about aurora borealis.

I snap to attention. Everywhere it is black, but I hear a slight hissing sound just outside my bedroom window. I have forgotten to turn off the water main hooked up to the garden hose, which is exactly what my father had asked me *not* to do, as it tends to leak a little and he is concerned about water getting into the basement. I wrap myself in a blanket and head out into the midnight chill, and when I do, I see that the sky is alive with the northern lights. Right above me is a point radiating out in all directions; its faint purple and green striations are dancing over the chicken coops. I go back into the house and creep up the creaky stairs to get Emelyn, who had asked me to wake her up should I see anything interesting in the sky tonight. We are both shivering under our blankets as we walk on the cold wet grass to the far corner of the farmyard, as Cousin Greg suggested, and we look up in wonder at the show.

I won't wake up my sleeping girls, although Emi was looking forward to seeing the flashing purple and green lights I had tried to describe to her earlier. But never mind, I tell myself, they'll have plenty of time to admire this heavenly dance. I think back to the road trips I took as a child, the nighttime ones; with their stars and radio static — and northern lights, too. I remember them now. The memories are coming back. I am reminded of so many things, and the feeling is bittersweet.

CHAPTER 15

Survival

1929 STARTED WITH AN EARLY SPRING. Seeding started around April 23rd. I had some wheat but thought I would sell some of it after seeding. I could have sold it in winter; the price was around $1.10 a bushel. As I was about through with seeding, the price plunged to 60 cents a bushel. Barley was 35 cents and oats, 25 cents. Beef and pork dropped to 15 cents a pound. Everything dropped. The grain exchange did this purposely in order to knock the Pool out. And the stock exchange, where there were millions at stake, took its toll. Traders that were millionaires one day were beggars by November.

A lot of these people could not take it. Some even went as far as committing suicide. It all started with the New York Stock Exchange and the Chicago Grain Exchange. It hit the farmers the most, as a lot of farmers had bought expensive land and now there was no hope of ever paying for it, and a lot of them lost their own land. The crop was fair that year, but the price of grain dropped some more. Even the Pool, which was backed by the government, could not pay more either. Beef, pork, and poultry prices were down, and it was really hard to make a living. But farmers, who had their vegetables, meat, and milk, and did not have debts to pay, made a fair living. In this disastrous year we had another increase in our family. We had enough milk and other produce for all of them. It was a nice big healthy boy and we were quite happy to have him. We named him Leonard.

In 1930, there were two events of importance. There was the federal election in which R.B. Bennett of the Conservative Party defeated the Liberal government of Mackenzie King. There was also a provincial election, and the Progressives were elected for a third term. The election of the Conservatives to govern Canada was a disaster. Times were getting bad, but that was nothing compared to what happened later. Despite all the surpluses and cheap food a lot of people were hungry. Beef and pork were plentiful, so was butter, poultry and eggs. I sold one steer and two heifers weighing about 1000 pounds each for $27 for all three of them. I sold a 450 pound hog for $4.50; 40 ten-pound turkeys for $38, or nine cents a pound; eggs nine cents a dozen; butter 12 cents, and that was for as long as the Bennett government lasted. The crop was good, but the price of grain hit a new low when they were elected.

In 1931 we got more of the same. I bought two cows for $10. Hogs were one cent a pound. Those that had a Model-T Ford took the motor out and attached a pole into the car and hitched the horses to it. They nicknamed it the Bennett Buggy. I had one standing on the scrap heap but hauled it away last year. I wanted to forget the nightmares of the thirties. The price now went as low as 35 cents for a bushel of wheat. You can imagine what the other grains were worth. I forgot to mention with the $4.50 I got for the 450 pound hog, well, I needed a pair of shoes so I bought a pair of shoes. I still had to pay 25 cents more than I got for the hog. If you went to the City and told your friends about how you have to give your produce away, they told you that you were still lucky to be on a farm: You have all the meat, eggs, butter, and vegetables. We don't get that here. All we get is stale butter, eggs, and spoiled vegetables. And meat that has more muscle than a prize-fighter.

— John James Schreyer

AND WE'VE GOT CUTWORMS in the beans. Or at least I think that's what we've got. I survey the garden this morning and look down at my beloved rows of beans, which are doing the best of all — next to Uncle Leonard's spiky green onions, of course. I am not pleased; the holes in the leaves, which I had dismissed as nature's whim a few days ago, have gotten bigger. I look around the rest of the garden; quack grass, dandelions, and thistle-like weeds are growing thickly between the rows despite my thrice-weekly attempts to hoe them out; there is a mountain of dead weeds and grass composting nicely in the summer heat at the end of each row. I am vexed by the three rows of quack grass growing neatly where the leeks, carrots, and Chinese cabbage ought to be. When I shared my concerns to my father and Uncle Leonard, and to Laurie, they all assured me that carrots take a long time to come up. That thought had sustained me, but now I am ready to admit that they are probably not going to surface. I have to face the fact that our garden is not turning out the way I had planned.

As my neighbour suggested, I go into town to the *Miracle Do It!* Centre and ask for some something to get rid of cutworms, or whatever it is that is eating up the leaves on my beans. The helpful woman behind the counter explains that cutworms chew the plant down at the stem. Okay then, I don't have cutworms, but something else, and I pay for a bag of powder that is going to save my beans — and also promises to deal harshly with potato bugs, too. The woman suggests I wear a mask when I administer the powder and so I buy one of those. I drive home dejected, my big plan turning into mediocrity after only a few weeks. And I think of Uncle Leonard's garden, and so many lovely gardens I had seen in these parts; perfect rows of green separated by black earth. Not one speck of a weed. Not one errant blade of quack.

I sigh, and look at the mask beside me on the car seat. I never thought I'd have to deal with one of those again. I can't escape the mask, not even here on the farm. It makes me think of when SARS had just had its first major spike in Hong Kong; 80 new cases in one day. A few days later, I could feel myself starting to panic, as many of my friends had already left Hong Kong, or were busy packing. And just at that time, Emi came down with a fever. She had never been so sick. At first I didn't want to think it was any more serious than the usual — although Emi rarely had a fever. But as an uncharacteristic lethargy took over her, and her whole body became so hot I could feel it though her clothes, I knew she needed to see a doctor. Having kept her close to home since the schools were closed a week before, I didn't want to take her to a doctor's office; it was one of the very places we were being told to stay away from if at all possible.

The doctor's waiting room had been relatively empty, but the few people that were there — as well as the three nurses at the desk — were all wearing surgical masks. Emi clung to me as we signed in. I looked at the box of surgical masks on the counter. Until that time, I hadn't worn one, even though my husband had brought a dozen home, thoughtfully provided at cost by his employer, the Airport Authority of Hong Kong. For me, donning the mask was like admitting that the danger was real, and I couldn't bring myself to do it. I didn't want it to be true, even when I knew there were tens of people coming down with the disease in my city every day. I looked at Emi, and the masks, still hesitating. Then I reached gingerly for two masks from the box, and sat down with my sick girl in my arms.

"Hey Emi. Let's play masks," I had said to her, as cheerfully as I could. I grinned and began to put one on my face, but Emi reached for my arm to stop me, her eyes wide with fear, saying nothing. She shook her head and I removed the mask, hugging her tight. The people in the waiting room were watching us and I knew they were not smiling behind their masks. They could see how sick my daughter was, and they were afraid.

My mind flashes forward several weeks, to early May. The mood had changed. Hong Kong was emerging from the darkness, rallying, recovering. We had finally beaten back the monster — or the monster was dying its natural death — and we were gaining confidence from that, even as we grieved for those who did not make it. Concerned by the high number of SARS cases among hospital staff, the English language daily, the *South China Morning Post,* had started a public appeal to buy Barrierman suits for all the hospital workers. The public raised 14 million Hong Kong dollars in three weeks (about three million dollars Canadian). We had helped to protect our front line when the government couldn't. Emi was back at school, recovered from a bad bout of tonsillitis, and was showing off her recently-acquired knowledge of the alphabet; that was something good that had come out of her month-long unscheduled school vacation. But the epidemic was not over; people were still getting sick, the death toll was still rising. I hadn't ventured into Hong Kong Island for six weeks, and didn't want to, but two days before we were scheduled to come to Canada, Emi needed to see the dentist due to a playground injury. As I was heading out the door with Emi, I stuck two masks into my handbag. When we got on the ferry, I saw that most of the people were still wearing them. I sat Emi down, not sure what to do. I opened my bag and looked at her. She looked at the masks in my bag, then at me. She smiled, "Let's play masks, Mummy. I'm not afraid anymore." Those words still play over in my mind, and every time I hear them, I can't help but be grateful. To hear them from the lips of a three-year-old! Life is beautiful.

[On this day, the World Health Organisation gives the all-clear to Hong Kong. When my husband buys the morning paper over there, this is what he will read: *These [eight] people died fighting a disease that struck down 378 of their colleagues. In total, 1755 Hong Kong residents were infected . . . and 296 died. 1262 people were put in isolation, 13,300 jobs were lost and 4,000 businesses folded. A WHO travel advisory was in place for 52 days, 13,783 flights were cancelled, 3,600,000 fewer travellers crossed at Lowu [the border crossing with China], 1,000,000 foreign tourists stayed away. Today, 104 days after the outbreak began, we are free of SARS.*]

By the time I have run through my most beautiful sars memory again, I am turning onto the driveway of the farm, and the issue of holey leaves or potato bugs, or quack grass, is suddenly no big deal. It will be great if we have some bounty to share at the end of the summer. It would be even better if the garden could look as neat and tidy as so many others I've seen. But at the end of the day, if the garden doesn't turn out as I'd envisioned, we will survive. I laugh as I grab the mask and bag of bug-killer. Besides, if I think we are in danger of starving, I'll just take the kids for a visit to see their Great-uncle Leonard. I see that Emi and Blaise are already in the garden with Emelyn, and they run to me with open arms. I approach my garden with a new attitude; the blessing is not in the results, but in the opportunity to achieve them, I think to myself, and I tend to our vegetables until the sun is high in the sky.

After lunch, Emelyn and I pack the girls into the car and head north again, to Victoria Beach this time.

"Hey Emi! Look! A bridge! What river are we coming to?" I ask as we approach Greenwald again.

A silence. And then: "The — *Mighty*head."

Emelyn and I start to laugh. Emi joins in. Even Blaise.

"*The Mighty Brokenhead,* Emi."

"Yes. *The Mighty Brokenhead.*"

By the time we get to Victoria Beach, a 15-minute drive past Grand Beach on Lake Winnipeg, the wind has picked up considerably. Victoria Beach is deserted, wild and rocky. I gaze at the fir trees along the shore and I pretend that the land hasn't been touched in a hundred years. The girls and Emelyn and I are having fun enjoying this wide open space that is, so far today, ours alone. We have to chase our sand buckets down the beach when we forget to weigh them down with sand, so strong is the wind. I dream of having a cozy cottage somewhere, someday, for my girls, and I think that there could be no nicer place than this. This beach does not look familiar to me, though I know I spent a lot of time here as a young child. Both my parents like to remind me of the time that I gave them a real fright by disappearing on my tricycle here. They found my wet clothes neatly hanging over a cliff, and me, quite naked, riding my tricycle down the path. I was Emi's age at the time. I find myself looking once again at the beach to the north; my heart beats faster as I survey the shoreline of boulders and sand and evergreens. It is a landscape so Canadian to me that my body remembers it — even if my mind has forgotten the specifics. Yes, I would love to have a place here to bring my girls, a place they can call their own. But again, I am reminded that things are not so simple. In their father's country of England, there is an equally lovely, though very different, sort of cottage country; the quaintness of the Lake District, or the Cotswolds, or Darrel's own Yorkshire Dales. And I know, to be fair, it is part of my mission to give my girls the freedom of choice. Eventually, we will have to spend time in England, too.

Emi and Blaise are both fast asleep within minutes of getting back in the car, so Emelyn and I decide to take a longer drive back to the farm. Instead of heading south on Highway 12, we follow the water, keeping left, to see the place where the Winnipeg River flows into Lake Winnipeg, and the small towns of Fort Alexander, Pine Falls, and Powerview. I don't ever remember being there, although I know I must have been at least once before. There are several dams on the Winnipeg River, and therefore my father is often up this way — and no doubt we would have come along on one of our summertime road trips.

At Powerview, I turn right, following the sign which points to a place called Stead, and wonder if it was named for Robert Stead, the author of *Grain* and other works about prairie life, and one of my father's favourite writers. The drive is breathtaking; expanses of flat farmland, green and unbroken all the way to Milner Ridge, which marks the beginning of the Canadian Shield and its equally singular beauty.

We get home in time for a quick dinner, then it is off to the Beausejour's baseball diamond to watch Andy Baker play. But when we arrive at the field, it appears Andy is not playing tonight. We stay for the game anyway, and Emelyn especially enjoys rooting for the team with the flowery shirts. After the game, we take another scenic drive. I try to find the village of Green Bay my grandfather mentioned in his memoirs. In doing so, I come to a small bridge that seems quite familiar, although I cannot remember why. I think harder, and the story surfaces; I had just driven over the very bridge where my father drove over a car battery many years ago. He and I had gone canoeing, with a dear family friend named Steve, to experiment with my father's new toy: a five horse-power electric motor (and battery). I remember sitting on a fallen log in the middle of the Brokenhead River, as my father and Steve tried to lift the empty canoe over the log that was blocking our passage. And then the sight of greenish pool of battery acid on the gravel road, and my father's chagrin — to put it mildly — directed at Steve for putting an electric battery behind the car, and not letting the driver know. Next time I see Steve, I'm going to tease him about that.

We drive down another gravel back road, trying to recognize our farm from a different direction. Emelyn sees it first. We see that there is some activity in a field behind our farm and I think I know why Andy might not have been playing baseball today. He is probably one of the men we see loading bales of alfalfa onto a huge flatbed truck. The sun is low in the sky. There is a bit of cloud cover, but it is clearing in the west; always a good sign.

We get out of the car and stand by the side of the road; listening to the dull whirr of the truck's engine in the distance, watching the men — and maybe women, too — doing their job. I look down at my two beautiful small blonde daughters, who are watching the scene with keen interest. "Emi? Blaise?" I say. They look up at me and smile sweetly. "This is your land. If you want to be a farmer, it can be arranged." Emelyn and I both laugh at the thought, but I am not trying to make a joke. It may never be true, in the strictest sense; I don't expect to see either of my girls farming the land that their great-great-grandfather cleared more than one hundred years ago. But I will — and I do! — tell my girls that they can be whatever they want to be. I thank God for our blessed freedom of choice, and — I freely admit — for a life that is easy, so easy, compared to the lives of those who made possible everything we were seeing in front of us.

CHAPTER 16

Stories

IN 1932 WE HAD THE BEST CROP of all time. The yield was an average 42 bushels per acre for wheat and all was sold for No. 1 Northern. But No. 1 Northern was an honourable mention – there was the honour but no money. The buyer gave the farmer a slip, No. 1, and the price per bushel was 22 cents, oats 5 cents, barley 10 cents. A hundred bushels of wheat would bring in $22. You could take 50 bushels in one load and if you wanted to haul 100 you had to make two trips, but whatever one got it had to be sold, so as to be able to pay your twine and repair bills, and so the Conservative government kept the farmer and worker in between life and death.

In 1933 things were getting worse. We not only had the Conservatives, but grasshoppers, and they too were bad. They were on the road allowance, on meadows, in the fields and even in the farmyards. We used hopper poison but that did not do any good. We were unable to spread the poison all over, we were afraid the cattle would get out of the fence and poison themselves. Some cattle did. The grass was very short, so the cattle had to graze close to the ground. And so with the grasshoppers and a poor crop and the price the same as 1932, things were not looking good. The Bennett government gave the farmers a bonus of 5 cents a bushel, but there were not many bushels that year.

The crop in 1934 was better, as we had more rain. The grass and grain grew faster and covered the ground. The hoppers don't like shade; they will hatch on bare ground and sunshine. There was more oats for the horses and we could work them; the year before the grasshoppers got all the oats. We also got most of our potatoes as last year the hoppers got most of them, too. But the price of grain did not improve, and neither did beef and pork. A rancher shipped some cattle and was told to pay toward the freight as the cattle did not cover all expenses when sold. But there were signs that everything was going to move a bit. By the fall of 1934, the grasshoppers got small red fleas under their wings and in a short time were mostly killed by this disease.

In 1935 we had an early spring planting. It started at the end of April, but the crop was not very good as we had a lot of rust. Not all the wheat was affected by rust. The later variety was good, but the old variety was rusted very badly. However, the grass was good, and we had a lot of cattle now that helped a lot, as this again was election year. Most of the farmers around this district worked hard to get the Conservatives out, and when election time came around they were defeated and the Liberal government under Mackenzie King was back in power, and the Conservatives, too, got the red beetles under their wings and passed on with the grasshoppers. And the last event in 1935 was that there was born to us our youngest son, which we were very happy to have, and we named him Edward.

We had a poor harvest in 1936 on account of dry weather and excessive heat. Our wheat crop was destroyed and also the early oats and barley crop had a very thin kernel. On July 6th, the Fahrenheit registered 105 above zero. We cut about six acres of a 40-acre field of wheat and threshed some of it. The seed was so small that it was unfit for feed, there being only the hull. We burned all the standing wheat. We did get some of the later oats; the sample was very poor, but with good hay. We managed to keep the horses alive and working until the following year. That same year we took out a permit in the Julius area for cutting poplar cordwood and we started cutting on December 4th. George and I were cutting until January 29th, 1937. At that time, we had cut 114 cords and hauled same out of the bush onto a road. We sold the wood for two dollars on the bush road. We also hauled 125 cords out of the bush on contract with the town of Beausejour for 50 cents per cord. Jack Hoban, the town clerk, gave me a cheque for $65. I tried to cash it at the bank. It bounced. The manager told me that the town was broke and did not have 65 cents in the bank. And that was the beginning of our wood operation for 15 consecutive years, until I retired from wood operations in

1951, and my son Anton took over the operation from me the following year.

These years, 1930 to about 1937, we called them 'The Dirty Thirties'. The Municipality of Brokenhead was broke and had no money to pay the teachers. A lot of the farmers had other places to pay off and could not pay their taxes. The school district of Cromwell was pretty paid up, but yet when we gave the teacher a cheque for $45 a month, he could not cash it. He carried the cheque in his pocket until it was impossible to read the writing on it. It appeared that we would have to tell the teacher that we could not expect him to teach the children if we could not pay him, and so we called a meeting to see what could be done. The teacher told us that he would like to teach, but we would have to pay his board and room. The Baker family, where he stayed, said that if the district would assure them that they would get paid as soon as there was money, they would board the teacher even six months. We, the trustees, assured them that when the first money was paid into the municipality, we would personally see that the teacher got paid, and so we kept our school open all through the thirties. It was not till 1937 that we got some of this money from the municipality.

There were other worries. The farmers had no money for buying clothing. The storekeepers cut their credit. A lot of the families that had large families were desperate. The youth had their frustrations, too. The young men were riding the freight trains, looking for work. But work was never found. They were given jobs in the wood or pulp camps, and given five dollars a month for tobacco. The men also received one shirt and a pair of pants together with five dollars from the provincial or federal government. The camp operators only had to put up camps in order to house the men. When the men came out of these camps in the spring, their clothes were full of vermin. There were only two things that they could do: burn the clothes or boil them in a boiler. Most of them got their clothes boiled. The burning part was impractical as they would have no money to buy other clothes.

– John James Schreyer

My father was born right in the middle of the Depression. I always knew that; I had done the math — and the history. I smile when I read of my father's arrival in the world in my grandfather's memoir. It's just like driving through Cromwell, or Brokenhead, or almost Ladywood: blink and you'll miss it. But I know it was something good in a bad time. Something to celebrate. Again, I am awed by the way the people lived with hardship. For me and my generation, the 'post-war boomers', we can barely make the connection. But I know we must try; I know that I must pass this understanding on to my girls. They need to know what their great-grandparents, and great-aunts and -uncles, and those just before and after, lived through, and how they survived. Having lived so long in Asia, I know that this is something that is especially difficult for younger Canadians to do; to make this connection to the past. Where I live in Hong Kong, even today, the remnants of history's upheavals are still quite apparent. Few families in Hong Kong have not been scarred by the cataclysmic events of recent Chinese history. Many lived through the anarchy of the Cultural Revolution, perhaps as part of the infamous Red Guard. They are my age. Those that are older may well have been its helpless victims, barely surviving what eventually evolved into the destruction of Chinese society. What greater fear, I wonder, than anarchy. In Brokenhead Municipality, the government may have been penniless, but there was order — and grace. The people may have been virtually penniless, too, but the will to help each other never deserted them.

We've come back to Winnipeg again — 'the City', as my grandfather called it — this time to help my father officiate at the season opening of the Witch's Hut at Kildonan Park, and to help raise funds for the German Society. It is also a tribute to the Grimm Brothers, who travelled the countryside collecting stories that have delighted children and adults for centuries. My father is asked to do this every year, and he gets a kick out of it. In fact, Emi and I had attended this little event before, two summers ago, when Emi was an infant and very fearful of the witch. But this year she is eager to go, and to help Grandpa give his speech. There is a contest for the best fairytale costume as well, so I dress both my girls in pink and fill their hair with peonies from my mother's garden. We try to think of fairy-tale characters they can represent, and settle for generic 'flower fairies'. During breakfast, Grandpa and Emi practise their lines; when Grandpa says *"Was sagst Du?"* Emi replies *"Wunderbar!"* and throws her arms up in the air: *What do you say? Wonderful!*

And she pulls it off too, at the appointed time, given a second chance from a patient grandfather. Emi is pleased with herself for her successful performance, and so am I. After the opening speeches, Emi helps her

Grandpa cut into the ceremonial cake, and then eagerly joins the rest of the children to watch a reenactment of the Hansel and Gretel story. She is having a *wunderbar* time, but when the crowd dies down and we head to the witch's hut to take a look inside, she balks. The permanent display shows a little boy behind bars under the stairway. There is also a rather evil-looking cat in the kitchen upstairs next to Gretel. Emi knows what's coming from her previous visit and wants none of it; I have to carry her up the stairs. Blaise, however, is fearless as usual. She looks at the cat and her mouth is an O of surprised delight.

I think about the Grimm Brothers 'backlash'; the idea that their stories are all too — well — grim; unsuitable for young children today. Examine the general subject matter of our well-loved fairy tales: kidnapping (Hansel and Gretel), family dysfunction (Cinderella), poisoning (Sleeping Beauty), kidnapping again (Rapunzel), gambling, blackmail (Rumpelstiltskin), death and murder (almost every story). But it's good that children understand that bad things happen. Life is not easy. It's true; life may have become more comfortable for some of us in the world, but the world we live in is not an easy one. To pretend to our children that it is would be a disservice. So, I tell my girls about Hansel and Gretel, how they got caught by the witch when they were not paying attention, but they used their creative-thinking skills and escaped from the mean old witch, and told the authorities — and aren't they smart, just like you. Blaise nods her head and smiles and giggles, Emi nods her head and pulls me out of there, in the direction of the balloons and the face-painting.

Later in the day I am in my father's own 'cave'; his workshop, a converted garage. I am poking around some more boxes. My father enjoys carpentry and is always grateful for a project. As I look around, I marvel at the assortment of power tools. I spy some jam jars and take a look at what's inside; nails and screws, other bits and pieces. All of them used. For some people, humble beginnings are something to cover up, to deny, but for others, it is simply a part of them, part of who they are and always will be. My father was a child of the Depression and I can see it even now, in those jam jars filled with used nails. My beginnings were not so humble, and very different. During my own fairytale teenage years, I lived in a castle (Rideau Hall, in Ottawa) and met space heroes (Joseph Engle and Richard Truly), king and queens (Hussein and Elizabeth) and even a wicked witch (Elena Ceausescu). But all that is not nearly so much a part of me as the place where I was born and lived my first 13 years, north of Winnipeg; and the farm, too, surrounded by the growing wheat and my grandmother's abundant flower and vegetables gardens. Literally, the land kept me grounded. And now, as I learn more about just how much of a struggle life was for my family, I am humbled.

I start scanning the boxes and come across one box labelled *Grandma Schreyer* — my father's mother. The box contains an odd assortment of Bibles and hymnbooks, old *Life* magazines and scrapbooks, as well as three rosaries tucked away in plastic boxes. My grandmother was very devout. I remember her coming to visit us, when I was perhaps eight years old. She walked into the kitchen where I was, with a smile on her face and holding something unusual in her hand. She came over to me, still with her big smile, then proceeded to hit me with the floppy thing, a palm frond. That's how I learned about Palm Sunday.

My father comes into his workshop and I tell him the story of Grandma and Palm Sunday. He smiles. We look through the box of his mother's things together. My father gingerly picks up one old leather-bound volume, its cover hinged precariously to the spine. "This is the Bible I was sworn in on as governor general," he says simply, then puts it back in the box and walks off to look for whatever had brought him this way in the first place.

I pick up the book and hold it in both hands, the Bible that my great-grandfather had brought with him from a village called Beckersdorf, somewhere in the Austro-Hungarian Empire, in 1896. It's in German, with that heavy gothic style of typeface that I remember in the pages of a book of Grimm's fairytales a long time ago. Even the scrawl I see handwritten on the inside front cover of this Bible is in German: *Nach Canada ausgewandert den 19 Ap 1896.* Landed in Canada April 19th, 1896, I assume. There is some other writing as well; a century's worth of family graffiti. Within the pages, the children's names and birthdates are all listed, under a heading marked *Kinder.* I think about the lives of the people whose names are written on these pages in fading ink: Anna, the daughter who never came to Canada; Caroline, whose gravestone I believe I saw briefly at the cemetery in Ladywood; Elizabeth, who, I was told, is buried beside my grandparents, although I don't know why; Jacob; Margareth; Joseph; Petter; John; George — the last of my grandfather's siblings. I study the list of names a little longer; something is not quite right. Something is missing. Why are Anton and Catherine not listed? Tears blur my eyes when I come to the obvious answer; they had died before this list of names had been written, and whoever wrote this list decided not to include them, for that reason. It makes me sad to think that all I know about them is how they died: Anton from gangrene, the result of that accident with the oxen team in 1896; and Catherine in the Spanish flu pandemic in 1918. They were 15 and 26 years old when they died. They have their story. I don't know those stories, though. And so I look for consolation in what I believe is a tangible relic of their existence. Perhaps they held this Bible in their hands, too. I make a mental note to find them, Anton and Catherine, my great uncle and great-aunt.

I close the Bible and stare at the cover. *This is the Bible I was sworn in on as governor general,* my father had said. I lay my right hand over it, as I imagined my father did on Jan 22nd, 1979. He didn't say where this book was supposed to go. Well, this is one item that will be staying in the family a little longer, I decide, and I put it on a pile I call 'me and mine'. There is another old Bible in Grandma's box; an English one. Great! It is better when these things come in pairs — like the royal pillboxes — so I can give one to each of my girls. As I carry my treasure-trove back to my room, I feel a little bit guilty about stealing what some may think is an important artifact of Canadian history. I can appreciate that sentiment. The Bible will be appreciated, too. It is, after all, a piece of the continuing story of my daughters' existence — the 'prequel', in contemporary parlance — and I want them to have it, at least for a time.

But I want it for me too, this Bible, brought by ship from the Old Country, and held by the grandson — prairie born — as he swears an oath to uphold the law of the new land. It is, to me, physical proof that our Old Guard was right. Old Anton had guessed correctly. He had brought his family to a land of promise. Our wishes, hopes and dreams are in our children — no matter where we go.

CHAPTER 17

Plain hard work

WE STARTED OUR WINTER WORK in 1937 with the hauling out of
50 cords of wood. Then, on February 10th, 1938, I started out
with George and Henry, 17 years and 15 years old, with the
sleigh and horse loaded with oats and hay and food for
ourselves. We were to find a bush camp, which was described
to us as Sigurdson's camp, but knew not where it was as we
were not yet that familiar with the eastern part of Manitoba.
It being such a cold day, we drove the horses until about ten
o'clock when we drove in to a farmer's place, fed the horses,
and went into the house to get warmed up. And the good lady
of the house gave us each a cup of tea, after a meal. We again
started out towards Seven Sister Falls. Here the road became
heavy as it was stormy and was drifting snow, but we kept on
going into the bush in order to find a place for the horses and
ourselves. We were getting tired and cold – and the horses too
– when finally we saw a light. We were really happy to see that
light. We went in to see if there was room and were told that
we could stay in the camp and there was also room for a team
of horses.

I will never forget that night in the camp. We kept our
clothes on all night and we had felt socks. We could not sleep.
We put all our covers on the bunk, and even with our clothes
on we just about froze. We did not water our horses that night
as we had no water. The next morning we took the horses to
a creek. I chopped about three foot deep in order to get to the
water. We watered the horses and went back to camp for
breakfast. We made some tea and a meat sandwich but could
not get warmed up. We left our horses at the camp and went
to look for the Sigurdson's camp. We walked about four miles

to find another camp, which was occupied by other bushmen. They told us to go back another mile and turn north. It was hard to find the road as it had been snowing, but we found the camp we were looking for. There was a stove in this camp and also a barn that was big enough for six horses. We made a fire in the stove and shut the drafts up and went to get our horses and sleigh. When we got back we put the horses in the barn and went to camp and it sure was nice and warm as we came in. We had supper and tried to sleep but I was so chilled that I got a cold and coughed all night.

The next day George and I went across the Winnipeg River to see if we could find some spruce logs. We started out both at the same time. Each went a different way and agreed that we would meet at the same place when we got back and so we each found sawing logs, and in the afternoon we went out with team, saw, and axe, and by the evening we had 25 logs on the river. We worked another two days and George and Henry were cutting logs and I hauled them on the river. By then we had about 150 logs on the river, but I had to quit as I was getting very sick. I left the boys and walked to Seven Sisters Falls, from there I got a ride to Beausejour and then home. I was sick for a week. George and Henry stayed another day and also came home, with team and sleigh. We stayed at home for a week.

In the meantime, one of our neighbours also wanted to go to the bush to see if he could get some sawing logs. He had hired an extra two men and wanted to go as soon as possible but I told him that I could not go back until I got better, that would be in about four or five days. I gave him the directions by drawing him a map. He left a day sooner than we did. We got to the camp early the next time as we knew where we were going. When we got to the camp we were greeted by the neighbour and his men and he had a nice warm meal and soup, which warmed us up for the evening. They told us they cruised the timber for logs and that they had found none. I assured them that there were enough logs and more than we needed.

The next morning we crossed the Winnipeg River with our team and were followed with their two teams and five men. We started cutting down trees and sawing them into logs. I hauled one load onto the river and came back for another. Our neighbour was having trouble; one of the hired men would not work with any of them as he said that none of them knew how to use a saw and axe and that he was going to leave and work for me. But I told him that I did not need another man. The neighbour came to me and we talked it over about how best to get the logs cut; we decided I would supervise the job. So we put the men who knew how to handle a saw and axe with George and the hired man of his. Two boys were put to making roads, and the other two were put to drawing the logs to a pile where we could load them onto the sleigh.

We made four trips to the river each day, and later when the hauling got farther we made three trips. We stayed eight days and by that time we had 1020 logs on the river. It took us all day to find booms and bring them onto the ice. Some were two feet in diameter and 40 feet long. Most of them were 36 feet long. We needed 16 booms. We chained them together by boring a hole with two two-inch augers in each one. We left the camp early the next morning. We had to leave in a hurry, as there was barely any snow left on the roads for the sleighs.

— John James Schreyer

A WEEK GOES BY and my girls and I are back in the big city again; this time to celebrate another very important occasion. Our dear friend Steve — the one who, among other things, joined my father and me on our canoeing adventure down the Brokenhead all those years ago — is retiring today, after 30 years in the Manitoba civil service, most of them as an analyst and speechwriter with, as he likes to say, the Dee-part-ment of Ay-gree-cul-cher. He follows this up with a farmer-like snap of his (imaginary) suspenders and the quip: "You want hogs? We got hogs! You want cows? We got cows! You want chickens?. . ."

My father and mother met Steve when he was assigned to drive my father around the province for official functions, when he first became premier back in 1969. Trouble was, Steve was a bad driver, but my father had discovered rather quickly that this young man knew everything there was to know about, well, almost anything, and in particular the things my father likes to know about; such as Manitoba geography, geology and anthropology. So my father ordered Steve into the back seat of the car and told him to start telling everything he knew. I find it reassuring to see that some things never change; whenever Steve is travelling with my parents, he is in the back seat.

Steve's imminent retirement is big news. The festivities are being kicked off today, with luncheon at the tony Winnipeg Winter Club, hosted by his colleagues from the office. Non-office friends, such as myself and my parents, have managed to get hold of invitations, and there is talk that none other than the minister of agriculture herself will be there to help mark the occasion, as busy as she is; having just been appointed deputy premier, in addition to resuming her post as minister of ay-gree-cul-cher, which she had held before the election.

On the way to the luncheon, my parents and I talk about the things we intend to do over the summer, and how things are going at the farm. My father is especially interested in how our vegetable garden is progressing. I think he is interested in making comparisons with his own garden, which, I must admit, seems to be doing better than my own. It's quite a bit drier on the farm, for one thing, but I also suspect my father has been cheating a little with the use of fertilizer and pesticides. Emi, Blaise, Emelyn and I checked out his vegetable patch when we drove in this morning from Beausejour, and while there are a couple of weeds, I can find no evidence of bugs. As for myself, I used the white powder once, but was put off by the whole thing — mask included. I swear I won't be using the stuff again, especially with my girls around. *We* are growing *organic*.

"I have a 'to do' list, but it's not getting done," I tell my parents. It's true; I put pen to paper last night and wrote down: Go to Stonewall to pick raspberries and rhubarb — make rhubarb cobbler; go to Oak Hammock Marsh — show Emi and Blaise the Canada Geese; find out where Great-uncle Anton and Great-aunt Catherine are buried; swimming lessons for Emi; check out Lake Manitoba; visit *everybody*. . . . It is a ridiculously long list.

"I want to see a fortune-teller," I add. I know it is an odd thing for my 'to do' list, and I am hoping my parents don't pooh-pooh the idea. I had seen a fortune-teller ten years ago, before I was off to Japan, and looking back I can see that she was spot-on in many ways, although at the time I was trying to puzzle it out. She knew I was off the next day to a place far away, and she said I wouldn't marry a Canadian. And the man she went on to describe was, in many uncanny ways, the one I married. Of course, now, as a mother, I want to see a clairvoyant because I want to get a glimpse of my future with my daughters. I want that elusive — impossible — assurance that their lives will unfold as I am hoping for; which means nothing in particular — just general health and happiness. Can't I know that? My husband, always the realist, however, was of a different mind. How would I feel if that assurance was not forthcoming, Darrel had wanted to know when I told him my idea over the phone.

"They don't tell you the bad news," was my reply — but later, by myself again, I had to admit he had a point.

In any case, it turns out my parents are not against the idea of my seeing a psychic. "I did that once in Winnipeg. Twice in my life," my father says from the passenger seat next to me.

The comment surprises me. I know about R. Ramakrishna Sarathy, the astro-palmist my father had encountered while on a trip to India. In fact, I had tried to contact the clairvoyant myself, after my father returned from that country puffed-up with the knowledge that he was going to live a long and healthy life (an excuse he would trot out whenever we asked him to quit smoking, which he finally did — cold turkey — three years ago). The reply to the letter I wrote explaining myself and asking for clues to my future came in the form of a delicate airmail letter and the request for my date of birth, which I eagerly and quickly supplied. After that — nothing. But who might my father have seen in Winnipeg? Is he or she still around?

"Dad's talking about Madame Red," my mother explains. "She was at the Metropolitan Hotel. That was a long time ago."

My father laughs. "I went to see her when I was an MLA. I was 23 at the time. When she started looking at my future, she seemed to get quite confused. She said to me 'I see a lot of paper. There is a lot of paper in your life. And animals — I see animals in your life. No, I see only one animal, but I am seeing it over and over —' "

"Did she say what kind of animal it was?" I interrupt him, laughing.

"She couldn't figure it out. It was a strange animal, apparently."

My father stops and I think that's the end of the story, but then he continues. "And when I became premier, I had to sign thousands of letters and memos. Rietta [my father's secretary] would bring in those big memorandum files, and pile them on my desk, every day. Letters, all kinds of letters, on Manitoba government letterhead — and every single one of them had a big buffalo on it." The bison, or the North American buffalo, is the official animal of the province of Manitoba.

By now we are all choked with laughter, just as we arrive at Steve's party. It is a lovely gathering, and we are entertained by Steve's colleagues, who are just as witty and erudite as the man himself, and I am starting to wonder if one needs to be this way to get a job in that particular dee-part-ment. I know there are many people, including myself, who are dying to say a few words to mark the occasion, and to show how much we care about the guest of honour. But this luncheon will not be stretched into the mid-afternoon. After Steve unwraps his gold watch and feigns surprise (he chose it himself), the speeches, and handshakes all around,

Steve and his colleagues head back to work. The truth is that these people are working hard dealing with several issues plaguing Manitoba's farmers this summer: drought, pestilence (hoppers), disease (BSE). In fact, Steve has mentioned to me that he will be staying on at work for several weeks after his official retirement date, because he is needed. Duty calls.

On the way back home, my mother and I think up ways to help Steve cope with the transition to retirement. My mother decides she is going to teach him how to cook, and I am thinking of ways I can surprise Steve by redecorating his flat, since I expect Steve will be spending more time there, in his next career as a screenwriter. When there is a lull in the conversation, my father tells us a story about his grandfather, whom he spent a lot of time with as a young boy. When my father was born, his grandfather was already 85 years old — and lived to the age of 100 — and in that busy farming household, it fell upon the youngest and the oldest to keep each other company, and out of trouble. My father tells us how his grandfather had a habit of leaving notes around the house. On one of these notes, he expressed wonderment as to why everyone was working so hard. But even Old Anton kept on working after he became too old and too weak for farm chores. He was the postmaster for the area until our farmhouse ceased being a post office, sometime during World War Two. His duties as postmaster meant that the farmhouse became the place to be on mail day; people came from all around — many on foot — to the farm on Fridays and lingered long, waiting for everyone to get their mail. Getting the mail was a major social event in that day. Apparently, this was a source of annoyance to his son John, my grandfather, who saw all these people milling about the farm and wondered why they had nothing better to do.

When I read this entry, I feel for my grandfather and Uncle George and Uncle Henry and all those men (and women, too, employed as cooks in these bush camps) out in the cold and the snow. But our work makes us who we are. When my Uncle George retired from farming and from his implement dealership, he started a meat-processing company. I had wondered, *why meat?* But after reading my grandfather's memoirs I believe I have an idea. Meat was important for life; there was no such thing as vegetarianism when you were trying to survive through a winter logging the bush. None of my uncles were ever afraid of hard work; all of them became successful — as farmer, businessman, soldier. In my Uncle Tony's case, he took over my grandfather's logging operation and from there became one of Manitoba's larger road-construction contractors. As for Uncle Henry, he chose to be fearless on foreign soil; in the battlefields of Europe and Korea, where he was gravely — almost fatally — wounded.

Uncle Leonard was just fearless, plain and simple. I guess that's just what happens when you know you're the strongest person around: tough on the outside; soft as mush on the inside — like my youngest daughter, Blaise.

At the end of the day I am back at the farm. As I carry Blaise up past the rickety second step, with Emi in tow, I vow that I am going to show them the example of all my grandparents and aunts and uncles. For one thing, I am ready to get back to work in the garden with a new attitude, inspired by the fighting spirit in all of them.

CHAPTER 18

Legacy

WE GOT HOME FROM THE BUSH on the 1st of March, 1938. We rested the horses, and we too took a rest, but not for long, as seeding started early that year. It was March 28th, the earliest that I could remember that we ever planted our wheat. But later we got a heavy snowstorm and wet weather that lasted for four weeks. The oats and barley were seeded late that spring. It was a wet spring and a wet summer. It was during the latter part of July that George and I and the neighbour hired a boat and went to see if the boom was still there as the river rose quite a few feet. We had about 500 logs in the boom, the others were on the bank. Everything was still there, but going back, the rapids just about broke our boat in two. We left the boom until September 25th, at which time the water was down and there were no rapids. We brought the boom to the sawmill by water, and had it sawed up in the next two days. Our total lumber from those logs was 51,000 board feet.

Our winter operation for 1938 started by building a camp and barns for about 20 men and ten teams of horses. We made an agreement with the Garson Store for hauling out 9000 cords of poplar at 50 cents a cord. It was seasoned poplar and we had two teams of our own and hired 11 more teams and men. We hauled out 7500 cords and had to stop as our agreement ran out; the other party ran out of funds and could not pay. We terminated our hauling on February 15th, 1939 and were home and rested until seeding time. Seeding started around April 25th and it was a fair crop. The wheat was well filled; a No. 2 and No. 3 Northern. The barley and oats were good, too.

War broke out, and a man could hardly bring himself to plan farm or bush work. It was hard to concentrate. Our winter work in 1939 was on the Bird River at Rosseau Camp. It started in the fall, as soon as we were through ploughing. We started around October 28th. We had six teams and we drove them with the trailer down to Bird River the first day. We hired a truck and semi-trailer to haul out hay, oats, sleighs, and other camp equipment. We had to unload it all later, as we couldn't get it to the camp. We had to get a smaller truck to bring the hay, oats and equipment to the river, as the river was not frozen. But to bring it to the river – there were two boys who had a ton truck with a rack on and we loaded half the bales and some oats – the road was so narrow and twisted that the bales and bags hung on to the trees and we had to stay overnight in the bush. We broke through the bridge and the next morning we lost the crank and had to go to Bird River to see if the blacksmith could make a crank, which he did. By that time, I and the men were hungry, as George had taken the food across the river with the trailer and we had had nothing to eat for 24 hours. We went to a settler and asked for something to eat. She gave us a cup of coffee and a butter sandwich and charged me two dollars for four sandwiches and four cups of coffee, which was a lot of money at that time.

We then walked back to the truck and got it out of the creek and brought in the load to the river, unloaded it, and drove back for the balance of the hay and oats. We had the same problem with the trees pulling our bales and oat bags off and spilling them so that it took us all day long until dark. I still had to unload the hay and oats. George sent a man with the trailer to drive us back to camp, which was about six miles. I sent Henry across the river to stay with the man and to tell him to wait for me. I helped the men to unload and paid them two dollars for all their work, which was little enough. By the time I looked for the horses, men and trailer, they were gone back to the camp. I was tired and hungry and it was dark. I had nothing to defend myself with, so I borrowed a hatchet from a settler and started walking. I walked about a quarter of a mile when I sensed that something was following me. I guessed it was a deer, as it was afraid of the wolves. They were with me all the way; kept howling all the time. So I stopped when I got to an old slab pile. I made some kindling and then lit the pile and sat down to rest and smoke a cigarette. When I got up to go again, I glanced into the bush and noticed that there were small lights like candles. They were only visible once in a while and it was getting too dark to walk, so I picked up two pieces of slab and held them together and had a light and could see where to walk and that's how I got to the camp. This also helped to keep the wolves at bay.

As I was walking, I was thinking of what I was going to do to the boys if and when I got to the camp, but when I got there they were still waiting for me, and had my supper kept warm for me, and I could think of nothing better to do but eat as I was very hungry so I forgot everything.

It took us two days to build camp and barn. We started swamping out eight-foot logs for railway ties after we had the barn built, so I left George in charge of the men and I left for home to get some meat for the men. I butchered a hog and also a steer. I took my daughter with me, as I wanted her to cook for us that winter at camp. We got a ride in a car, starting early. But we had to leave the car at the river and walked the next eight miles. We arrived at camp at 11 o'clock in the evening. All the next month, November and up until December 20th, we hauled out 5000 cords of pulpwood and skidded out more than 3000 ties. We finished our work by December 20th and were home for Christmas. After Christmas and New Year 1940, we drove to get some firewood from bushes not far from home. We hauled our wheat, and the wheat price was a lot better as the war was changing food markets and prices.

We had a good crop in 1940, and we had good weather for our harvest. This same fall we again started our bush operation on Bird River and with the same man, Rosseau. There were four teams less and we had more work. We hauled out 1020 cords of pulpwood and 10,100 ties; got 65 cents a cord and 6 cents per tie. We started work on December 17th, 1940 and got through with the skidding of ties and hauling of wood by the February 10th, 1941. We did not draw very much money while we were working, only for mitts and socks. We left most of the money to be sent to the bank at Beausejour. We were notified by the bank that there was $1300 in the account. The bank manager could not believe that in these hard times there was so much money around. That winter was the hardest for me as I did most of the hauling myself. That same year we got an afterpayment for wheat, to the extent of 90 cents per bushel. The Dirty Thirties had come to an end in more ways than one.

Now we could build a new barn, buy a new tractor, and complete the changes from horses to modern farming.

— John James Schreyer

SUMMER IS DEFINITELY HERE in Manitoba, and thanks to a brochure from Travel Manitoba I have set my girls firmly upon a weekend treadmill of fun things to do and places to see. It's a great diversion from the weeding. The girls love puttering around the farm; even hoeing up weeds and making piles of them at the end of each row is a game for them, but in my rigid, goal-oriented mindset, those weeds represent something not going to plan. I am glad to focus on something other than my lacklustre gardening skills.

Canada Day is coming up next week. It falls on a Tuesday this year, but it is Friday today and already people — and towns — are starting to celebrate. After lunch, we head off to Lac du Bonnet to participate in some of their early Canada Day festivities. My Travel Manitoba brochure lists every summertime country fair from Churchill to the International Peace Gardens, and we intend to see as many as we can. My girls love these small-town fairs, which are so different from the overblown, overcrowded theme parks that are a city-dwelling child's only comparable form of entertainment. I love the fact that my girls can have fun in a petting zoo, get their face painted, and ride on trains made from old oil barrels, but it is the bake sales that most interest me. In Lac du Bonnet today, I am overjoyed to come across a table laden with homemade fruit pies, and I buy one each of apple and rhubarb for dinner. It is raining on and off, and in between sunny patches, when my girls are on the midway rides, we retreat under the awnings around the games of skill and chance. By the end of the afternoon, both Emi and Blaise are dripping with glittery plastic necklaces and fluorescent feathers, won by Aunty Emelyn and myself.

Grandma and Grandpa are coming for dinner again, along with the soon-to-be retired Steve. We greet them in the drive as their car approaches, and lead them to the garden — rather mucky today — for inspection. In fact, it has been raining quite a bit this week, which has put our hoeing on hold. And it shows; the garden does not have the green-and-black striped look to it, but is more a blanket of green blotches covering a black background. Our guests inspect the garden thoughtfully, not saying much. I am doing most of the talking. I make excuses for my absent carrots and Chinese cabbage, and the corn — which I thought was doing well but now, after having compared it to a few of the neighbouring gardens — seems rather weak-looking. But I quickly direct the guests' attention to our potatoes, peas, beans, and prized onions. At least they are all looking impressive   a few holes in the bean leaves notwithstanding. We talk about gardening in general, and I tell them how nice the neighbour's garden is up the road towards Ladywood, and that I see a man in that garden every time I drive by. The last time, I had felt compelled to honk, and he stood up and waved at us. I have no idea who the man is, but my father does. "Oh yes, they've always had a nice garden," he says. For the last 50 years or so, I'll bet. I console myself with the thought that the man is probably cheating with chemicals.

The rest of the weekend is taken up with trips to Grand Beach; and to Birds Hill Park, which is hosting a festival called Bison Days. After a swim in the man-made lake at Birds Hill Park, Emelyn and I have fun taking the girls on a horse-drawn hay ride and making Indian bannock on skewers. As Emelyn keeps the girls at a safe distance, I am coached in the art of spear-throwing, and the girls clap at my attempts. Then it is Emelyn's turn, and I take pictures of her in action for her scrapbook. Soon the girls are so worn out they fall asleep in the shade of a tree, and I am able to enjoy a peaceful moment watching them curled together on the blanket. Having a child was the best thing I ever did — until I had the second one. Watching Emi and Blaise interact, I have at times been awed by acts of the purest, tender love — while, at other times, their actions have had me convinced that sibling rivalry is an inborn, animal instinct. At this moment though, watching them sleep, all is bliss.

*   *   *

Canada Day has arrived. By a quirk of history, it is also Hong Kong's comparable day with the rather bureaucratic-sounding — not to mention long-winded! — title of 'Hong Kong Special Administrative Region Establishment Day'. Once you've said all that, there's hardly time left to celebrate, so I am glad we're in Canada this year. Blaise wakes up first, and from her cold bed on the floor, she rouses me with a plaintive cry, followed by 'um-um-um', which is, strictly speaking, a call for her pacifier, lost somewhere in her blankets; but which really means, "Hey, why am I here alone? I'm cold and hungry and lonely. The nerve!" Half asleep, I reach over and hoist her into my bed, making sure that she is tucked safely in the crook of my arm, since she is on the outside edge of the bed. I need to be in the middle, the barrier between my two semi-sleepy girls, who will otherwise sense each other's presence and wake up ready for fun. I am still too tired to start the day, and I hope that the sleep-inducing warmth of Mama and a fluffy comforter will outweigh Blaise's hunger and her desire to start the day. I feel Blaise's body relax and lay still, and just as it does I feel a stirring at my back. Emi is waking up now. I look at the clock and sigh. Canada Day is going to start at 5:48 in the morning this year.

"Mama," I hear. "Mama?"

"Yes, sweetie?"

"Is Dada coming back today?"

The question throws me off. That won't be happening for another three weeks or so. "No, sweetie, but today is a special day. We're going to a birthday party."

"Whose birthday is it?"

"It's Canada's birthday," I whisper over my shoulder. I feel a hand grab it and pull, and then my chin. My body is being twisted 180 degrees. With my neck stretched at an unnatural angle, I can see that Emi is sitting up on her knees behind me. She is looking down into my face.

"Canada's? Canada doesn't have a birthday!" Emi is smiling, but I know I am being admonished.

"Shhh," I say, quietly. And then I make the big mistake: "Yes, Emi. Canada *does* have a birthday. It's today."

"No!" Emi cries out. "Canada's *doesn't* have a birthday! Canada is not a . . . *people!*"

My eyes flit to Blaise. I hold my breath, waiting for her eyes to open. Nothing happens. I slowly let out my breath in relief and am ready to turn my attention back to Emi. In that moment, I feel the two chubby legs at my left side rise up and kick off the comforter. The eyes fly open, and are staring straight at me. A big grin. I melt and smile back. "Good morning, Blaisey-Daisey. Happy day!" says Emi, her usual morning greeting to her sister. That does it; I am energized once again.

I get up and lift my two girls so they are seated together in the middle of the bed. On my knees in front of them I begin to sing: *Happy birthday to you. Happy birthday to you. Happy birthday Dear Canada. Happy birthday to you,* and point at my girls when I say 'you'. I ask them to sing with me, and Emi happily obliges, while Blaise keeps time with her arms, bouncing herself on the fluffy bed. I realize that I should really be pointing to myself; after all, I am, technically, the only Canadian in this bed. My Hong Kong-born daughters have British passports, a concession I made quite readily when my husband broached the subject, within minutes of Emi's birth. In spite of a drug-induced haze — or perhaps because of it — I came to the conclusion that the advantages of having a British passport, allowing unfettered access to job opportunities in the whole of the European Economic Union, outweighed the advantages of a Canadian passport. But now my head is clear, and I am not so sure. Getting them Canadian citizenship has been on my 'to do' list for some time now.

We have a busy day planned. After stopping by to see Grandma and Grandpa (and sneaking some of Grandpa's bacon while we're at it) we head off to Lower Fort Garry. It's Open Day, and there will be a lot of things going on to amuse little children. The grounds are spacious, grassy, and inviting; families are milling about between the museum building and the original fort site; some are barbecuing their lunches already, or simply lounging on blankets. Green space everywhere, and the Red River meandering lazily next to us. A cool breeze and a warm summer sun. I try to think of a setting in Hong Kong as lovely as this is at this moment; fresh, relaxing, invigorating, peaceful — educational, even. Do Manitobans really know how much they have?

We walk into the crowded museum, and are greeted by an enormous Canada Flag birthday cake. It looks so perfect that I feel strangely compelled to take a photo, and as I do, through the camera's viewfinder I can see a hand reaching for the bottom-right corner of the cake. I gasp, and reach out blindly with my free hand, the camera still fixed in front of my face. I was right; the hand was Blaise's. Through the viewfinder I am watching my hand pull her chubby fingers away from the cake. Blaise is indignant for not being allowed to make her mark in such an irresistibly pristine thing, and proceeds to throw a tantrum. I can hardly blame her.

I scoop up her flailing arms and legs and head outdoors, to a green grassy space where Scottish dancers are preparing to entertain. Emi spies the women in sleek white dresses and the men in kilts and runs toward them. We find a shady spot under a nearby tree and settle down to watch them dance. Emi, a dancer herself, is watching with rapt attention.

After the dancing, we head over to the original site of Lower Fort Garry, to the 'Great House', where the governors of the Red River settlement once lived. There are some guitar players sitting on the front porch, and people milling around on the front lawn. The staff, dressed in period costume, are standing by the door. I snap a photo of my girls sitting on the steps by them. I would have liked to tell my daughters that I once lived in that house, too, when I was a teenager, and when their Grandpa was governor general of Canada; my father had had the intriguing idea of living at Lower Fort Garry for two weeks during our usual summer stay in Manitoba. I wonder if my daughters would believe me if I tell them. I tell Emelyn instead and she looks dubious.

As we follow along for the guided tour through the house, the rooms cordoned off to prevent the tourists from getting too close to things, I try to remember the experience of living in this place. I remember the room I slept in, and look now at the bed; it is a pile of straw about two feet high. They must have given me a regular mattress when I slept there, I tell myself. Things are getting harder for me to remember, but I do recall having to get up early enough to get my own things out of the way before the first visitors came through on the guided tour. The basement of the Great House had been modestly upgraded for our arrival, in order to fit in a serviceable kitchen. I do remember how hot it would get down there — and feeling sorry for the cook. Some administrative space was set aside there as well, for the aides-de-camp and other administrative staff who are a part of the entourage of any governor general, and I seem to recall that I spent a lot of time swatting flies and joking around with the aides-de-camp, who were not too happy with their new office situation. At one point, we also had held an open house, and my family, like the rest of the staff of this living museum, dressed up in period costume from Parks Canada. Mine was a floor-length pink dress with multi-layered skirt and black trim. It fit me well and I liked it.

We exit the house and make our way to the front again, where the governor and his wife introduce themselves to the small crowd. He asks those sitting on the grass to stand up. We are going to take a reaffirmation of the citizenship oath. Upon seeing the others stand up, Emi gets to her feet and helps her little sister to do the same. I repeat the oath along with the rest of the crowd, and then everyone is singing the national anthem. I look at my daughters and both of them are standing straight and tall, arms at their sides. They seem to know, at their young age, that something special is happening and they must pay respectful attention. I am almost embarrassed by how I feel; there are tears stinging my eyes. I feel like I want to put my hand over my heart like the Americans do, but Canadians are known to disparage such public displays of patriotism, aren't we? Perhaps it's one way we can be different from our southern neighbours. Well, having not been in my country for so long, I think it is a pity.

Afterwards, the governor and his wife hand out parchments with the oath of citizenship, and I take one and show it to my girls. "Look, Emi. Look Blaise, at what we've got. This is the Oath of Canada. This is what we said." They look at the paper, but I don't know what they are thinking. They are only three-and-a-half and 17 months, after all. I smile and tuck it away in my bag. Maybe one day they will become Canadian. And then I decide that getting them Canadian passports is going to go right to the top on my 'to do' list when I get back to Hong Kong. Still, I know that the paperwork is not what that makes one Canadian; I know my daughters are feeling Canadian now. My motherly mission is paying off. When my children grow up, they will have to choose where they want to live, and I am glad to be able to provide them with the option of coming to Canada.

Freedom to choose. I know that's why my great-grandparents came to Canada, and all the people that came here with them over one hundred years ago — as Robert Stead said: *coming from the land of 'May I' to the land of 'I will'*. But it didn't come cheaply. They paid for their freedom of choice with a lifetime of sweat and blood, and we are reaping the reward. I am hoping my girls are drawn to Canada, but maybe they will go to England — or stay in Hong Kong, a place which I know my girls see as their home, and which I have grown to love as much as Canada. It is, after all, the place I came to for much the same reasons my forebears came to Canada; for a chance to start new and make my own way in the world. And I am so pleased with my choice. Coming to Hong Kong gave me what I have now; my family. As for where my daughters end up, it won't be my choice to make. Maybe they will someday have a Hong Kong passport with the word 'Chinese' appearing in the place marked 'Nationality'. The wheels turn slowly in China, but they are turning nonetheless. Hong Kong is a place of immigrants, just as Canada is. When I read the story in the newspaper about the young Indian girl, born in Hong Kong, who became the first non-ethnic-Chinese to receive a Hong Kong passport with the word 'Chinese' indicating her nationality, my breath caught and my mind soared. What a blessing it is to live in a place where you can be anything you want to be; where being different means no difference at all.

For my great-grandfather a hundred years ago, to be anything you wanted to be meant self-employed farmer instead of indentured serf. For my daughters, it will mean being a CEO instead of the secretary; or being a prime minister, when their great-grandmother had to fight for the right to vote — or even to be considered a person. Or being Canadian or British — or even Chinese. If my daughters really work at their Cantonese and Putonghua, there is no reason they cannot become the chief executive of Hong Kong; after all, Adrienne Clarkson was born in Hong Kong, too — and she became governor general of Canada! What a blessing is the freedom to choose and to try.

CHAPTER 19

Sons and daughters

THE SPRING OF 1941 we planted about 250 acres of wheat, 120 acres of barley and 60 acres of oats. We had 200 acres of our own and rented 400 acres from several neighbours. We summerfallowed about 180 acres. We bought a new John Deere tractor and a used 28-cylinder Minneapolis Minnesota Separator, or thresher. We had four other farmers' crops to thresh. We started on August 13th. We finished all our wheat then started threshing for our neighbour. We threshed about 2000 bushels of wheat and 3000 of oats, then wet weather set in. It was so wet we could not drive on the fields. We kept going from one farmer to another, threshed a few bushels wherever we could haul the sheaves to the thresher. It took us about two months. We threshed the last when we got a frost so we could drive in the field. We did not do any fieldwork that fall, as it was too wet. At the same time, Henry joined the army and George was conscripted, so I went to see the chairman of the selection service board and told him that one of my sons had already joined the army and that I needed one of them to help me on the farm, but he still insisted that the one that joined probably would stay home. I told him that Henry was under age and would take him out of the army. He then agreed to postpone the calling of George till 1944.

Our 1941 pulp operation started the first week in December. There were no other teams, just our two. We hired two men, and I started hauling pulp with one, then drove home and got Tony and one of the men to take my job, as I had work at home. This time we boarded with the contractor and got seven cents for skidding ties and 75 cents for swamping wood. That operation, they swamped out 1500 cords of pulp and 1000 ties were skidded, and were through March 19th, 1942. One day, while they were working in the bush, they found a bear sleeping by a waterfall. He had made himself a nice bed of hay. They let him sleep until Groundhog Day to see if he got up. When they came to see what happened he lay the opposite way. He had turned around. But they did not let him sleep. They had two rifles and made bear meat out of him. They took him to their camp, skinned him, and made a rug. They also melted some fat for harness oil. I have never seen anything that fat. They cut a hole with a jackknife on the ribs and he had about two inches of lard.

Seeding that spring was very slow and all the land had to be either ploughed or cultivated, and it was still wet and muddy from the fall before. We attached oak cleats to the rear wheels. These kept the wheels clean from mud so that the wheels had traction. We worked from early morning until late at night every day and seeded about 400 acres of wheat and barley. We had a fair crop of wheat that year and the barley was very good. Our barley averaged 50 bushels to the acre. We had a fair crop and the price was good, too, as there was a demand for all grain. We ploughed our fields and cultivated all of the sum- merfallow and were ready for the bush again beginning in November 1942. We again worked at the same place and with the same contractor. This was our last winter operation with S. Rosseau and also for him. He stopped contracting after that year.

That winter we skidded out 5000 ties and 500 cords of pulp. I got another man to help Tony skid ties, as George and I were away for 10 days to cut logs and haul them to the sawmill. We cut poplar logs. When cut into lumber it was about 14,000 feet of lumber. George cut the trees down and cut them into 12-foot lengths, and I had a two-mile haul up to the mill. After that we went back to haul pulp. Our man had to go home, so we had to bring in son No. 4, Leonard. He was always so strong and wanted to be in the bush so he got his chance. He was still going to school. He was in the bush for about two weeks at which time the other two boys did not need him there, and he was glad to get home.

He had quite an experience in the bush. He was working with George skidding ties. At the end of the day, they would pick up the hay the horses left and wrap the blanket around it and also the lunch pail and put them on the horse's back, mostly on the quiet horse. But this time they put it on the bronco's back. When Leonard got on to ride him, he picked up one rein and before he could grab the other, the horse was gone, with Leonard and the lunch pail beating against his ribs. All George could do was tell him to hang on. There was about three miles of bush road. By the time George came back with the other horse, there was no horse and no rider. When he looked into the barn to put his horse there, the bronco was eating as if he had never seen hay for a week and was still shivering. He was not cold, he was scared. When he got to camp Leonard was sitting on the bunk and he too was shivering; not cold, just scared.

We finished our operation on about March 1st, 1943 and rested our horses and got everything repaired for spring work.

— John James Schreyer

I HAVE TO LAUGH out loud when I read this entry. I can't imagine Uncle Leonard being scared. He is the tough one of the family — just like my Blaise. Although six years separate my father and Leonard, this brother was the closest in age, and they seem to spend a lot of time together even now. My father has a lot of stories to tell about how he was always seeming to get on this particular older brother's nerves. Fortunately for my father, it seemed that Leonard was always prevented from seeking revenge on his pesky little brother by the sudden appearance of another older brother or a sister — or their father, who would settle the score with the oft-heard 'Leo-NAAAARD'. My father heard this so often he can do a good impression of it — and likes to, judging by the number of times I have heard it so far this summer. I can hear it now: 'Leo-NAAAARD!' followed by my father's boyish laughter. My father was well-protected from Leonard, and he knew it. Because of this, a certain pattern of behaviour evolved between the two boys that exists to this day.

My father still likes to antagonize Leonard, but these days the torment is more or less relegated to the golf course. When my husband Darrel returns from a golf game with the two of them, he will invariably have a wide smile on his face, and tell me in hushed tones about how Leonard was, as usual, keeping diligent score, while my father was secretly (or so he thought) playing two balls. My father would win the game and the competitive Leonard would, grudgingly, accept his defeat at the hands of his little brother. And little brother would find other ways to antagonize: a loud noise — such as that of a golf bag falling to the ground — just as Uncle Leonard was swinging the club — for example. More than one relative has remarked how my father seems to take on the little brother persona in the company of my Uncle Leonard.

I love having a big, extended family. When Darrel was first introduced to the family at a gathering in Canada before we got married, I got a kick out of how he was able to spot the uncles. George, Henry, Leonard — he got them all. He was even able to spot of few of the male cousins, too. They all look alike, but in different ways: Henry and my father have the same eyes, from their father; George and my father, the same gentleness of face, and smile, from their mother; and with Leonard, there is an obvious connection but I can't put my finger on it. Swagger, maybe?

*   *   *

Today I am taking Emi to the other side of the Red River, for another big family gathering: Christy's wedding shower. We stop at my parents' house on the way to fetch my mother, and I decide to ask my father about his brothers, and how they got along. From my own experiences, and from watching my two girls, maintaining a harmonious sibling relationship is something that gives me increasing concern.

"Did you have any — you know, sibling rivalry?" I ask my father, when I find him in his garage. He is doing something to his lawnmower.

My father looks up from his task, and I notice that he does not seem surprised by the question, which has really come out of nowhere. "There wasn't much of that growing up — at least as far as I am aware," he says. "Don't forget, when I was a pre-schooler, the rest of my brothers and my sister were already in their teens, away working summer and winter, as though they were adults. Except for Leonard."

Hmm. Sounds like an honest answer, and not the least bit damaging. "Who's your favourite brother?" I want to know.

My father laughs a little, as if to tell me that I have asked an odd question. There is a pause, but only a short one, before my father indulges me anyway with an answer. "George is the kindest," he says. He doesn't need to think long about it. I know he looks up to his eldest brother.

"But who do you *like* the best." A pointed question, not a fair one, I know. But my father is used to this kind of thing from me — which is not to say he approves of it.

He obliges nonetheless. "Well, I suppose I see Leonard the most," he says, by way of response. I understand that: all those golf games — and foursomes of cribbage and whist with their wives.

"Who was Grandma's favourite?"

"Henry," he answers, also without hesitation. Our war hero. The restless one. That a mother would feel something extra for the troubled one is a common pattern, I think.

There was Tony, the handsome one, with the white-blond hair that set him apart from the rest of his siblings. His grandfather Anton's favourite. He was the athlete, too, blessed with the grace and coordination, rather than brute strength. He took me to Winnipeg Jets hockey games when I was a kid, and played hockey himself. It was acknowledged that he was in the best shape for his years — all the more cruel, perhaps, that his vigour, along with his mind, would be taken from him at an improbably young age by Alzheimer's.

Of course, there is Eleanor, the daughter her parents were so thankful to have. I know that there had been a girl born before her, Rosalie, who died in infancy, but my father only told me once — the simple fact of her birth and death and brief existence. It wasn't something I had learned from my grandparents — not even from my grandfather's memoirs. For them, the pain of losing a daughter had been too unbearable to want to even remember. As gruff as he may have seemed — as men of his time and place usually did — my grandfather had a soft spot for little girls. Even I sensed that as a child. I have a fond memory of my grandfather telling my sister and I in no uncertain terms that we were the boss when it came to dealing with 'the boys'. I don't even think I was ten years old at the time. That was the closest thing to a girl-power (or a birds-and-bees) conversation that either of us ever received from any of our grandparents.

And how does my father fit into this scheme of things? Well, he is the baby, and as most babies are, he was the coddled one. Or perhaps it was just that he was simply too young to have had to spend time in the bush. He just missed out on that era. Instead, by dint of his time of birth, his labours went towards academic pursuits instead of a life on the land. My father tells how his oldest brother got a raw deal; how his aptitude and personality was suited for a life of intellectual endeavour, not only the hard life of a farmer and logger. But the arbitrariness of birth order didn't stop this brother from being involved in education; Uncle George was a school trustee in the Selkirk region of Manitoba for 50 years. He had found a way to his passion — or one of his passions, anyway; just as my father had found a way to be close to the land, as a premier and as an energy minister, too. These days, my father continues to be close to the land through a variety of civic organisations, such as by being a board member of the newly-formed Lake Winnipeg Stewardship Committee, the Sierra Club, Habitat for Humanity — and by tending his own vegetables (he does not attempt to compete with Leonard when it comes to the garden). I look at the brothers and the sister and see no rivalry, just a total pride in each other for who they are — and who they are to each other; brothers and sister more than anything else.

It is fascinating, and sometimes — as in the case with Uncle Leonard — hilarious to see how these siblings interact. I hope my two girls can grow up to be like their grandpa is, with his sister and brothers, and I think it is one of the biggest parts of my mission to try to guide them along this path; to make them see that they are each others' best friends. So close in age, I wonder how I will be able to help them resist the rivalry. I can see it is already here; when I find myself trying to hoist a 14-kilogram girl in each arm, both scrambling for purchase somewhere — anywhere — on their mother's limbs. I smile every time I find myself struggling under the load of their vying for my attention; their emerging personalities seeking room to grow, separate from the one person they are almost always with. Ultimately though, whether or not they are friends in adulthood will be their choice.

I hope I can tell this to my cousin, someday, I think to myself, as Emi and my mother and I head to Cousin Christy's bridal shower. But I suppose, right now, she needs advice on coping with culture shock — as regards both marriage and Japan. In a couple of weeks' time she will get married and move to Japan to teach English. (As it turns out, after the wedding, both bride and groom returned to their parental homes laid low by pneumonia, recovering just in time to catch their flight to Japan — and how's *that* for a wedding story!) When it is time to give gifts to the bride-to-be, I present her with my old Japanese-English dictionary, confident that it will be the best, most useful gift she will receive — despite the raised eyebrows of some of the older women in the room.

And at this bridal shower, some other, wonderful news is shared; Cousin Penni, the daughter of my Cousin Bev (the eldest daughter of Uncle George), has just had a baby. A girl. And we will get to see them in August when they drive in from Calgary for the annual family-reunion golf tournament.

"Emi — a new baby in the family!" I say when we are told the news. I look down at my little girl and remind myself that, up to this moment, she and her sister represented the newest additions to the Schreyer family — the youngest of all of us, with all the special attention that comes along with that position. And now, my two girls, at the ages of three-and-a-half and 17 months, will have to give up the spotlight; not only for a new little baby girl, but to make way for the beginning of a whole new generation.

"Uncle George is now a great-grandfather," I say, but more to myself than to Emi. This fact astounds me. My Uncle George is a great-grandfather, but my own great-grandfather died more than 50 years ago.

But Emi does not understand the significance of this fact; she wants to know about the new little girl. "Where is she? Can I see her? Now?" she asks. Emi is excited. She is the picture of grace.

CHAPTER 20

Empty nest

IN 1945, AT OUR OPERATIONS and camp, we had our daughter
Eleanor as cook, and we had a couple named Reichert – just
married. He came to cut pulp and had nowhere to leave his
wife, so we asked him to bring her along. She helped Eleanor
as Cookie and we paid her wages. We finished that operation
around February 26th and then we all rested until seeding
time. Our daughter Eleanor worked hard all winter and I
promised her that when we got through with our winter work
we would go for a trip. So when Easter came we were invited
to Minneapolis, Minnesota by my brother who lives there, and
my daughter and I made the trip by train to that city.

George took us by car to the station in Winnipeg. He had
time to look around while we were gone. He was now 24 years
old and wanted to get married and settle on a farm. As he was
walking along Main Street, he noticed that there were notices
of farmland for sale. There was a place not far from the city,
about 12 miles out. He tried to get the exact location, but that
being Good Friday the office was closed. So when he got back
home, he told his mother that he had probably found a place
for himself, provided it would not be sold before Dad came
back. We were to stay a week at my brother's place, but I only
stayed three days as I had nothing to do and there was so much
to do at home.

I left Eleanor with them and I started for the train and home.
I started by train at five o'clock in the evening and arrived at
the Winnipeg station at 9:30 in the morning. I walked out of
the station and met a neighbour of mine and he was ready to
leave in 15 minutes for home, so by 11:30 I was at home.
Everybody was busy working around the barn and the house.

They could not believe that I was home already. Most happy was George. He told me all about that advertisement and by 1:30 we were back at the real estate office in Winnipeg.

The man at the office gave us the location of the place and told us that at present it was rented out and that there was a three-roomed house and a 20 x 30 foot granary and a small barn on it. We went out of the office, got in our car, and drove back the same road we came on. We came to the place and noticed that it was one of the old river lots in the St. Andrews district. It was three-and-a-half miles long, and about 800 feet wide. It started on Main Street, then in about ¼ mile the CP Railway runs through it, another ¾ mile Highway No. 8 runs through it, then in another ½ mile there's a big drain running through it, another 1¾ mile there's another big drain running though it – then there is another ¼ mile of land. We walked all the way around it. We had knee-length rubbers and, as it was spring, there was water after ½ mile all the way. However, we thought it was still a good buy at that price and drove back to Winnipeg the same day and gave the real estate man a deposit of $1,000 on the land. The owners were miners in Flin Flon.

In the meantime, the man that rented the land was anxious to buy it, too, and he offered them more money. I should have mentioned that there were 290 acres at $27.00 an acre; $7,830 and we were to pay half in cash and the balance in three equal payments, but they wanted cash up front and said that if we could pay them in cash they would consider dropping $1,000. We told them we would be glad to do that so the deal was for $6,830. We were given about three weeks to get the money ready. We borrowed about $3,000. When we came to close the deal, the mortgage company kept $40 for the paperwork so we were $40 short and we were only given three more hours to come up with all the money. We began to worry as it was too late to go back to Beausejour. As we talked this over we went to our automobile where my wife was waiting. She asked what the trouble was and when we told her she said that she had more than $40 and would let us have that amount. She had saved it as she was going to shop for clothes for the children, but said that we could give her the money when we got back to Beausejour. And that's how George got his farm and house.

As for my own farm, we wanted to build a new building every year starting in 1939. The old barn and house were old and leaning over and had to be torn down. We started with a granary. In 1940, we built a hog barn for about 30 hogs and a hen house for about 300 hens. In 1941, we tore down the old barn and built a big barn, which still is in good shape today as it was built right, and a new house in 1943 all with No. 1 Fir. Every 2x4, 2x6, 2x10 and all the boards were No. 1 Fir. It was eight rooms and a full basement.

At that time we needed a big house, as we had a large family. But in a few years they were all gone. We are left, the wife and I. We would have enough with four rooms. But it's good to have the space sometimes; when the sons come with their families there is room. In a small house they would have to stomp on each other's toes.

— John James Schreyer

WE'VE GOTTEN SOME MORE RAIN this week at the farm. Drizzly, dull days are not so much fun with two little kids in an old house, and Emelyn and I work overtime trying to keep them occupied: having a video machine helps. But I am glad that the garden is getting watered, and hopefully — I still have hope even though I know it is futile — those carrots and leeks, and the cabbage, will finally present themselves. In any event, the garden is too damp for hoeing, and the most popular activity; swimming at Grand Beach or the Pit by Ladywood, or mucking around in the Brokenhead River, does not have much appeal today. Instead, I decide we will explore the house. I want my girls to remember it, the way I do. Of course, our memories will be different — the house itself has changed considerably since I spent time here as a child. But I want them to have an image of every room, every interesting nook and space — even the scary ones — that will stay with them.

Someday this house will stand no longer. It is already 60 years old, and my father has been talking about having it moved off the premises; handing it over to the Beausejour-Brokenhead Museum, perhaps even turning it into a writer's retreat. I had been intrigued by the idea at first, although the longer I live in the house, the more I wish it could stay where it is. I think what I really am wishing for is that the house will exist for all time; that those fir two-by-fours and two-by-sixes will never weaken; that the breath of life will always keep this place warm. Over the summer, my girls and I have come across too many of the old, long-abandoned 'ghost houses' of the area and seen what fate may befall our farm. Not to this house, I hope. Not to our house.

As children, my oldest brother and sister and I would often spend time here during the summer. Our parents would drop us off and we had no idea where they went; it could have been an evening out, or a trip to a foreign country. They were pleasant times, but nothing too exciting: fun in the garden, with the dog, going to church; the usual quiet routine with grandparents on a farm. The kitchen was the heart of the house, where my grandmother felt most comfortable. Make no mistake, she could take charge in many places — not just the kitchen — and often did. Looking about the same kitchen today, I can see that so much has changed; the cabinetry, for one thing, is all different; a light brown woodgrain veneer, instead of the handmade doors with a thick, glossy paint the colour of cream that I remember. Even so, I walk over to the corner cupboard and open it, hoping to see the big newspaper clipping of the Dionne quintuplets that my grandmother had pasted to the inside of the door at least 50 years ago. Back then, I never knew who those five identical faces were, and I don't think I ever asked; I was familiar with my grandmother's penchant for clipping pictures of young children and pretty young women — Breck girls — from magazines and newspapers. It was only much later, years after my grandparents were no longer living in the house, that I discovered the identity of the five smiling faces and their unhappy lives; made wards of the state because they were identical quintuplets. I don't know if my grandmother had thought about their lives, or simply pasted their picture on the door because the happy faces appealed to her; but as I stare at the blank inside of the cabinet today, I miss them. I miss them all.

I carry both of my daughters into the living and we sit on the sofa, facing a disconnected cast-iron stove, something that Cousin Greg recently bought after having spent a fortune last winter on his electricity bill, trying to keep the place warm. "This is where your great-grandpa used to sit," I tell Emi and Blaise, pointing to the new cast-iron stove. "There was a big chair here when I was your age — the biggest chair in the world. Because Grandpa's daddy was a great big man — big and tall. He liked to sit in his chair at the end of a long day."

"Like the man on the stage," Emi adds knowingly, and I laugh, delighted and awed by her association with the lieutenant governor at the convocation ceremony in Brandon.

"Was he bigger than Grandpa?" she asks.

"Yes. *My* Grandpa was a big tall man. Bigger than *your* Grandpa," I reply. It comes out like familiar childhood repartee, although it is not at all what I had intended.

My grandfather was one of the biggest men I ever knew, with a push-broom moustache that suited him, and which my eldest cousin — Cousin Brian, son of Uncle George and the patriarch of my generation — has to handsome effect inherited. All my uncles are tall — my Aunt Eleanor, too. Some have the broad build that says power, some more graceful. My father was the shortest, apparently; Aunt Eleanor whispered this bit of information when she told it to me years ago, and had asked me not to repeat it. Even though my grandfather was larger than life, with his dark suit, and severe moustache — often wearing the ubiquitous black fedora of the day (I *never* saw him in a farmer's cap), I was not afraid of him. His grandchildren brought out his gentleness. He taught my brother and sister and me to play Go. He would draw the board himself with a pen on a piece of cardboard, and we would use coins for markers. I wonder if he ever knew the game is Chinese.

Perhaps there is one instance when my grandfather's strength scared me. He and I were standing outside the back door of his house one morning during a visit, and I noticed a bird on the grass in front of us. The bird looked injured; it was not attempting to fly off.

"Look Grandpa, a bird," I said with concern.

My grandfather saw the bird and moved in on it. I assumed he was going to make things better. "A sparrow," he said contemptuously. He picked up that broken bird and threw it. What I remember is that he threw it so hard the bird hit the barn door a hundred yards away. I was scared — and confused. I didn't understand then what a sparrow represented to farmers; a pest, a threat — like grasshoppers and other things.

I remember when my grandfather died. Not long after his funeral, various uncles, aunts and grandchildren came back to this house. I remember watching my grandmother hugging his big chair, crying disconsolately, and an aunt hugging her mother-in-law's heaving shoulders. For a moment I stare at the cast-iron stove, seeing through it. I see the big easy chair, and my grandfather filling it, sitting after dinner with me on his knee, while my grandmother is still bustling around in the kitchen. The feelings are so strong inside me that I feel I have brought him back to me, for a moment, and I struggle to hold onto it as Blaise and Emi both start to squirm in my arms. They are bored.

"Let's go upstairs," I whisper. "To the *secret room.*"

"What secret room?" asks Emi. She immediately stops wiggling and grabs my leg. She is all eyes and ears now.

"There is a *secret room* upstairs. I'll show you."

Both girls follow me, absorbed in our new mission, and as I open the door that leads to the stairway, they are doubly excited. I haven't allowed them upstairs yet, although once Blaise did get away on me and I found her, just two minutes later, looking down at me from between the railings on the second floor, with a grin that was both triumphant and mischievous. There is a tiny doorway at the top of these stairs that opens into the attic. It had been a place filled with boxes and interesting things when I came to visit as a girl, and I spent quite a bit of time in it playing hide-and-seek. But when I open the door this time we are hit with a waft of hot air, and I notice the walls are covered in pink insulation. It is not a useful attic anymore, no longer a serviceable secret hideaway. I turn to the girls, who look as disappointed as I feel.

"Never mind," I tell them cheerfully. I have to think fast. "I'll show you something else. Come this way." We walk past the alcove where my brother and sister and I used to sleep. It is now a walk-in closet for my cousin who, it appears, is a bit of a clotheshorse. We continue to the end, to the main bedroom, where my grandparents slept, and where Emelyn sleeps these days. It no longer has the enormous bed covered in my grandmother's homemade quilts that I remember; just a run-of-the-mill bed, nothing interesting or magical about it.

"Look," I tell my girls. I am pointing to the window with its northern exposure, excitement in my voice. The girls head to the window.

"What, Mummy?" Emi asks. Blaise, too, is looking at me expectantly. We are looking out at the barn.

"It's the barn, Emi. The *magic* barn. And the *garden,* too. The *magic garden,"* I am desperate. Emi looks at me and raises an eyebrow. Why did this house hold such magic for me as a youngster? The most interesting room, the summer kitchen just off the main kitchen, down the rickety stairs — and certainly my grandmother's favourite place, judging from the amount of time she spent in it — is now gone; moved next to the barn and now overgrown with grass. The bathroom, with its sink and tub marked red by rusty well-water, scares me as much now as it did back then. But I know the magic was there once and, I am starting to realize, it is here still. It's just that the performance has changed. I am the magician now — conjuring up the mysteries to be found. I see magic in the photos of my daughters standing in the growing wheat. I feel it when they are asleep in my arms in the bed downstairs. It's even in my daughter's raised eyebrow at this moment.

But perhaps these are my own feelings, and not my daughters'. We stare out the window, but all we can see is the dullness of the day, which is sapping our spirits, and my daughters' imaginations. There is one more place we can go, although I hesitate to take my girls there. In fact, I had avoided the place all this time. "Okay, there is one more secret place," I say, and I lead the girls down the cellar steps very slowly and carefully, not only because these ones, too, are rickety, but because I was never allowed down them as a girl. But the smell — that damp, musty, wet cement smell — that came up from the cellar and filled the summer kitchen where as a child I was allowed to stand and peer down into the darkness, is still there.

Emi is afraid. She is pulling back on my hand. Blaise, in my arms, is looking interested. I duck down at the bottom of the stairway and look into the dim cellar. I am surprised to see how clean it is; the floor has obviously been swept, there is little in the room but a pile of firewood and a stack of newspapers. So this is it, I think. No bogeyman man here after all. I guess that's all I need to know. "It's all right, Emi," I say. "It's just a room. Nothing scary." But she will not be convinced, and she pulls me back up the stairs.

*   *   *

The drizzle has lessened, and I decide to take the girls into Beausejour. First stop is the library for a read, and then we go to the playground at the town's elementary school, where Emi surprises us all with her strength in the arm hang, as she goes from bar to bar the entire length. I am very impressed. Emi and Blaise are a good match on the see-saw and they love it. (We don't seem to have those in Hong Kong.) Their giggles are infectious. We stop at the Co-op for some groceries and they have fun driving the shopping trolley that doubles as a truck (another thing I have never seen in Hong Kong). But Emi's mood turns sour when we head home. She wants ice cream, but it is not an ice cream kind of day, I have decided, rather arbitrarily. She is putting on a tantrum as good as I have ever seen and to put a stop to it, I do something I am always ashamed to do. I play upon her fear. The timing is right; we are just coming up to a 'ghost house'; this one just north of town and very tidy-looking; weather-worn but not tumble-down. I turn off the road onto the drive that is almost non-existent, and slip a CD into the player. It is my daughter's favourite singing duo, Scotty and Lulu. One of the songs is called *There's a Ghost in the House* and Emi always instructs me to pass it over. This time, however, I am playing it, and we inch our way closer to the ghost house in the car. Emi gets the picture and quiets down in a hurry.

The effect wears off as soon as we get home, however. Emi is stomping around the living room, and the whole house is reverberating with each footfall. "Shhhh! You'll wake up the monster!" I tell her.

She stops mid-step. "Where's the monster?" she asks. I look down at the floor in the corner of the living room, and motion my girls over. We peer down through the ornate iron grill to the basement. "Down there," I whisper. Emi, Blaise and I peer down, holding our collective breath.

"Tell the monster to go back to sleep," Emi instructs me. I obey.

That evening, we are playing together on the living room floor. I am hugging Emi in my lap. We are talking and laughing with each other, when I feel her stiffen suddenly.

"I see something dark go past on the floor," she says. I hear the anxiety in her voice.

"Oh? It's nothing," I say automatically. But I admit to myself that I thought I had also seen 'something dark' move across the floor yesterday. I had dismissed it at the time, not sure of what it was, if anything.

At that moment, the mysterious 'something dark' takes the opportunity to erase any doubt as to its presence. A mouse scurries straight across the room, inches from our blanket on the floor where Blaise and Emi and I are sitting. The little mouse heads to the wall by the windows, then makes a beeline for the sofa. Emi is clutching me around my neck, blocking my windpipe. I emit a strangled scream. Blaise has become airborne; in one fluid motion she goes from sitting next to us on the blanket, to clamouring to stay in my already-occupied arms. Emelyn comes running in.

"Did you see the mouse, Emelyn?" I ask, after loosening Emi's grip.

"Oh yes," she answers. She does not sound at all alarmed. "I feed it."

I am not sure I am hearing her correctly. "You *feed* it?"

Emelyn nods. "Yes. I feed it. I feed it rice."

"But — *why?*"

Emelyn looks at me as if I ought to know better. "I feed the mouse *so it won't bite Blaise.*"

I feel confused, but I decide that is as good a reason as anything I am likely to hear. And Emelyn's serene response to the rodent is making me feel like a scaredy-cat. "Okay," I tell her, then turn to Emi. "Never mind. It's just a mouse — like Maisy. Yeah, Emi, like Maisy Mouse. And Mickey, too." I can see Emi is brightening at the thought. She loosens her grip on my arms. She smiles. " What do you want to name it, Emi?" I am drawing on something I learned in parenting class: *Giving the child control over an unexpected situation will lessen any anxieties he/she may have.* As Emi thinks about a name, out of the corner of my eye I see the mouse moving stealthily from behind the sofa into the kitchen and, I hope, down the rickety second step and out the door, or to the basement — wherever it came from.

"Curly," says Emi, with a satisfied grin.

"Huh? What, Emi?" I have been distracted by the mouse; I don't know what Emi is talking about.

"We'll name it — Curly."

Later that night, as I carry the girls to bed, I reflect upon my feelings about this house — and my parenting methods. I'm not sure if introducing my girls to the monster sleeping in the basement was the right thing to do. But, between the monster in the basement and Curly the Mouse, there is certainly plenty of magic left within these walls — enough to last another generation, at least.

CHAPTER 21

Restlessness

GOING BACK TO THE SUMMER of 1945, we had a late spring, and we had a lot of rain. That spring, seeding time was about two weeks late. The wheat generally headed about June 25th; but that year it headed July 10th. Threshing was later, too, about two weeks. The crop was fair and the price was good. We had a hard time with the threshing, though; our stook teams were driven by young boys and girls. We helped them as much as we could. When they drove their loads to the separator, George, who was looking after the threshing outfit, mostly unloaded the sheaves for them. It was tiring for all of us, and we were glad when we got through the threshing that fall.

We were just finishing, it was the last day, when I delivered some wheat to the elevator. On the way, I went to the post office to get my mail. With it was a telegram from Henry, who was overseas in Europe during the war. The telegram said AM IN HALIFAX WILL BE HOME SOON. We were all happy, as we had not heard from him in a long time. I might mention that he was wounded by shrapnel in 1944, was at the hospital for three weeks and back to the front lines after that. I inquired when he would arrive in Winnipeg, and when he came with a trainload of soldiers we all went to meet him, even his grandmother, who was almost 90 years of age. She too was happy that he came home with all his limbs.

When he got home he was very restless and wanted to be on the move all the time. He was mostly home for the night, but during daytime was mostly in town, namely Beausejour. As winter came, we again started looking for winter work, and we contracted with a contractor named McIntosh. We were cutting pulp on Mile 8, close to the Point du Bois railway track.

As George was already married, I agreed to let him run the camp. I supplied the oats and the hay and the two boys, Tony and Leonard, who were strong and hard workers, even though they were just teenagers. We were to divide the profit 50/50, if any profit was made. I also told Henry to go to load car or cut pulp so as to get him to do something and lose that restlessness which was bothering him. He did go for a week to help the boys load pulp in the car. He came back for a few days, but then went back again to the bush and stayed till they finished that winter's pulp work, which was on March 10th, 1946.

In the spring of 1946, I told Henry to go to the Veterans' Land Board and get a farm for himself, as the government bought land for those who wanted to farm. I went with him. The board did not question him, as they knew that he was working with me. He got 120 acres, which was summerfallowed by the farmer whom they bought the land from. He seeded it all with wheat and got a fair crop out of it. He should have paid off more on the land, but he had 25 years to pay and was in no hurry. So he spent the money on something which he did not need. This happened in 1947. Later, there was a house and three lots for sale in Beausejour. In order to make better use of his money, I advised him to buy that house and the lots. He did, and paid $1500 for all, but still he would not settle down. He decided to go to British Columbia and wanted to sell the house and the lots, so I bought it all for $2,200 and gave him a $700 profit. The house did come in handy three years later, when my youngest son Edward moved into it at the age of 14 years, so he could attend high school in town.

Henry did not stay in British Columbia, and later had no money left. He had given up farming his land, so I worked it for him. I summerfallowed half the land and the next spring he rented the land to Tony and he again joined the army to fight in Korea. He was there for three months, mostly on patrol duty. The Koreans ambushed his patrol and practically wiped them out. Henry was badly wounded by rifle fire in the stomach and was also shot through the lungs. It took him quite a while to get better, but being young he did get healed. He came back to Beausejour, but never farmed again. I kept on working his land with young Edward's help and made sure that his payments on the farm were kept up to date.

– John James Schreyer

THERE IS DEFINITELY a streak of restlessness in the family. I inherited it. That restlessness is what had me begging my parents, at the age of 17, to let me loose in Europe. Upon graduating from high school (early; in January), I spent six months backpacking through Europe. I sometimes cringe at the situations I found myself in: sitting in the middle of a road on the edge of Florence, Italy, next to an old woman who lay dying after being hit by a truck; being accosted by perverts on the Paris Metro and at the gift shop in the Centre Georges Pompidou; having a rifle pointed at me by a zealous Albanian border guard, while I pretended to be an intrepid photojournalist and fearlessly (stupidly, I now think) continued to take photos across the border into that closed, mysterious country. These are just a few examples — the ones I think I told my parents about.

My father was against the idea of me roaming around Europe by myself, but he agreed that some time in Paris could help improve my French language skills. And so it was I lived with a French-Canadian family in Paris's Septième Arrondissement, a rather deluxe neighbourhood near the Seine, with Yves St. Laurent as our downstairs neighbour. The father of the household was employed at the Canadian Embassy, and I enjoyed exploring the city with the family, which included the couple's two children. They were most friendly, realizing that I was terribly homesick, although they probably never knew just how much. In those first few days I regretted begging for my freedom and wondering what I had gotten myself into. But returning home was not an option, and the discovery that homesickness eventually fades as wonderment takes over is one I'll not forget.

My French lessons at the Foyer International d'Accueil de Paris were in the mornings, which gave me the rest of the day to explore the incredible city, and I spent hours in art galleries, parks, and museums. I also spent an equal amount of time sampling the delicacies of French cuisine — or at least those that I could afford; basically eating my way through every *pâtisserie* and *charcuterie* between Montmartre and the Arc de Triomphe. After a couple of months, my expanding waistline told me that it was not safe to stay in Paris. My confidence as a traveller was also expanding, and I learned the ropes of the backpacking circuit. I moved farther afield; as far north as Helsinki, and as far south as Santorini, before it was time to head back to Canada to start university.

Restlessness has come over me again here in Manitoba — and the girls, too. We are heading for Neepawa, to the annual Lily Festival. Emi and Blaise are aware that Grandma is going to officially open it, and now, just as Emi helped Grandpa at the opening of the Witch's Hut at Kildonan Park, it is Blaise's turn to help Grandma. Blaise Lily is named after her grandmother (Lily), and the name is especially fitting today. Of course, this doesn't sit too well with Emi, and I placate her by telling her she can help her sister. I ask Emi to write Blaise's speech. But Emi is too clever for that; she reminds me that her little sister cannot talk. I laugh. Emi grimaces at me, aware that an attempt to trick her has just been foiled.

We are zooming down the Trans-Canada Highway; the opening of the Neepawa Lily Festival is in a couple of hours. Emi is in the car with her grandparents and Steve, and I follow behind with Emelyn and Blaise. I look at the car ahead of me and wonder if they are practising Grandma's speech. We arrive shortly before the opening at one o'clock, and my mother is a little unnerved by the surprisingly large crowd assembled under the marquee. To kick off the proceedings, some local young ladies are dancing; Irish jigs and Scottish flings, and, most incongruously, some contemporary dance — to Christmas music! Never mind; Emi is spell-bound by the vision, and disappointed when the dancing stops so the speeches can begin.

Emi listens with the rest of the crowd as her grandmother talks about her granddaughters, about her flowers, and how therapeutic gardening is to her. She has the crowd laughing by explaining how opening the Neepawa Lily Festival had been a dream of hers for years, and how disappointed she was when, each year, the festival would come and go without an invitation to open it. And how this year, however, her daughter (that's me) had phoned the organizers and asked if she could attend, tired as I was of her complaining. The first part is true. I know I had taken great liberties, but sometimes you just have to make things happen; like getting married and having children, even if you're afraid of what you don't know. Or, in this case, giving a speech, even if you are nervous about public speaking — because you want give something back to the flowers.

Hang on, Emi. Hang on, Blaise. It's almost time. If your grandmother professes to be afraid of public speaking, she sure is enjoying it, if length is any indication. Emelyn and I have our hands full trying to keep the girls' restlessness under control. Finally, the ribbon-cutting ceremony has arrived. The emcee announces that the two granddaughters will be joining their grandmother on stage. Emi knows this is her cue, and she insists on leading her toddling little sister up the stairs all by herself. I hang back in my seat and watch, worried, but they clear the stairs without incident. I vault onto the stage later when I realize that my mother is not going to be able to cut the ribbon, guide Emi with the scissors, and hold the chunky Blaise Lily all at the same time. I hold Blaise in the same football-like grip that I saw Emelyn use before, and guide her hand to rest on her grandmother's. Emi is standing in front of all of us, and she pulls her grandmother's hand down so she, too, can get a hold of the scissors. We are ready for our photo-op.

"I declare the Neepawa Lily Festival officially open," I hear my mother say. I see three hands holding the scissors, and then watch a pink ribbon waft gracefully to the floor. Applause. Emi is looking up at Grandma, and then at me, her face is full of pride. Blaise is kicking. She wants out of the indignity of the football grip, and I am quick to grant it to her. Mission accomplished.

But, actually, there's one more thing I feel compelled to do. The opportunity has presented itself, and I'm going to take it! I make my way to another speech-giver, Inky Mark, the member of parliament for this area. I am dying to know how he got his name. I have seen it before — not in *Hansard* (I don't read it), but in one of my daughters' favourite children's rhyme books, *Round is a Mooncake*:

> Square is a checkerboard in the park
> Square is my name chop's inky mark

A name chop is a special stamp everyone in China and Japan once had, and was used in place of a signature, for official purposes. Although the practice is now obsolete, when I lived in my village in Japan, for instance, I made my inky mark each time I went to the bank. And so, I go and introduce myself and we chat about flowers for a little bit. When I ask Inky Mark about the origin of his name, he is vague.

We spend the weekend in Wasagaming, on the shore of Clear Lake in Riding Mountain National Park. This part of Manitoba is my mother's territory. She was born and raised on a farm straight north of here — in a place called Grandview — about 50 kilometres west of Dauphin. She is the Canadian-born daughter of immigrants: Germans too, but from an enclave called Friedenstal, in Bessarabia — part of what is now Moldova.

In fact, the village where my maternal grandparents grew up changed hands several times between Romania and Russia. It was this political instability that caused my mother's father to decide to leave his relative wealth (his father owned a large farm, and he himself owned a horse and therefore had a position of some importance in the Romanian cavalry) and come to Canada. He brought his wife and Herb, his first son, then a toddler, and settled in Grandview, several years before the communists took control of the country that would eventually become home to one of last century's most brutal regimes, under Nicolae Ceausescu.

Some family members that stayed behind met a tragic fate; at the end of World War Two, my grandmother's sister, along with four of her children, spent 11 years in a labour camp in Kazakhstan before finally making it to Canada in the 1960s.

I am reminded, again, of an official state visit to Romania that my father made as governor general. I had lobbied my father hard again, and he allowed me and my sister to come. I remember being thrilled to be in a real communist country; the word 'communist' still carried some weight back in the early 1980s. I remember landing at Bucuresti-Otopeni International Airport and noticing two enormous portraits above the terminal building. One of them, I knew, was President Nicolae Ceausescu himself; the other looked oddly familiar. It took a few seconds for me to realize that the 10-metre-high portrait was of my own father. His features had been given a strangely Russified appearance; stern look, bushy eyebrows, a little jowlier than real life. In fact, the rendering was a morphing of my father's face with Leonid Brezhnev's, and at the time I thought it was pretty cool. Later, my mother said that at the state dinner, she had told Elena Ceausescu that her own parents came from a place that had once been a part of Romania. Elena smiled at my mother through yellow teeth and replied, "We are just like sisters, then." Years later, after studying the Ceausescu regime in university, and when the whole world is still uncovering the truth about their regime and of their brutality, her remark still chills me.

I realize that I have been so wrapped up in my paternal grandfather's memories and his life, that I have not yet introduced my girls to the other half. This is my chance. We will drive to Grandview tomorrow and, while we're at it, we are going to climb Baldy Mountain, Manitoba's highest peak — or rather, its highest place. But I am not fussy; I love to climb mountains: the tallest mountain in Japan (Mount Fuji) and in Australia (Mount Kosciusko) and the tallest mountain in South-East Asia (Mount Kinabalu) are some of the peaks I've climbed, and I have plans to, someday, accompany my daughters to the top of Mount Kilimanjaro, the tallest mountain in Africa (which is, I understand, more climbable than that distinction would make it seem). If I can climb Kilimanjaro at 50, my daughters will have to climb it at 13 and 15. My youngest, Blaise, I am sure will have no trouble when the time comes. This summer we will train on Baldy Mountain.

As we leave Riding Mountain National Park the next morning, I am smiling: this will be the girls' introduction to my other half — but could it be the *better* half? Growing up, I often heard my parents engage in a little good-natured teasing about each other's backgrounds: Catholic vs. Lutheran, who spoke better German, who was the more able on a horse. I had come through this same area last summer with my parents and, not remembering having seen it before, I had marvelled at how the gently rolling farmland looked, somehow, *richer* than the flat, stony plains of the Rural Municipality of Brokenhead. Mom laughed. Dad was grimacing at the effrontery of the comment, but he did not deny the truth of my observation. I then teased him by bringing up another difference I remembered between my two quite distinct sets of German grandparents: I have clear memories of Grandma Schulz tempting me as a child with delicious fruity candies imported from Austria, wrapped in lovely paper with exquisite pictures of the fruit inside, proffered from cut-glass bowls. By contrast, a visit to the Schreyer farm would soon have us all seated around the kitchen table, bowls of dessert placed before us. It didn't matter if a meal was hours away; we knew that we must eat whatever was in those bowls — and sometimes it was hard to tell what it was. Most of the time, though, it was boiled pumpkin covered in chocolate sauce. Or boiled rhubarb, which I quite liked and would happily eat — until I came to the slice of day-old bread underneath it. Sometimes these desserts came with a scoop of ice cream on top — almost always Neapolitan; its stripe of strawberry looking wonderfully neon. I knew my dad was not a fan of his mother's cooking, but this did not prevent him from carrying out his filial duty.

As for myself, I didn't mind eating any of this — for the most part — being just a kid. I still don't; making rhubarb compote for my girls is high on my 'to do' list this summer, and despite its humble origins, I happen to know that boiled rhubarb is also the dessert of choice of some pretty high-up people. It was during a state dinner, on an official visit to Germany, that I had the opportunity to eat rhubarb compote with vanilla sauce, while seated next to the German protocol officer; one Graf (Count) Fink von Finkenstein. As the dessert was being served to us in silver bowls, the man leaned over to me and said under his breath, "Rhubarb compote — bah! This is peasant food. But it is *the president's favourite.*" I am not sure what the Count was implying about his president, and even now I can't actually remember if that was indeed the protocol officer's real name — or if my recollection of it has been tempered by my impression of him. In any case, I ate all of the rhubarb compote with vanilla sauce and it was very good indeed.

Teasing my dad about his mother's secret recipes and her general inventiveness in the kitchen would also bring a grimace, but no denial, and he would sometimes shoot back by reminding me that his mother's sister, Mary, was the best family cook of all, with which I readily and wholeheartedly agree. But my father could give as good as he got: he liked to tease my mom about her German. It was, according to him, the 'low' kind — while his family spoke 'high' German. For me, even after sitting through forced German lessons as a child (and later secretly signing up for two years of German in university so I could finally figure out what my parents were talking about when they didn't want their children to know) I still am not clear what these references to high and low German mean. Perhaps it's time I looked it up.

Grandview, Manitoba is a small farming community; the kind that has a one-street main-drag kind of feel. Grandview is also the gateway to the Duck Mountains, and the smoothest route to Baldy Mountain. Despite its small population, less than one thousand, there is an inordinate number of hunting and fishing outfitters based here. The locals seem to have a good sense of humour, too; I read the following when I looked up the Grandview home page on the Internet before heading out this way: *While the town has its own RCMP detachment, they are not often occupied with crime issues. Crime in Grandview Manitoba is something you see on TV, happening elsewhere. If anyone committed a crime here, he or she might be excluded from of the coffee clutch or miss a bonspiel — a fate worst than any fine or jail term!* It takes us more than an hour to get to Grandview from Wasagaming, and as I drive through with my children, I decide its time for a 'wee' stop.

We park the car next to the only place that seems to be exhibiting any sign of activity; the local Chinese restaurant. I walk in with Emi and ask the proprietress if I can use the washroom. Her young son is watching us, and I hear the mother talking to him in Cantonese. I say *jo san* to the boy as I head to the washroom, and *m'goi* on my way out, thereby utilizing virtually all of my Cantonese, a fact that does not make me proud. The boy's big eyes go bigger as they follow me and Emi out the door. I wish I could sit down and ask this Chinese family: *How did you get here? Where are you from? Do you like being Canadian?* I want to tell them that I am from where they have come. *My children are Chinese. Just as you are Canadian. It's all pretty wonderful and incredible, don't you think?* But I cannot speak their language while they, no doubt, are going to be spending a lot of time and effort learning mine. I feel ashamed.

I get some gas, then tell Emelyn and the girls we need to make tracks to Baldy Mountain. Although the sky above us is clear and blue, there is a ridge of black clouds to the west and they are heading our way. We continue north, straight as an arrow, and after 40 minutes have entered Duck Mountain Provincial Park. Within minutes we are driving up to a telegraph tower and a fire tower. I am disappointed. This is not a mountain at all, but a parking lot in the pines. My father had warned me, though, when I had told him what we were going to be doing, that any talk about climbing mountains in Manitoba will inevitably lead to disappointment. How right he was. I get out of the car and look up at the darkening sky, then over to the fire tower. My children cannot climb a ladder, but even if they could, the first several rungs are covered with a plank and secured by a lock. I look around me and cheer up immediately; through the trees, I can just make out another tower, this one with stairs.

All is not lost. I grab Emi, Emelyn grabs Blaise, and we head up the steps — 61, Emelyn tells me later — to the top of the lookout tower, to look out over a vast green tree-covered escarpment and golden plains beyond. Emelyn, Emi, Blaise and I celebrate being at the top of Baldy Mountain. We take some photos and punch the air. We giggle and scream. *We did it! We did it! We did it!* Then we race back down the stairs and into the car, and watch and listen as the clouds open up around us. We are out of breath and a little wet, but thrilled nonetheless: for a moment, we were the tallest people in Manitoba; for a moment, we were the kings of the world.

CHAPTER 22

Legend

WE DID NOT EXPECT to go back to the bush in the winter of 1949, as the paper mill at Pine Falls did not do much cutting. There were one or two contracts, so they operated the camp themselves. But we could not sit around doing nothing. Operating a pulp camp was in our blood, and so we went and took a small contract from another contractor. We started about the first week in December, 1949. We had four men cutting and we had a man and team to haul it to the road, and one of my boys trucked it to Pine Falls, a matter of 35 miles. We got through in the latter part of February, 1950. We did not make much but we made something. We got home again and prepared for the 1950 seeding season. We planted wheat and flax and barley. We had a good crop of wheat that year and after harvest on October 4th, 1950, my father passed away at the age of 99 years and two months.

1950 was my last winter pulp operation. We had a choice of working with a contractor at Great Falls or at the Manitoba Pulp and Paper Co., which was later a subsidiary of Abitibi Corp. We chose to work with the M.P.P. Co., as the hauling of the wood was closer in this case. It was not heavy timber but, it being close to Pine Falls and a short haul, we made out fair. We started cutting about December 5th but in the meantime had to build a barn for two teams, and we pulled up a lumber camp which was about a half mile from the main camp. We started hauling pulp onto the ice about the 10th of January. We had one team there already. We had a team at home but needed them for bringing hay to the cows and other young cattle, and also for hauling out the manure. We bought a team from Henry Hintz, and then had two teams for hauling.

I left it up to the boys to decide what teams they wanted to drive, and they decided that Tony would drive the old team and Leonard was to drive the one we just bought. All went well when they hauled the wood on the ice at a place where it was not too steep and the bank went down gradually. But Leonard thought he could save a lot of time if he could bring the wood onto the ice at another place, which was a lot closer. I told him not to try it, that it was too steep, but while I was gone home to bring in some beef, he got a bulldozer to make the road there. Well, he tried it. It did work twice while there was still deep snow, but on the third load while he still had the bear trap on, while going down the bear trap broke and the horses could not hold back the load. The smaller horse ran ahead. The bigger horse tried to hold it back and the load forced the horse against a tree and stood the horse straight up against the tree.

The sudden stop forced Leonard to go flying over the other horse, luckily into deep snow, as he would have had the same fate as the horse otherwise. When he got out of the snow he grabbed the axe and cut down the tree. The horse fell, but it was dead. He later unloaded the wood and put the other horse in the barn, and came home for a horse that we had at home. I might mention that the horse that was left got sick from shock or whatever and was unable to work. Leonard came for the horse we still had at home and we finished our hauling. We cut and hauled out over 1000 cords and came home March 10th, 1951. That was the last year of my pulp camp operation, although I had a spring cut agreement with the Manitoba Pulp and Paper Company. I left Tony to do the cutting and supervising and that same year, 1951, Tony started his camp operations, which went on for quite a few years.

In this year of 1951, everything changed. The family that had worked together now parted. In the summer of 1951, on the 23rd day of June, Leonard got married and moved into a small house we had on Lot 15 in St. Andrews. They were living alone and quite happy and then tragedy struck. His wife got rheumatic fever and she was four months in the hospital, first in the Saint Boniface hospital in Winnipeg. Then he brought her to the Beausejour Hospital where she stayed another two months. She got out of the hospital and it took her some time to walk, as she had been in bed for four months. We were all happy when she was able to walk again. It had been especially hard for Leonard, as he was busy with harvest and had to cook for himself and keep house until Elsie got well again.

In the fall of 1951, Tony started his pulp operation on the same place and the same camps. He started cutting, but as he was getting married that fall, he had to come home and arrange for the wedding. He had George to look after the cutters while he was getting ready for the wedding. I remember I went with him and his bride to Winnipeg to get the permit and also beer for the wedding. The highway was so icy that we could not go faster than 25 miles per hour, but we did get everything settled and on December 1st, 1951 he got married to Lillian Rattai. After the wedding, he and wife both took their truck and left for camp. That winter he cut around 950 cords of pulp and made out quite well. That started him as a pulp operator, and with the money he made, he bought a brand new T.D.9 Caterpillar. He bought a plough that summer and started ploughing and custom land-breaking and made good.

I might mention that when he took over the cutting and operation of pulp, I turned over the team of horses, the truck and two heavy sleighs and camp equipment that was necessary for the operating of the camp. After 15 winters operating pulp camps, I could not do without going to see how Tony was doing, so I still went to see and mostly brought beef and pork and sold it to Tony, as I could sell it a lot cheaper. He also bought the oats and hay from me.

— John James Schreyer

EVERYONE HAS THEIR STORY. The first time I ever heard that phrase was at an all-candidates meeting in Vancouver's West End, and a bitter young man had just finished demanding of one of the candidates what she was going to do for him and all the other unemployed young people who were feeling they had nothing to hope for. "Everyone has their story," the candidate began, by way of response. Judging by her tone of voice, I think she was saying that his particular situation was no more compelling than anyone else's — to stop feeling sorry for himself, in effect. But before she could speak any further and offer up the inevitable list of party promises, a group from the AIDS awareness organisation ACT UP (The AIDS Coalition To Unleash Power) stormed the venue, marching around the room, singing to the beat of their drums and tambourines. It was good optics for ACT UP — they certainly got everyone's attention — and the acoustics were not bad, either. But it was that phrase, uttered in a cynical tone: *Everyone has their story* — that has stuck with me ever since.

I also believe that everyone has a story to tell, but I believe it in a good way. Every family has its stories and legends. They need to be told. They need to be passed down and remembered. We need to learn to listen, too. We need to not be afraid to share our feelings. Otherwise, our family histories are in danger of being watered down or rewritten altogether, no different from the way it had been done in China during the Cultural Revolution, for example, when people standing in old photos next to Mao Zedong were airbrushed out of existence. Looking back, I had often heard my aunts and uncles talk about their time in 'the bush'. I had even been to places along the Winnipeg River where I was told my grandfather and his sons and daughter and daughters-in-law had spent their winters hard at work. I had just assumed that it meant they were cutting down trees. In 'the bush' means so much more to me now. It conjures up different feelings and emotions: awe and profound gratitude, instead of mild interest; pride — and a bittersweet feeling that I can't put a name to. *I'm sorry you had to walk in the cold and the dark. I'm sorry you went hungry. If I had been there, Grandpa, I would have helped you.*

Like in a game of Chinese Whispers, stories get altered over time if they are not put down. Case in point: for years I was under the impression that my grandfather was 'the first pioneer baby born in western Canada'. It was a point of pride with me and I had told many people. Then I made the mistake of mentioning it in passing to my father, who asked me where on earth I had come up with such a story. Still, I argued the point; the amount of time I had believed this untruth had me convinced of its veracity. Now, having read my grandfather's journal, I think I can pinpoint the very place where the facts took flight; my grandfather was, in fact, the first baby *in his (pioneer) family* to be born in (western) Canada. My father concedes, however, that his own father was probably one of the first pioneer babies born in what was later to become the Rural Municipality of Brokenhead. For me, this is just as awesome. And here's at least one story that has not been disputed, at least in my lifetime: Legend has it that my Uncle Leonard was so strong he won a tug-o-war match with his horse.

I never questioned it myself. But this summer, after learning the truth of my grandfather's birth, I feel compelled to find out if the tug-o-war story is accurate. "Dad, is it true what they say about Uncle Leonard?" I ask my father during a phone call.

"What — about the red dress?"

"Uh . . . no — not that. The story about him winning a tug-o-war with his horse." I can hear my father chuckling, and then chuckling some more. And then some more. I wonder if I will get an answer.

"Well, those who were there insist that is an exaggeration," my father begins, and I can tell he is smiling at the other end of the phone line. "The harness tore, and so the event ended in a draw." I am laughing so hard it takes a while for me to get out a thank you to my father for setting the record straight.

This summer I have heard stories of my grandmother's psychic abilities. The first was back in June, on the way to Steve's retirement party. I told my parents that I had visited a psychic in Sedona, Arizona, during the road trip my husband Darrel and I had taken with them several years ago. Right away the clairvoyant looked at me and stated that I had a bit of psychic ability. I was pleased to hear it, seeing it as expert affirmation of what I had been wondering for a long time. My particular skill is to have a sense of something — a person or scenario — in the morning, think nothing of it, and by nightfall that 'something' will have eerily presented itself in some way. In other words, I can see the future, but I don't know it is the future I am seeing until it becomes the present — so what use is that? What's more, I sense a lot of things in the morning, most of which do not present themselves in any way. I must also admit that I felt this particular psychic was of dubious ability herself; she told me I was pregnant with twins, which I found hard to believe, as thrilling as it sounded. Three weeks later, however, I discovered that she was half-right: I was pregnant with Emi.

"Your grandmother had psychic abilities," my father told me matter-of-factly, after I finished telling my parents this story.

"You're kidding. She never told me that." I was intrigued, and disappointed that my grandmother had never shared this special talent with me.

"She never spoke about it."

"Why not?"

There was a pause. "I think — it was because of her religion."

I understood. For my grandmother, it was better to rely on faith and hope rather than to try to get a clear picture of the way things would be. To me, this was an indication of the strength of her beliefs. There was nothing more to say. But then my father started to tell me the story of my grandmother and the night Uncle Tony almost died.

"It was in the middle of the night. I was sleeping in the room next to my parents, and then I heard my mother begin to wail. She got up, and started to pace the floor, she sounded delirious, more than hysterical —"

"Dad, what did you do?" I interrupted.

"I stayed in my bed. I was only about nine years old. I must have been scared," he replied, then continued. "She was crying, and pacing. I heard her say 'Tony! Tony!' Then, sure enough, a half-day later, Tony came home. His truck had fallen through the ice on the Winnipeg River. He had managed to escape unharmed, but he was of course badly shaken."

My grandmother's innovativeness is also legendary — and not just with regard to her 'imaginative' cooking. She liked to spend time in the kitchen, but this may have been due to an interest in chemistry rather than home economics. During World War Two, my grandmother was making some soap in the kitchen and the materials she had chosen to tackle this particularly tough job began to bubble up in what was appearing to be a potentially dangerous chemical reaction in the aluminium pan. Quick as a flash, my grandmother grabbed the container and raced out the door, flinging the contents on the grass. She brushed herself off, then proceeded to write a letter to the government of Canada, telling them of her discovery and its possibilities with regards to munitions and the general war effort. And she wanted the patent, too. She did get a polite reply from Ottawa, thanking her for sharing her findings, and letting her know that they were already in possession of this information.

Her creativity was also evident in her parenting methods, as demonstrated by the 'red dress' story I had learned about just a few weeks earlier. When my Uncle Leonard was a very young boy, it was a lot of work to keep him from getting into trouble on the farm. All hands were needed for the farming chores, and childcare was a luxury no one could afford. Uncle Leonard's particular habit was to walk out on the highway, which was only about 100 metres from the house. This was a constant worry for my grandmother, until she came up with an effective measure to keep her boy from wandering. When she sent him out to play, she dressed the strapping young Leonard in his older sister's bright red dress. Even at such a tender age, Leonard knew that he did not want to be seen on the road wearing it. The choice was his to make. And Uncle Leonard chose to stay well away from the road, although later he would choose to remove the offending red dress and hang it on a fence post, but as he didn't want to be seen running naked on the highway, he still remained in the yard. My father finished telling me this story by saying, "Those who know him best say that, even to this day, your Uncle Leonard is easily annoyed by red trappings."

My grandmother was ahead of her time in many ways. I was reminded of this in Neepawa, while looking at a quilting exhibition in conjunction with the Lily Festival. My mother and I, who also like to create with our hands, marvelled at the display. The craftsmanship and artistry were inspiring. A couple of the quilts were especially intriguing; they had been made using photo-transfer technology. These pieces were not only precious quilted heirlooms, but family photo albums as well. As a quilter myself, I looked at these and decided that I would give it a try someday.

My mother had been thinking the same thing. She said, "Do you remember how Grandma used to type sayings and poems onto fabric?"

Of course she had! Memories were coming back. She was an avid quilter; making so many that she was always able to respond to a request for one for a church raffle, and gave many away. But hers were not simply made with fabric swatches; she made her mark with fabric paints as well, and many of her poems would end up sewn in the quilts, written in brightly-coloured paint, or typed with her ancient manual typewriter. I admit that, at the time, I thought it was funny; the typeface was crude, you could even see the smudge of ink from where the ribbon had been pressed down around it. But now, I don't have one of my grandmother's quilts, and I wish that I did. Her artistry included interior design as well, and she was brave with colour. The walls of the farmhouse were painted in an assortment of bold colours and patterns; yellow circular dabs on a robin's-egg blue background in the living room, which she did all by herself. From all the TV decorating shows I have seen here in Manitoba this summer, it is a technique and a use of colour very much in vogue at the moment, and my grandmother was doing it 50 years ago.

My grandmother had strong opinions about what was good for her grandchildren, and again, she proved to be ahead of her time. When my siblings and I spent time at the farm during summers, my grandmother would wipe our arms with a piece of cotton wool soaked in hydrogen peroxide. When our parents came to pick us up on their return from their travels, we would run to our mother, eager for her embrace, which she just as eagerly returned. But quickly her attention would be focused on our complexions. Our arms and faces, made pale by the nightly swipes with peroxide-soaked cotton wool, lead my mother to believe that we had spent our entire holiday indoors. I assured her that this was not the case, and told her that Grandma just liked to wipe some stuff on our arms and cheeks before bed. At that time, tanning was the done thing; with all sun products meant to enhance the sun's effects rather than counteract them. My grandmother would also insist we wear long sleeves when we went out to play, an unfair request in the heat of the day, I had always thought. But now my daughters wear bathing suits made in Australia, with three-quarter length sleeves and legs that go down to mid-calf, reminiscent of 1920s bathing suits. These days, at the swimming pool where I have enrolled Emi in lessons, mothers stop to ask me where they can buy one like it, and that they have never seen them available in Winnipeg shops.

I would do anything to see my grandparents again; to show them my daughters. I'd do anything to ask them for their advice and helpful parenting hints; they've obviously done a good job. Instead I must keep them alive in our hearts and minds, and I intend to do so by writing up the legend of their lives — and not just *their* lives but the lives of those who came before and after. This is not something that can be done in a finite amount of time; it is a project that I will endeavour to do as long as I am alive, and which will, I hope, be continued indefinitely. It is starting this summer where, here in Manitoba, I can choose from a number of legendary figures for my daughters to connect with every day. Maybe today, for example, we'll drop by and see my Uncle Leonard. Why not? We'll see how his garden is getting along, maybe even give him some of our own onions, which we have started to pick and eat and enjoy. Maybe, if we're lucky, we will have lunch with a legend. Maybe, if we're lucky, he'll show us the legendary bright red dress. My daughters would love that.

CHAPTER 23

Light

IN 1952, AFTER LIVING IN BROKENHEAD district 55 years, we finally got Manitoba Hydro lights and power. A lot of us had been working and holding meetings to get farmers to sign up for the utility. The town of Beausejour had had electric light for a long time. But it was hard to get farmers to sign for power, the excuse was that it would cost too much. But with a house-to-house canvass we did get about 90 percent in favour, and now the farmers are getting the power. It was the nicest thing that happened in this district.

I remember when the Hydro men were working the lines, and asked them when they would start the lights and power. The electricians were just through with putting the electricity in the barn, as my house was already done. They told me that it would be the next day. The next afternoon, I visited my brother, four miles away. I had forgotten that the electricians were to put the light on. I stayed at my brother's until it got dark. As I was going home, I noticed from about three miles away my house lights were all on, the barn lights were on and even the pole light was on. When I got home it sure was a beautiful sight to see.

That evening there was only one farm light – that was mine. But the next evening all of the district was lighted up. My dad, who passed away a year earlier, always said: I would like to live to see the lights before I pass away. But he died a year too soon. The telephone, too, had been started in 1951, but not all of the farmers installed them until 1955.

In 1953, for the first time, I bought a new car. It was an eight-cylinder Buick, a popular car, and brand new. I had driven automobiles since 1917 but I was disappointed with this new car. I had a six-cylinder Pontiac before, which had about 120,000 miles on the speedometer, and it still had better springs and was more comfortable than this new car, so a new car was not always the best. I traded it for a used one, and the used one was a lot better car. I have had it for a long time, and still had no expense except batteries and muffler. As for wheat and livestock prices, they were getting lower as the Liberals made no effort to sell wheat to the Russians. The livestock, too, could have bought a better price if we had traded with the Russians. It took another six years before the government, under Prime Minister John Diefenbaker, let us do that.

— John James Schreyer

I HAVE THE PHONE to my ear, and Emi and Blaise are pulling on my legs. We are all frustrated; the girls want to go out and play, and I want to find Great-uncle Anton and Great-aunt Catherine, whom my Uncle George told me were buried at St. Mary's Cemetery in Winnipeg. I have been trying to make contact with someone at the cemetery's office, because I know that, if I have a name and a year of death, records can be found, and burial places located. I had already been there once with the girls, on the way to an 'ice-cream fun-run' along the Red River, and had walked along the rows of gravestones with them, trying to find these two relatives myself. But I was unsuccessful; so many gravestones — and many of them so old they were unreadable now. No one is picking up the phone — again. I have already left a message. I hate phones. What was a vital convenience, as well as a novelty, in my grandfather's day, has morphed into the 'automated messaging service'. We have created a monster! I slam the receiver down. Emi and Blaise give a cheer.

Despite my feelings about telephones, I like this entry about the day when light came to the farm. My grandfather's thrill is infectious. We take our utilities for granted now, like so many things. I am surprised to learn there was no electricity at the farm until my father was well into his teens. He would have been old enough to appreciate the difference, then. Perhaps this is why energy — specifically, sustainable energy development — was my father's great passion and still is, perhaps more now than ever. My father was, for seven years, an energy minister. I suppose that being premier of Manitoba and, concurrently, its energy minister (and finance minister, too, for a time) was a bit of an anomaly, but such was his desire to see the province develop what he saw as its assets. He saw water power as Manitoba's comparative advantage in what is, in other ways, a 'have-not' province; without Alberta's oil reserves, or the manpower and markets of central Canada.

My father got into trouble for his dams in the past. Government policies go in and out of fashion, it seems, as quickly as clothing styles. But this year, what I am hearing most is how hydroelectric energy is Manitoba's cash cow. What an asset! Aren't we lucky! And Manitoba is making good selling it to Minneapolis and other places. Throughout the summer, I have been following the continuing debate in the Winnipeg newspaper over proposed dam projects along the Nelson River, in Northern Manitoba. On one day: 'Clean and renewable' says the Manitoba premier, and also Premier Jean Charest of Quebec, whose province is also blessed with this asset, who has come to visit the Manitoba premier to talk about how best to utilize it. I am encouraged. But on another day, I read that the dam projects will be an environmental disaster. 'Not true!' says a proponent. What to believe? In any case, I wonder what the opposition think the alternative is. Candlelight? Coal, perhaps? In that case, I invite anyone to spend a day in Chongqing — or any city in China — then blow his/her nose. And then ask themselves if they would like to raise their children in *that*. Alternative sources of energy don't have a chance of becoming viable as long as Big Oil's solution to depleting oil reserves is to pump it out of the ground that much faster. Who wants to freeze in the dark now? Well, perhaps with global warming, at least we won't freeze. I always felt that if we were sending the world down the toilet, Manitobans would be the last ones standing. After all, Manitoba has arable land, water, and a cold climate that, with global warming, will warm up enough to lengthen the growing season. But who wants *that?* Who wants to be the last one standing?

No, I don't want to think about the future, I want to dwell on the past. And so, in remembrance of the day that light came to the farm, and also in honour of the work my grandfather and uncles and aunts did in clearing the Seven Sisters reservoir area of trees in 1949, I decide to take the girls to the nearby Pinawa Dam Provincial Heritage Park. My father had brought me and my husband here before, during his first visit to Canada, and now I understand better the attraction the place holds for both of them; my husband is a civil engineer and my father wishes he were. During that first visit, my father had told us how much time his own father and all his brothers had spent here toiling — backbreaking, terrible work — clearing the place for the 1950 dam construction. But this work helped to ensure their survival.

It's a sunny day, hot and breezy, perfect for a walk. There is a hiking trail that includes a suspension bridge over the Winnipeg River, a part of the Trans-Canada Trail project under construction, and I know it will impress and delight my girls. I am not sure how easy it is going to be to navigate the trail with a stroller, but life is for the brave. We park our car next to a Lutheran graveyard near the trailhead and away we go. In less than a minute, we reach the suspension bridge, which is not as long as the one in Souris, but the beauty of its surroundings more than makes up for that. Emi starts walking, and I follow close behind with Blaise in the stroller. This is a suspension bridge, so I show Emi what to do; we start to wiggle and jiggle, and Blaise giggles and wiggles in her stroller. The suspension bridge wiggles and jiggles along with us. We are all laughing, and I can't think of a more beautiful place to be doing this.

When we cross the bridge I discover a lengthy staircase, and proceed to unbuckle Blaise from her stroller so that I can carry her down. But what to take first, the stroller or the baby? The staircase is narrow and I can't take both at the same time. I look around me, then at the bridge. I see that the bridge is constructed with strong fencing; there are no gaps. So I tell Emi to stay on the bridge with Blaise as I race down the stairs with the stroller. I race back up the stairs to get hold of my daughters — just in time to see Blaise commit her dummy to the Winnipeg River. She is holding onto the fencing and, with a mighty blow, the pacifier pops from her mouth. Time is suspended now; we all watch as Blaise's dummy flies, clears the wires, and arcs gracefully down to the water about 30 metres below us. We continue to watch it float away until it is a small blue and white speck. Emi is chortling. I look at Blaise. She is giggling, too, but I know that she will be regretting her actions soon enough — and so will I; I didn't bring a spare.

We push on down the narrow stairway. I buckle Blaise into the stroller again, and then off we go along the trail, into the trees and scrub of the Canadian Shield. We abandon the stroller after 100 yards; the trail, despite the sign that welcomes bikers, is impassable with it. What was I thinking, anyway? I hoist Blaise's bulk onto my shoulders and engage Emi in a game of "How many different coloured flowers can you find?" I make the mistake of giving the white flower a name (I call it Dogwood) and must now invent names for all the others whose names I don't know. Emi's questions are, as usual, incessant, and she is finding more flowers than I ever thought existed: blue, purple, yellow, more white flowers — pink ones, too. I show her some birch bark fallen on the ground. I'll write her a secret message on it later, like the Ojibway and Cree did, I tell myself. We round the corner in the path and come to a clearing. There is a large pond to our right, and we are now walking on the rocky outcrops that are so distinctively a part of the Canadian Shield landscape.

We sit down on the rocks and look out at the pond. I pretend I see a beaver dam on the far shore and tell my daughters about beavers. Of course, they have never seen one, that quintessential Canadian animal. Beavers are awesome, but I know they are pests. My father complains about the beavers living on his property north of Winnipeg. Once, years ago, he even showed me the trees they had cut down. It looked like an open-and-shut case, those thin stumps gnawed to a point, but I found it hard to believe that there were beavers in the exurbs of Winnipeg — until I saw one crossing the street last summer. I was returning home one afternoon, and saw that several cars were stopped on the road in front of our house. When I drove up, sure enough, there was a beaver waddling across the road, making its way to the Red River. There are rabbits, chipmunks, squirrels on the property, too, and earlier this summer Emelyn said she saw two deer helping themselves to the lettuce in my father's vegetable garden.

I sit with my girls on the rock, looking out over the pond, hidden, and yet protected by the nature around me. I pretend it is unchanged and undiscovered land, and I wonder if a beaver or a deer might make themselves known to us. I especially like the silence. Hong Kong has incredible hiking trails that meander along seashores and over mountains, and through rainforested areas, too. This is one of Hong Kong's best-kept secrets. But no matter how far you can get away in Hong Kong, there is always the ambient noise of the rest of the world. Here, by this pond next to the Winnipeg River, there is none of that. I beg my children to be silent, to simply listen for one magic moment. They give me about 15 seconds, and I take it gratefully. *Listen to sound of nature. It is the most beautiful sound in the world!* Someday my girls will understand that. And they will know where to find it, too. Then, just as we get up to return to the car, we hear a splashing noise in the pond. A beaver maybe, but more likely a fish. I stand up and look around me one more time, trying to commit what I see to memory. I won't bother taking a picture — it would never come out right. I say goodbye to this place, looking forward to bringing my girls back to this spot when they are older, and more willing to appreciate the solitude.

Our next stop is Pinawa Dam, which, as the Travel Manitoba literature says 'rises like ancient Roman ruins' out of the Pinawa Channel. As we stand overlooking the site, I can't help think the simile is apt; it is impressive, even in ruin.

"What is it?" asks Emi.

I don't tell her it was built in 1906, and what she sees before her are the remains of Manitoba's first concrete hydroelectric dam. "It's a *ghost dam,*" I say. She raises an eyebrow at me, and then at the dam.

I read the information plaques as we make our way back to the car, which explain the intriguing history of the dam, and its life — and how it was abandoned in the 1950s when bigger dams were built on the Winnipeg River. It was a feat of engineering in its day — and it is still remarkable, I decide, as I drive out of the park to the road. I wonder, if it was operational in 1906, why did it take another 40-odd years for the lights to go on in my grandfather's house? I am saddened by the fact that my great-grandfather, Old Anton, did not get his wish; to see the lights on in his home.

Tonight will be our last night at the farm. Tomorrow Daddy arrives, and so tomorrow morning, we will move back to Winnipeg. My daughters' other grandparents are scheduled to arrive by train the following day, and Darrel and I had decided it would be easier for everyone if we all stayed close by each other in the Big City of Winnipeg. I am both surprised and pleased to see how hard Emi is taking our imminent departure, and I remind her that we will be returning to the farm regularly to look after our vegetables, and maybe we will even see Curly again. This puts a smile back on her face. But, right now, there are chores to do; packing our things into the van, and also cleaning up after ourselves. Emelyn and I decide to put on a video to occupy the girls, while we get busy packing clothes and toys, and boxes of food. I clear the bedroom first, and my heart skips a beat when I find Cousin Greg's hunting rifle under the bed we had been sleeping on so soundly all this time. I leave the room and shut the door behind me, lugging a huge suitcase.

It's such a warm evening, and our last, to boot. So after dinner we head to the Pit in Ladywood for one last muck around. Blaise unilaterally decides to take her clothes off, and I let Emi do the same. I roll up my overalls and stand up to my knees in the murky water. Emelyn starts chasing some crayfish and ends up waist-deep and fully clothed. But we've got three crayfish. Do they kill mosquito larvae? I wonder. We will take them to Grandma and Grandpa's house and perhaps find out.

By the time we get back to the farm, the sun is low and the girls are exhausted. But there is still one more thing I want to do before I leave — goal-oriented as I am — and I am hoping my girls will be able to stay awake long enough to participate. I want to watch the moon rise over the farm. I am not sure why I want to do this, although a dozen years living in Asia must have influenced this idea. Moon-viewing is an important summertime activity in most Asian cultures. By the time the moon is ready to show itself, however, my girls are long asleep. I guess this is one thing on my 'to do' list that won't happen this year. *Yes, it will,* I tell myself a moment later. Emelyn helps me steal my children from their beds, and we carry them to a blanket I set down on the grass next to the wheat, which is now golden and taller than Blaise. I think about where I am and what is all around me: I look behind me to the house, the lights are on; my girls are asleep in my lap; I am looking up at the moon, lit up in the velvet night sky. *It sure is a beautiful sight to see.* Here is a ritual born; a memory that will last my lifetime — and, I hope, maybe longer.

I see several shooting stars before I head back inside.

CHAPTER 24

Destination

THE YEAR 1954 WAS FOR THE MOST PART quite uneventful, not many farmers got any crop off as the rain came very often in that fall season. Most of the farmers had just started swathing their wheat, but did not harvest it. It was just left in the swath for the winter. Some farmers thought that they would harvest it in the springtime when the fields dried out. I happened to have all my grain swathed but did not harvest one bushel. In the springtime there was just chaff left; the mice followed the swath and got all of the grain. There were coyotes in winter that followed the swath to get the mice. And in the spring there were a lot of owls and ever so many young owls; we just had to accept it. It being dry, we all worked our field and made a lot of summerfallow for the year 1955.

Our road was built in 1950 and 1951. There were roads before, but just mud, and a bit of gravel on them. But after a heavy rain it got so muddy, so after 60 years of narrow mud roads we now had a wide road. The government bought another 15 feet on both sides to make it about 130 feet wide. And for the first time it was asphalted.

But the farmers around here ran into problems. On Saturdays and Sundays the city people would drive to Grand Beach and Victoria Beach, and so there was a steady stream of cars. If you wanted to cross the road you would have to wait a long time before there was an opening, and it wasn't long before there appeared holes in the roads, as the roads were not built right. The asphalt was broken through all over the road so the road boss was forever repairing the roads. He had his own little machine to dig holes with, and then brought some stone to fill the holes, and that was a continuous job. The road boss made money, because the then government of the Liberals did a poor job in the first place. But when the people started complaining, a second coat of asphalt was put on and since then that place is the best of all of the 22 miles.

1956 was also the beginning of the end of the federal Liberals. It was the Trans-Canada pipeline affair that helped to put the Liberals out of power. With the leadership of the Conservative Party – John Diefenbaker was a westerner which the western people supported and also a lot of eastern Conservatives – it looked that the Conservatives would have a good chance beating the Liberals. The federal Liberals were in power from 1921 to 1926, out for a month or two in 1926, then back in power until 1930. From '30 to '35 the Conservatives were in power, but lost in 1935 as that Bennett government was the least liked in Canadian history. The Liberals were in power for 32 years while the Conservatives were only in for five years. But a government that is that long in power becomes weak, as through those long years they become arrogant and believe that only they are supposed to govern, and this was the case in 1957 when they were put out, not only by the Conservatives but by the CCF too. And that was the first time in history when we had a member for the CCF party representing Springfield, a man by the name of Jake Schulz. He was well known because of his being the president of the Manitoba Farmers' Union.

The Conservatives had no majority, but held the most seats. The Liberals wanted the CCF to join them, but the CCF refused, so it was up to the Conservatives to form the government. All went well while it lasted. But the Conservatives knew if they could give the people a few goodies and call an election they could get a majority government, and then just take it easy for the next four years. And that's exactly what they did. They called an election in 1958 and won 208 seats. The Liberals were left with 47 members, the CCF with only eight, and the Social Credit were knocked right out. Great men like Stanley Knowles and M.J. Coldwell lost their seats, and John Diefenbaker had the biggest majority of all time, with 208 seats.

Well, the Conservatives were safe for the next four years. Farm prices began to worsen. The Liberals had left $900,000 in the unemployment kitty, but this was gone in a very short time as unemployment was the highest of all time. The Prime Minister rode elephants in India, while here everything at home went wrong. The next four years were like any other, just like the previous Conservatives were running the country, Borden, Bennett, and then Diefenbaker.

— John James Schreyer

JAKE SCHULZ IS MY OTHER GRANDFATHER. My grandfather doesn't mention that Jake's campaign manager was his own son, Edward, and that Jake's daughter became his own daughter-in-law. I wonder what they felt when they met for the first time, these two men — if they sensed what was in store for them both, in terms of both the personal and the political. How could they know they would someday be related — through the marriage of one man's daughter to the other man's son?

This entry brings to mind an event that occurred years ago, when my father was attending to an awards ceremony — as governors general do. There are several different kinds of ceremonies and investitures that are a part of the duties of the governor general, such as the Order of Canada, and the Order of Military Merit, and the presentation of credentials from foreign diplomats. These are all very interesting to observe, but for me, the most compelling is the presentation of the bravery awards. They are held twice a year, in the ballroom of Rideau Hall, the official residence of the governor general. When I lived there, I made a habit of reading the accounts of those who were going to be receiving honours — the Medal of Bravery, the Star of Courage, or the Cross of Valour — at the upcoming ceremony. Reading the stories of these ordinary Canadians and their extraordinary courage invariably brought tears to my eyes, and on more than one occasion I skipped school to watch the presentations. I don't think my parents ever knew, because I did my best to hide behind pillars or blend into the crowd. The ballroom would always be packed with honourees and their families, as well as the media, so if my parents ever saw me there, they didn't let on.

At one such presentation, one of the recipients was Bob Butterworth, the owner of a fuelling dock on the Fraser River at Steveston; a popular, touristy place just south of Vancouver. A customer had been fuelling his boat, and while it was filling up the boat caught fire, causing the tire fenders of the fuelling dock to catch fire as well. Knowing that there was well over 300,000 litres of fuel underneath him, Bob had to act quickly. Using an aluminium pole, he tried to pry the boat away from the tires that lined the dock, but the pole broke due to the intense heat. The only other option was to push the boat away from the fuelling dock with his bare hands. Bob helped the boat owner and his son off the burning boat and pushed the boat away, and received second-degree burns in four places. A passing boat then towed the boat out into deeper waters where it eventually burned and sank and a calamity was averted.

I wonder what Mr. Butterworth and my father felt when they met. As Bob received his medal; one man's pride, another man's admiration, perhaps. But was there more? Of course, neither of these men knew it at the time, but they, too, would someday be related through a marriage — or, rather, two marriages. Their children would marry cousins; cousins who were, at that moment, simply living out their childhood together among moors and dales; far away in Yorkshire, England. . . .

And so it is, that I find myself waiting at Union Station in downtown Winnipeg, for the arrival of my daughters' British grandparents; my British mother- and father-in-law. What follows is two weeks of non-stop activity, which includes birthday parties, trips to Lake Winnipeg, to assorted family gatherings, to more swimming lessons, to the Western Canada Summer Games, to a Habitat for Humanity Build, to the St. Pierre-Jolys Frog Follies — and every festival in between. Those first lazy weeks of our special summer have sped into a whirlwind. *Where is the time going?*

On this day, I get up and take the girls to the gas station down the road to buy the morning paper. It is not something I do regularly, but my husband did it when we stayed at my parents' place, and the girls have come to expect it. Their Daddy has gone with my father and his own parents — and Emelyn — to a place beyond Bird Lake, for two days of fishing. I am looking forward to spending a little quiet time at home with the girls. At the gas station, I buy the newspaper and some milk. The headline on the right side of the page catches my eye — in particular, the words 'United States', 'visa', and 'suspended'. With growing concern I scan the article and realize that the US has just suspended the visa waiver program which had allowed people from certain countries visa-free transit through American airports. My heart is beating. Emelyn had been given that blue placard at the airport in Minneapolis on our stopover there, with the letters TWOV on it. *Transit Without Visa.* Could it be. . . ?

I calm myself down. All right, worst-case scenario: we need to do a little paperwork, spend some of our precious time waiting in a line somewhere. I can do this. As soon as I get home, I drop the girls off in front of their morning children's television programming, then sit myself down at my father's desk. I call the United States consulate in Winnipeg to find out their hours of operation, determined to sort this matter out quickly. But my calm turns to disbelief when I am informed that "the US consulate in

Winnipeg does not do consular work, such as the issuing of visas". Then I hear the word 'Calgary' and start to panic.

"I don't mean to be persnickety," I interrupt, "but if you don't do *consular* work at your *consulate* — what *do* you do?" Despite my growing despair, I am truly curious about this, and I am relieved that my query is received as such, and not as some kind of sarcastic, frustrated barb.

"No problem," is the cheerful reply, "we are primarily a diplomatic post."

"I see," I reply meekly. My question has been answered, but I feel like I am arms akimbo, beseeching the heavens. I end the call without any complaint or smart remarks, not sure whether I should be annoyed on behalf of all Manitobans by the inconvenience of having to drive 800 miles — each way — for a stamp in a passport, or flattered that the United States considers its diplomatic relations with Manitoba of such importance that it warrants a dedicated diplomatic outpost. The preposterousness and the inevitability of the situation is starting to sink in — but still I will not give up hope; during the course of the conversation, the woman on the phone admitted that she was trained in diplomatic relations, and *not* in what I surmised was the lowly art of consular services. As such, she has claimed not to know anything about the new visa requirements and has suggested that I contact her colleagues in Calgary to confirm the situation. So this is what I do.

"Perhaps those who were allowed transit without visa on the way *into* Canada will be exempt from the new rules for the return leg of the journey," I suggest to the new voice in Calgary.

"Not at all," is the prompt American reply, delivered by a voice remarkably similar to the one in Winnipeg. "Your nanny will need to come here right away for an interview — but if all goes well, it will only take one day."

I sigh. We just have to accept it. My motherly mission is being sabotaged; the shoe thrown courtesy of the United States Department of Homeland Security. I reach for a pen. "What do I need?" I ask, and proceed to write down the list of things that are to accompany the application; photo on white background (2 x 2 inches), us$100 (cash only), onward airline ticket, proof of residence. I hang up and turn on the computer so that I can download and print out said application form. I stare at the monitor. Right now, the screensaver image is a photo of my girls standing up to their necks in golden wheat, with blue sky and red chicken coop in the background. It looks like heaven. I sigh again. I wish I didn't have to put my girls through such a long road trip, but there really is no choice here. I will put one foot in front of the other — we all will — and before a minute goes by, I am absorbed in the tourist websites of Saskatchewan and Alberta. I call Emi and Blaise over from their cartoons. "Look here, girls. Look where we are going. *Calgary.* We are going to go to the top of this big tower — the *Calgary Tower.* We are going to see the *Rocky Mountains.*" *We are going to make lemonade out of this big fat lemon!* And we don't have much time; the annual Schreyer golf tournament is in ten days and I don't want to miss it.

The next day, my mother, the girls and I drive out to Flanders Lake, beyond Bird River almost as far as the Ontario border, to join the fishing party, and I tell everyone about our upcoming trip to Alberta. Emelyn is clearly excited; she shouts and jumps with glee (although this may be due, in part, to the fact that she caught most of the fish). By now, I am excited as well, but everyone else in the cabin is incensed that anyone should have to drive for five days just because the United States government says we must. I remind them that Cousin Christy and her new husband had to drive even further, to Edmonton, to get their work visas for Japan. I remember that when I needed a work visa for Japan 12 years ago, there was a Japanese consulate in Winnipeg. But not anymore. In its heyday in the 60s and 70s, Winnipeg boasted as many as 30 consulates; it was the city of choice for a country's presence in the prairie provinces. But over time, these consulates relocated to Alberta or pulled out of the prairies altogether. Perhaps the us outpost is the only foreign diplomatic presence left here in Winnipeg. How the mighty have fallen.

When we get back to Winnipeg the next day, I take Emelyn to a photo studio in the north end of town. We need a two-by-two-inch photo on white background and it is proving to be a more difficult task than expected. This is the second place that we have gone to, and I have phoned first, asking the photographer if he can supply what we need. He said sure; and asked if it was for an American application. As we enter the photo studio now, I notice that many of the large portraits on the walls are of the same family, taken over the years, and I am not surprised to see, once inside, that the man behind the desk inside is none other than the man in all the family portraits. He asks me what I need and I remind him that we spoke on the phone earlier. He nods and looks at my girls, and he starts to smile.

"You have little angels," he says in a thick Polish accent. As he sets up Emelyn in front of the camera, he continues to talk. "People will tell you that they grow up too fast, and you will not believe it. But it is true. They grow up too fast."

Blaise is hugging Emelyn around the legs and I reach for her. "Never mind, she's okay," says the photographer, "Just let her hug you and keep your body still. She will not be in the picture."

I like this man. I know from the photos on his walls that his children are already grown. I thank him and pay for the photos, and as we leave he gives my girls some candies. As I help my little girls scramble into our van, I am aware that what I am feeling at this moment will be no different from what I will feel when they leave my home for good. Then I drive away from the photo studio, and take one last look at the front window of the shop and the chronology of that kind man's life.

On the day that my in-laws leave to return to England, we visit the farm early in the morning. Emi and Blaise had showed their visiting grandparents the farm and the garden the day after they had arrived, but since then we have been so busy, we haven't been to the farm in over a week. We are shocked by what we see. Grasshoppers have been eating the greens off what was left of my prized onions, and every leaf off all the beans and potatoes. We get out of the car and walk toward the garden slowly, with disbelief. Grasshoppers fly up and around us all with every step, like clouds of dust. Emi screams and demands that I carry her.

"What happened?" she asks. She is the first to say anything.

Once I am over the shock, and after a closer inspection, I feel surprisingly serene about it all. The grasshoppers may have liked the leaves, but they obviously don't like the beans and peas themselves. There are quite a few hanging on every plant, and we set to work picking the remains: two shopping bags full of yellow beans and green peas. I dig up the last of the onions; some of them still have green stalks. There are loads of onions; I can return to Uncle Leonard a fine supply of seed onions for his garden next year, if he should need them. I also will drop off a bagful at the home of Cousin Barry, who happened to mention that he loves to eat raw onions (just like Nellie McClung) — and also to the man living in the church up the highway; he told me the same thing. I snap a few photos of Emi and Blaise standing among the naked stalks of potatoes, which look like stands of bleached coral. I pull up a stalk: not bad, a few small new potatoes are clinging to the roots. There is more where they came from.

"Will potatoes grow without leaves?" I ask. No one seems to know, not even Emelyn, so we compromise; pulling out half of them and leaving the rest. It has been dry lately and we will be gone for another week on our road trip to the foothills of the Rockies. As I head back to the van with the bags of vegetables, I notice a paper stuck on the side door of the house. I walk over and see it is a note from Uncle Leonard and Aunty Elsie. *Greg,*

Will drop by another time it says. They have been here. Uncle Leonard must have seen my garden. I can feel my face getting hot with embarrassment.

As we head back to Beausejour, we stop in at the Baker farm, where husband and wife are in the shade of a tree beside their home. Darrel and I step out of the van for a quick word. I am holding Andy Baker and his brother to the promise of a ride in a combine. I can see that harvesting has begun, and I need to know if it will still be going on when we get back from Calgary. Terry Baker is seated in a chair with a towel around his shoulders, his wife Laurie standing behind him. When Terry recognizes me he jumps up and comes over to us, and I introduce him to my husband. Terry gives me a big hug; this is the first time I have seen him all summer long.

"Are you giving your husband a haircut?" I say to Laurie over Terry's shoulder.

She is smiling at me, and holds up something in her hand. "Have you ever seen one of these?"

I focus on what she is holding and it looks — alarmingly — like a nit comb. I back off. It seems that my only embrace with a Baker Boy will be a brief one — and troubled, too. I think of how to respond, and remember something I read in my daughter's nursery school parents' manual. "Cool! Lice like clean hair, you know! So no stigma . . . eh!"

After a chat about the suspected origins of the pestilence, Terry assures me that they have at least another ten days of harvesting, so we won't miss out on our combine ride after all. I tell them we'll be back at the end of the week, then head back to Winnipeg to prepare for our drive west.

The next day, we fill the van and head out on the Trans-Canada Highway due west, and Grandma and Grandpa are along for the ride. Our first stop is Regina, for a Habitat for Humanity Build, one of four my parents are involved in this summer. It turns out my parents need to get to Regina, and then on to Medicine Hat, for two Habitat builds, and we are happy to be able to give them a lift. Lemonade from lemons, we're turning this frustrating endeavour into a pleasure trip of the Wild West. I've scouted out all the best kids' attractions from here to Calgary. We stay at hotels with waterslides, and eat copious amounts of subway sandwich. We listen to Scotty and Lulu, and ABBA, and the Bee Gees (Aunty Emelyn's favourites) one thousand times. The needed visa is, as promised, obtained in a single day, without much fuss, but with a lot of waiting.

In between the interview and picking up the visa, we have an outdoor lunch in Olympic Plaza, and come across none other than Nellie McClung herself, in bronze, along with the rest of the 'Famous Five': Henrietta Muir Edwards, Louise McKinney, Irene Parlby, and Emily Murphy. These women were the ones who successfully challenged the definition of 'personhood' in the British North America Act; thanks to them, women in Canada became — legally — people. I snap a photo of my daughters standing among them. *Thank you, ladies.* Later, we take the 'alligator', as Emi calls it, to the top of Calgary Tower. The view from the tower is going to be our one chance to see the Rocky Mountains — we simply do not have any time to spare to venture farther west — but the smoke from nearby forest fires obliterates the peaks and covers the sky in a yellowish haze. As we walk along the streets of downtown Calgary, fluff is suspended in the air, which I initially take to be from cottonwoods, as it is in Winnipeg, until I realize that there are no trees in the vicinity. Then it strikes me that it is ash from the forest fires, falling around us like a light dusting of snow.

We head south early the next morning, not wanting to take the same route home. We pass through Lethbridge, then a small town called Bow River, where we stop to take a photo of Pinto McBean; the giant, smiling, cowboy-hatted pinto bean that welcomes one to Bow River. The photo is an excellent addition to Emi's photo collection of 'Roadside Big Things' which already included a giant turtle (from Boissevain), a golfball (Gilbert Plains), a big Canada Goose (Lundar) a camel (Glenboro), and Chuck the Channel Cat (Selkirk, the catfish capital of Canada). We get back onto the Trans-Canada for an hour, then detour south into the driest nether-world of southwest Saskatchewan, to a tiny town called Eastend. There *is* method in my madness. Specifically, I want to check out Wallace Stegner House, the house where the famed writer and conservationist lived in his youth and which is now available for writers to live for a few weeks at a time. I had been entertaining the idea of living there, and want to see if it would be doable with kids. The new T. rex Discovery Centre has just opened in town, and I am optimistic that my girls would enjoy the experience of living there for a short while, someday.

Wallace Stegner House is even more lovely and quaint in real life than its photos on the Internet let on. The town, too, is a gem; a tiny green oasis in a big dusty valley. I park on the main street to make inquiries and as I exit the car, the desert heat accosts me roughly. I make my way to the constituency office of the local member of parliament, and I hear someone talking in the back office about Bovine Spongiform Enceph-alopathy over the phone. I head to the receptionist to pick up an application form for Wallace Stegner House, and before I know what's happening, the receptionist is handing me her telephone. I am talking with Sharon Butala, a local writer of national acclaim, whose books I have read and enjoyed. She is the one in charge of the program, apparently. I am nervous, spluttering, trying to explain myself, but soon into my explanation, Ms. Butala is telling me things that don't seem to make sense. Blackout in America. New York and Ontario. CNN.

"My goodness," I say, "Oh my *goodness!*" The receptionist looks up at me sharply. Eventually, Ms. Butala and I speak briefly about the application procedure and I return the receiver, letting the curious receptionist in on the major event that was just now starting to unravel out east, and ending the conversation by saying I hope to be back someday. I get back in the car and then head up to the Discovery Centre for a fascinating look at the Tyrannosaur bones unearthed in the area, although I have to present the museum as a Fairy Discovery Centre for Emi, who declares that she is afraid of dinosaurs.

We spend another night in Regina; at the same hotel with the water-slide, then spend most of the next day heading east on the Trans-Canada, getting into Winnipeg around eight o'clock in the evening. We have added the Saskatchewan and Manitoba province-welcoming markers, as well as a miniature grain elevator-cum-tourist information booth (Grenfell, Saskatchewan) and a rather politically-incorrect Indian head (Indian Head, Saskatchewan) to our photo collection of roadside big things. I am glad to get back to Manitoba, which I now appreciate as being a welcoming, emerald-green paradise, compared to the parched dun-coloured hills of Saskatchewan and Alberta that we have been driving through all week long. I am glad that the task of fetching Emelyn's visa is behind us with some fun along the way. But mostly, I am just plain weary from driving all those miles. Emelyn and Emi and Blaise and I take our leave of that van like four bats out of hell. I am back in time for the Schreyer golf tournament tomorrow, but as I crash into bed later that night, I wonder if I am going to be able to play.

CHAPTER 25

More politics

By 1958, THE PROVINCIAL LIBERALS were too long in power, since 1922, and they became too arrogant and wasteful. This was a provincial election year. They were asked to build a floodway but did not act upon it, so they, too, were voted out of office. Just like the federal Liberals, they wanted to have the CCF join them. The CCF, under the leadership of Mr. Stinson, would not join them, and so the Conservatives formed the government under Duff Roblin as leader and Premier of Manitoba, with 26 members. The Liberals had 21 seats and the CCF ten. It was the first time in history that a CCF candidate was elected, for the constituency of Fisher. And the constituency of Broken-head was formed for the first time, where my son Edward was elected for the CCF and at the age of 22 years, the youngest member ever to be elected in Manitoba. There was a fair harvest in 1958, but grain was hard to sell that year because of weak market demand.

In 1959, the provincial Conservatives wanted a majority and so they called another election. This time they elected 35 members. The Liberals had 12 and the CCF seven. The CCF leader, Mr. Stinson, was defeated, but came back to the legislature to help the boys, until Russ Pawley took over as leader. This time the Conservative government began to arrange for the building of the floodway. It took a lot of time and work and money. Some of the engineers thought if the Red River could have been dredged and the silt taken out south of the Lockport Bridge, it would have answered the same purpose.

In 1960, there was not much snow and no rain early in the spring. The farmers seeded quite early in the spring, and because it was dry, the grain sprouted and appeared out of the ground but did not grow. Weeds that had a root deeper than grain did quite well, so in about the end of June, the grain, weeds and grass were cut for hay which was needed to feed the livestock as hay was very poor that year The wheat that was planted on the summerfallow did well. It came up quite heavy, but due to dry weather the straw was very short. When the wheat began to head we got a nice rain. Although the straw was short, the kernel was well filled and we got about 30 bushels to the acre. The swathing job was the hardest after that rain; the wild oats began to grow. It was about 12 inches tall when swathed. It was hard to cut as the green oats would block the knives of the swather and would break the rivets in the bar. It took two days of work instead of one. But it had its advantages, too. We pressed the straw and the green oats in bales and it was very good feed for winter.

The delegates of the CCF went to Ottawa to formulate policies after that defeat of the 1958 election, and to vote for a new leader as Coldwell did not want to take the leadership after his defeat in 1958. There were two members vying for the leadership; Tommy Douglas and Hazen Argue, who held a seat in Saskatchewan. But the delegates picked Tommy Douglas. The other event of 1960 was that the delegates changed the name of the party from the Co-operative Commonwealth Federation to the New Democratic Party. At a CCF policy meeting in Beausejour, my suggestion was that the new name should be the Social Democratic Party of Canada. They did not follow my advice, but whatever the name, it is the substance that counts.

– John James Schreyer

"I SAW YOUR CORN," says one alpha-male cousin, barely able — or perhaps hardly trying — to contain his mirth. "I don't think it's ever going to grow any ears. You'll have to keep it growing for five years before you get anything to eat off of it."

How word gets around. I am more embarrassed by this teasing than I care to admit. Emelyn and the girls and I slept in this morning, and so I am almost late for the tournament. I have only just arrived at the golf course in Sandy Hook, on the edge of Lake Winnipeg, and already the teasing has started. I know there will be more to come; I am looking through the window of the pro shop and can see the rest of my uncles and aunts and cousins lining up their golf carts, ready to play, probably wondering where I am and looking forward to bugging me about my vegetables. All my uncles, and a good number of my male cousins, are of the competitive alpha-male variety, and I think they are going to use this as a chance to psych out their competition — namely me.

I humbly accept the ribbing before asking this cousin to pay for my green fees; I am out of cash from the road trip, it's a Saturday, and I have just received a lecture from the proprietor of the golf course about why he won't accept American Express. Alpha cousin — my White Knight — agrees magnanimously. He is known as the family jokester and perhaps he feels that he has gone a little too far in his gibes about my gardening abilities. But how can I shoot back? It's true; my garden looked pathetic last time I saw it, and I can't imagine what has become of it now. I'll be taking the girls to see it tomorrow, and I am afraid of what we will find. I am contemplating the sad possibilities when Uncle Leonard approaches me, with his trademark grin and swagger.

"Looks like your garden needs some help."

I nod, red-faced. "But I learned a lot, Uncle Leonard. The girls and Emelyn had fun. If I did it again, I would do things differently," I reply, somewhat defensively. "I'd till it a few more times first. A little Roundup before I plant," I add, trying to sound like I know what I'm talking about. My Uncle Leonard's response is to look at me, laugh some more, and then walk away shaking his head.

I have the satisfaction of beating Uncle Leonard at golf later in the day. My team — consisting of Uncle George (the Patriarch); Uncle Leonard's middle son, Cousin Jim (a former Mister Manitoba, a volleyball coach for the University of Manitoba, and our family's undisputed super-athlete); and the teenage son of my White Knight — has come in second place in this year's Texas Scramble. Moreover, despite playing golf only a few times a year, I was able to bring our team in under par by sinking a longshot putt when it was most needed. It was Cousin Jim's natural coaching abilities that got us through the game, however; his positive reinforcement was relentless. When I sunk that putt, I had all my team-mates cheering and giving me pats on the back. Even when we learned that we had to take second place to Cousin Brian's team — again — I was still puffed with pride.

That evening at the Awards Banquet (a euphemism for potluck/barbecue; the awards being anything anyone wanted to bring, ranging from baseball caps and T-shirts to picnic dinnerware and towels — most things looking suspiciously as if they had been acquired free of charge) many non-golfing family members show up, and I am thrilled to meet the newest baby girl in the family; the one who took over that honour from Emi and Blaise.

"Where are your kids?" asks a cousin, visiting from back east.

"Well, they don't know how to golf. They're at Mom and Dad's," I say, by way of a joke.

"Where *is* your dad?" asks someone else. "Why isn't he playing this year?"

I stop laughing; the annual family golf tournament is an important event, not to be missed. "He's in Australia — on business." It's true; he had flown there directly from his last Habitat build in Vancouver — that much I knew.

"What about your mom?" asks someone else.

"She's in Quebec City."

"What's she doing there?"

"She's christening an icebreaker."

The relatives nod. Some look like they don't believe me, though. But this is also true; my mother was asked to christen the *Amundsen,* which she had christened 20 years ago in its former life as the *Sir John Franklin,* a Coast Guard icebreaker, and which has now been refitted as an arctic research vessel.

"So — did you bring the plaque?" asks one of my aunts.

"What plaque?"

"Your dad hosted the tournament last year. He has the plaque. He was supposed to get the names of last year's winners engraved on it . . . he has the plaque."

I swallow hard. There are at least a dozen alpha-males looking at me — and even an alpha-aunt or two. I am actually quite nervous by now. I start to speak — I will be making excuses — but then someone starts to chuckle, and then a few more people. "Never mind, Karmel," says Uncle George in his gentle way. It's sounds to me like they are used to this kind of delinquent behaviour from my branch of the family — or perhaps from their little brother. I chuckle along with them. Dinner is served and, after filling up on Polish sausages, perogies, and corn-on-the-cob; and collecting my prize (a beach towel) I head home. I am thrilled with my performance on the course. But, more than that, I am filled with the knowledge that the kind-hearted, funny, strong, entertaining, competitive, intelligent, loyal people I just spent the day with are *my* people. They are my daughters' people. We may not see them much, but that's okay — we are still a part of this precious circle of friends.

Early the next day, Emelyn and Emi and Blaise and I head out to the farm. It is time to wind up our farm project. I get Emi and Blaise to help me dig up the few remaining potato plants, and the bone-dry earth gives them up to us easily. I wield my camera. Emi and Blaise hold the potato plants up in the air and shout, "We did it!"

Do potatoes continue to grow after the leaves have been eaten off by grasshoppers? I believe the answer is no. But it doesn't matter; I am looking at my daughters' triumph as they hold the dangling plants up high, proud of themselves and of what they have accomplished. The plants they have in their hands are nothing but desiccated, leafless branches, but the small potatoes cling tenaciously to them. "We'll cook them tonight, with a nice roast beef," I say to Emi and Blaise. Then, after inspecting the row of stunted corn (Alpha cousin was right; those ears are about the size of my own), we gather the last of our vegetables, which include a few more peas and beans and quite a few more onions, and place them on the picnic table to admire. There is enough for one final, wonderful, meal.

I think back to my relatives' teasing the day before, and I know it was worth it. I also got a lot of praise; from other relatives — primarily of the younger generation and female persuasion — who understood that my farm project was more of a learning experience, and not a competition. The garden was an absolute success; more than I had ever imagined it could be when I thought of it in the first place. I am proud of all of us. It's true I had imagined that there would be something to leave behind when we headed back to Hong Kong — our gift to the garden-less relatives — but this is not going to be. The girls and I give our garden one long, last look. How can we not feel proud?

Next stop is the Baker farm, to let them know we are back in town and hoping to make an appointment for a combine ride — perhaps in a few days. They are well into the harvest now; I notice that the wheat field by our farm has already been cleared. We drive up to the farmhouse and see quite a large gathering of Bakers at the side in the shade of the tree.

"Hi! We're back!" I say as I hop out of the van. "We're not too late are we?" I am assuming we're not. Terry had said it would be another ten days one week ago.

"We're just heading out in an hour or so," says Terry. "In a few hours we'll be caught up."

I nod. "That's good. So, can we come — maybe Tuesday?"

Terry smiles. "No, what I mean is, we'll be finished in a few hours —"

I am alarmed. "What? You mean you'll be — *finished?*" I look at the other Bakers assembled, it seems just like any other quiet Sunday morning with family. I would have thought that the moment a farm family officially finishes the harvest is a time of great celebration. Where's the Champagne? Something's not right. I am confused — and disappointment is creeping up inside me, too.

Clarence, Terry's father, comes over to explain the situation, quelling my unease. "We'll be finished with the grains today. The soybeans will be in a couple of weeks. And the sunflowers not until October," he says patiently.

We do not have to miss the harvest after all. But I have left my camera back in Winnipeg, and I want photos of this moment. "Okay then," I reply. "I just want to go get my camera. We'll come back after lunch." Blaise will want a nap after lunch, I think. "Say — around three?"

Both Bakers look startled. Terry's eyes are wide and he hems before he speaks. "No, you can't go back. Stay here. We're just going to get out there in about an hour."

I get the picture: now is our only chance. "We'll be back in an hour," I say. I run back to the van, and zoom back to Winnipeg to get my camera, pick some flowers and grab one of my novels to give to Alyssa as a gift. We make the trip in record time, I'm sure, but even so, by the time we get back, the Baker boys are already in the field. However, their visiting parents are on their way home and offer to lead us out to the field where they are harvesting the last of the wheat. I am surprised when they drive right onto a field, but I follow nonetheless, and we park our vans in one corner. We all get out and watch as two giant red combines make their way around the field and back to our corner. After the photo opportunity, Emelyn and Blaise climb aboard the huge machine and sit next to Terry — in what Clarence refers to as the 'banker's seat'. They are excited, and Emi and I watch as the machines slowly make their way again around the field. It is terribly hot, but I had heard that the cabins of these farm machines verged on the luxurious: air-conditioning, plush seating, and classical music piped in. I know Blaise and Emelyn must be having a grand time up there.

Emi and I continue to watch from the comfort of our van. At the far corner, I realize that one of combines, the one Blaise and Emelyn are in, is no longer moving. After several minutes of inactivity, I am beginning to suspect that the combine has broken down. Oh bother; Emi has already indicated that she is afraid of the big machines and will not go on, and I am feeling that we have already insinuated ourselves too much into what I now understand is an operation of military precision. The breakdown convinces me that we have made enough of a nuisance of ourselves. What I want to do now is just get my kid and get out of everyone's way. I put the car in drive and inch our way towards the stalled combine. About halfway there, I see Terry jump down from the cab. He is running towards my vehicle. I roll down the window as he approaches.

He is panting, but he manages a smile. "Gee, Karmel, the ground is so hot today, I am afraid you will start a fire with your muffler. It's very dangerous," he says. I think he is trying not too sound too alarmed, but I am alarmed enough for both of us.

"Oh my goodness I'm sorry. I just was coming to get Blaise and Emelyn. I thought you had broken down."

He laughs. "Oh no. We're full. I was just waiting for the truck to come and take what I've got."

I am relieved to hear that, but I am very nervous about the possible danger I am in the middle of causing. I explain that Emi is not ready for a ride and that I will just take the others back. Terry offers to take me for a ride in the combine once he has made his way around to our corner of the field. He is so insistent — and once again I am awed by frontier hospitality. I really want to — but no, it won't be this time. Not this year. Everything is starting to feel so rushed. Only ten more days to go. "Thanks," I reply. "I'll be back next year." Terry smiles and runs off to get Emelyn and Blaise. The truck has just arrived. Terry returns with Blaise in his arms, and Emelyn behind, then waves and races back to his combine. As I drive our vehicle back onto the road, a car pulls up, and Alyssa, Terry's daughter — and Emi's new friend — jumps out. She runs up to our vehicle with my book in her hand, the one I had given not much more then an hour ago.

"It's good," she says. She has started reading it already. She thrusts a paper into my hand and runs off to her father's combine, which is now emptying its load of grain into the truck. I watch the young girl running across the field, and I envy her: she will be riding high in a combine with her dad today, watching the grain be sent on its way, the tangible evidence of her family's hard work. It must be very self-affirming to see that, I think. I look down at the paper in my hand. I assume it is a thank-you note but it isn't. It is a story on one page; her creative writing, and I am touched, not sure if she is wanting some professional critique. As we drive back to Winnipeg, I begin to feel a little panicked. Only ten more days to go. So little time. Things half done; like participating in the harvest. Things not yet done — and perhaps too late now; like raspberry picking, or canoeing down the Brokenhead. Or finding Great-uncle Anton and Great-aunt Catherine. I didn't make rhubarb compote. I didn't see a fortune-teller; don't know what the future holds.

We arrive back in Winnipeg and spend the rest of the afternoon chatting with some visiting relatives who have come to Manitoba from out of town for the golf tournament. They are interested to hear about our stay on the farm, and impressed by the fact that Blaise has helped in the Baker harvest. They are also eager to see how my girls have grown; some see Blaise for the first time, and the girls know they are on show; Emi has changed dresses several times. Steve pops by and we talk about the effects of the power failure in the east on the chances of some dams being built in northern Manitoba. I, for one, hope the dams go through. I hope my husband can get a job one day on one of those projects, so that we can live in Manitoba.

CHAPTER 26

Change

As I'VE SAID BEFORE, nothing helped them. In the election of 1962, the once-majority Conservative government of 1958, the largest in history, folded like a stack of old straw; yes, from 208 seats to 116. The Liberals under the leadership of Mike Pearson had about 126 seats, or the minority, the Conservatives held 116 seats, and the NDP gained some seats. We got Stanley Knowles back.

The provincial Conservatives, under Duff Roblin, also called an election in 1962 in late fall, although they had another year to go. They thought the chances were good to get another majority and they did get a majority of 36 seats, with the Liberals 14, and the NDP were down to seven seats, the worst since the 1940s.

Times were getting better under the Liberals. They seemed to understand the farmers better by now. The Liberals continued selling wheat to the USSR and China, not only wheat but livestock, too. The next three years, nothing important was done. The Liberals had no majority and they were asked to do some things and they got annoyed. One of the ministers told the Prime Minister that if they called an election soon they could get a majority, so after three years, in 1965, the Prime Minister asked for dissolution of parliament and called an election. The result was that they won 131 seats. The Conservatives lost seats. But the NDP won seats. Our seat of Springfield was recaptured from the Conservatives. The Conservative member was elected in 1959 and re-elected in 1962 with a 6000 vote majority over the NDP. In 1965 he was defeated by Ed Schreyer, by 800 votes.

The provincial Conservatives were not doing much, but they were trying to get industry to come to Manitoba. They did not check who they were dealing with when they got these people from Switzerland. They were not interested in manufacturing. They were out to defraud the province. They started building a mill in 1965, and by 1970 it was still not done.

Another event in our life was that I retired from farming in 1964. I still kept some cows and hogs until the fall of 1965, when I sold the cows and hogs, as I thought and knew that I could not work hard as in some cases you have to lift bags, and that I could no longer do, and now I have a small tractor for working in the garden.

– John James Schreyer

I SENSE MY GRANDFATHER'S frustration with the calling of snap elections, as well as his feeling that, in 1962, the Conservatives got their just desserts. Too bad he wasn't around 30 years later; he would have been impressed by the enormity of that denouement, when that same party went from its highest number of seats ever, down to two. But I also see my grandfather's disdain for the cynical practice might explain why my father needed a little time to canvass the constitutional experts and mull things over when, as governor general in 1979, he was asked by Prime Minister Joe Clark to dissolve parliament. He did, of course, and an election was subsequently called; but from what I remember, some people thought he had taken a little too long to do it.

I also notice that mention of my own arrival on the scene has not made it into my grandfather's memoirs; by then he had probably lost count of the grandchildren. I was born in 1964, the same year he retired from farming. My grandfather had entered into one of the final phases of his life, marked by that rite-of-passage called 'retirement' — long before I even knew him. This gives me hope, because in all my memories of him and my grandmother, there is nothing that comes close to the image of a tired old retiree waiting out the days. My grandparents kept a garden, which my girls and I are now continuing; they grew their own vegetables, and flowers too. They would come to Winnipeg to visit us often, and I know that they boarded an airplane for the first time in their lives to come to Ottawa to babysit us — how's that for grandparental love? My grandmother was as civic-minded as her husband, although she may have preferred the church over politics (Uncle George told me this summer how she was not afraid to stand up during the occasional town meeting and give the bickering trustees a talking-to, even as she nervously fiddled with the handkerchief in her hands). She made her quilts and then gave them to away to people who needed them. My grandfather taught me how to play Go. He told me about boys. He was strong.

I stare at my grandfather's manuscript; there is just one more page and I feel a little uneasy. It is something I can barely bring myself to feel, but I force myself. It is as if, the more I learn about the man, the more I realize I never knew. I want to bring him — bring them both — all of them — back — if only just to say: *Oh Grandpa, Oh Grandma, I hardly knew you. And I am sorry.* My memories are full of gaps. I remember my maternal grandmother well enough, or so I had thought all these years, but this summer, every time I tried to recollect one conversation with her, nothing came to my mind. This realization had compelled me to ask my mother if Grandma Schulz spoke English. My mother was shocked by the question. "She spoke English very well," my mother had replied. There was a knot in my stomach when she said that. There is now.

I hardly knew you.

I want to grab my children and run. I will run to the nearest grand-parent, before it's too late. I am crying; they are not here. Two have gone home to Yorkshire. One is in Australia. One is breaking a bottle of Champagne over an icebreaker in Quebec. In a few days my daughters and I will return to the other side of the planet. *Come back! Hurry! We don't have much time.*

It is times like this when a little 'Disney Therapy' is called for. The term is my own invention, but I believe the practice itself is widespread. I coined the term when my children started watching videos, and I was glad to have an excuse to rent the movies of my own childhood, such as *Bambi,* which brought back my memories of snuggling with my mother and father in my pyjamas at the drive-in. Nor was I surprised when Emi informed me that Snow White was her favourite princess. You can't beat the old classics, but I do believe that Disney has outdone itself in recent years. Some of my favourite Disney movies are the story of the Chinese heroine, *Mulan* (great after a bad day at work, or when you are hit with a case of low self-confidence) and *Lilo and Stitch* (wonderful for reaffirming that a family can be many things — wonderful in every shape and form). Today I know what I need to see. After dinner, my girls and I will get into our pyjamas, snuggle down on the sofa, and watch *The Lion King.* We will learn, again, about how we know who we are — about the 'Great Circle of Life'.

Later that night, when the girls are asleep, I sit at my father's desk, and look at my 'to do' list. *Ich Weiss Dass Mein Erloser Lebt.* I still haven't made that call to Johann Wong's mother. Never mind, I'll try the Internet. I do a Google search for the German phrase, and in seconds I am reading an English translation: *I know that my Redeemer lives.* It is from the Bible, the Book of Job, and a traditional part of the Christian burial service, I discover. And not only that, it was inspiration for part of Handel's *Messiah.* I listen to it, on my father's computer — there's nothing you can't find on the Internet. The music is beautiful and familiar. I should have guessed. What does it mean, though, to know that my Redeemer lives? I am aware of the suffering of Job, but I continue to search; there are more than a few sermons published online that attempt to answer this question. I learn that Job made this declaration only when he had nothing left. It was his moment of clarity at his darkest hour. A defiant shout of hope. A measure of his faith. I would like to believe it; I want to understand.

*   *   *

I have special plans for this afternoon. It isn't something that was on my list; it stems from a conversation Emi and I had had the other day while in the kitchen, when she had asked for a drink of water. I pulled a mug out of the cupboard and noticed, as I was filling it, that it was a 'Brokenhead mug'. In this house, that refers to a mug with the official centennial crest of the Rural Municipality of Brokenhead and the words 'Birthplace of former governor general Edward Schreyer' on it. Our conversation went something like this.

"Do you know what that says?'

Emi studies the letters. I fully expect her to say that she does not. But instead, she nods.

"You know what this says?" I say incredulously, pointing to the letters. I am impressed and proud. Emi is a genius!

"Yes. It says 'Birthday of Grandpa'."

"Who told you that?"

Emi beams proudly. "Grandpa."

Ever since that conversation, I have wondered what Emi thinks of it all; these unconventional things going on around here, that Emi seems to take for granted. Like Grandpa's speeches; Grandpa and Grandma building houses; going on stage to help Grandpa open a witch's hut; helping her sister and Grandma open a lily festival; Grandpa's name on a school; a picture of our farm in a history book at the library; Mummy's surname (and her own, as well as her sister's, second middle name) on a postage stamp; Grandpa's name on a coffee mug. And, not to mention, she'll have a royal pillbox to put her baby teeth in when the time comes. I must admit to myself that this is pretty extraordinary. But I have never wanted to think of my parents as extraordinary. I have always determined that they must be ordinary people; ordinary parents, and now, ordinary grandparents. I can feel so much admiration for my parents' pioneer families, for what *they* accomplished, but when it comes to my own parents and their accomplishments, I realize I am have been taking them for granted, too.

There may have been one moment, however, when there was a lapse in that thinking. It was at Rideau Hall — the imposing edifice where I spent my teenage years — and I had invited some friends over for a party in the Tent Room. I remember dancing away and then noticing suddenly that the room seemed a little empty, so I turned to the doorway. I saw my parents; they had just come home from an official black-tie event somewhere, and were making a parental check on my party. My friends had gathered around them, everyone was talking; they were smiling, shaking hands. At that moment, I saw what my friends all saw: the Governor General of Canada, and the First Lady. I have never forgotten that moment, or the feeling that came with it — when they were not Mom and Dad, but someone else.

That was just one moment though, and it was 20 years ago, but there are still reminders. My father's phone rings alarmingly often. He's still busy giving speeches, going to meetings, helping people who need his help. People still ask him if he is Ed Schreyer; even my British husband is used to that — it has happened so often, even on the golf course. How much of this do I try to explain to my daughters?

I have decided to take Emi and Blaise to Manitoba's Legislative Building. "There's a big picture of Grandpa hanging up there," I tell them. My girls are missing their Grandpa and Grandma, and a portrait on a wall will have to suffice for now. As a youngster, I sometimes spent weekends at the legislature while my father worked overtime. Our friend Dave Chomiak reminded me earlier this summer that one of his memories of me as a kid was when I would go whizzing by his office door (where he worked as my father's executive assistant) on my skateboard, shouting, "Hi Dave!" I remember the security guards smiling indulgently too. I guess they knew who I belonged to, but I doubt if that behaviour would be tolerated these days.

Today, when I take my girls and Emelyn to 'the Ledge', we stop in first at Dave's office and although I am disappointed to learn he is in meetings,

I am delighted to be able to have a chat with one of his boys, who is keeping himself busy alongside Dave's assistants. Suddenly another young boy comes in and I assume the two are friends, but this is not the case; the boy is helping his mother on her mail rounds. The hallowed halls of Manitoba's seat of government are — and always have been, I decide — a wonderfully child-friendly place. But it's way too warm in here; there is no air-conditioning. "A political hot-potato," I am told. Hot, indeed.

We take a self-guided tour of the building; a photo-op by the Grand Staircase flanked by the two enormous bronze buffaloes — earlier this summer I had found a family photo with Santa, taken in what must have been 1970 in this very place — and then I lead Emelyn and the girls to the Pool of the Black Star, a lovely round foyer-like area, with a polished black and white floor. We do a quick song-and-dance and marvel at the acoustics. With that done, it is time to start searching for Grandpa's portrait; I know it's here somewhere, although I have not seen it myself. We wander the echoing halls and then, in some side wing, we see a series of large frames hanging at the end of a lonely corridor. My girls race ahead expectantly. But what's this? These names — and faces — do not look familiar to me, and then I realize that these are all Speakers of the House. So where are all the premiers that my grandfather mentions in his memoirs? Where's Bracken and Rodmond Roblin? Where's Duff Roblin, my father's favourite?

"Where's Grandpa?" asks Emi.

"I don't know, Emi. But we are going to find out."

We go to the nearest office and ask the people therein where the premiers' portraits can be found. "They are hanging in two separate meeting rooms, and the doors should be unlocked," they tell us.

"Thank you," I say. I smile at Emi and she smiles up at me expectantly, I take her hand and together we march over to the room next door. At first glance, I can see that the walls are lined with large oil portraits of unsmiling, bearded men. Sombre colours. Scary-looking men. These pictures must represent Part I of the premiers' portraits — the early years.

"Where's GRANDPA?" Emi puts her hands on her hips and shakes her head, exasperated. We hightail it to the next meeting room. It's locked. I go back to the people in the first room and and they phone the security station to come and unlock the door. "It should be unlocked," the woman says, mystified. I think so too.

We march back to the door and wait for the security guard, who saunters over with the key, and waits while we file in. I see the walls lined with more large portraits. Classic portrait poses, dark colours, but lighter, cheerier colours, too — and a few familiar faces. Howard Pawley's portrait looks very nice; a good likeness. He must be pleased with that. Some of the portraits in this room are rather unconventional. Sterling Lyon has a dog in his painting. That's different. Duff Roblin's portrait, next to my father's, is quite small; just a head-and-shoulders portrait. But my father's portrait is quite unlike the majority of the others. For one thing, he is not seated in a chair. Also, the colours are different; he is not in a navy suit, but rather, that icon of 1970s menswear, the tan sports jacket, with wide lapels. My father's likeness is not as good as the others; he is not smiling, and his features are stylized, impressionistic. It is different, that's for sure, but not unbecoming. The eyes are a piercing, almost unnatural, blue — at least the person who did the painting got that right. I conclude that the reason for this impressionistic rendering of my father is because he couldn't be bothered to sit for the artist.

But as I examine the painting more closely, I realize that this cannot be the only reason; the whole painting is an abstraction; based not on realism, but metaphor. My father is standing in front of two distinctly different landscapes: on his right, the prairie's patchwork of fields of grain; on his left, unmistakable Canadian Shield country. I understand the significance of this immediately; he is standing where he was born, in the R.M. of Brokenhead, the transition zone between prairie and shield; two geographical regions, so vast and significant to Canada's landscape that one can hardly believe there is a place where that change is noticeable, and can be pinpointed; like the Great Rift Valley in Africa where tectonic plates are being pulled apart. My father is standing in the middle of it all; a part of both. I wonder to which part he would turn if he had to choose. I think I know. Lucky for him he never had to.

And then I notice something else; the sky in the painting is filled with dark and swirling clouds. What's this? Has the artist decided to invest his own opinions of my father's government into the painting? I know that's things were pretty chaotic in those first few years, when my father and his cabinet were pushing through a lot of dramatic new legislation, like government-owned auto insurance, for instance. These days, people like their low auto-insurance premiums, and their low hydro bills. My father told me once how the mayor of Winnipeg, Steven Juba, would often say to him, 'Slow down, son.' And I remember that people were sometimes demonstrating on the grounds of the legislature opposing my father's regime. Even as a kid, when you see someone waving a sign that reads: *Send the Schreyers to Siberia!* on the evening news, and your mother's worried face, you know that's something's up. But then another realization comes to me as I stand before the painting: it's clearing in the north.

I get it. It's where Manitoba's energy comes from. *It was clearing in the North! Tomorrow would be fine!* I continue to examine the portrait, and admire my own clever interpretation of it.

"What's Grandpa holding?" asks Emi

"Those are blueprints," I tell my daughter.

"What's that mean?"

I am not sure if I know myself, but I will try to answer Emi's question. I kneel down and hug her, I whisper in her ear, "It means *plans,* Emi. Your Grandpa had plans for this place, plans for the future. Some of them even came true."

Emi looks up at her grandfather again. She nods. The guard is lingering by the door. From where he stands he cannot see the wall, so I grab a chair and hoist my children onto it, so that they are closer to their grandfather. I snap a quick photo, then look one last time at my father's official portrait as premier of Manitoba. How long will it hang on these walls?

"I like it," says Emi.

CHAPTER 27

Celebration

IN 1966 THE GRAIN WAS STILL the same price per bushel but it was still on quota and the market was not good, as there were no buyers, so that the farmers had to keep their grain over for the next year and then had no ready cash, so when they needed seed wheat and fertilizer they would have to borrow money to start their spring operation. The provincial Conservatives had to call an election as their four years were up. This time they came through with 31 seats, the Liberals with 13, the NDP with 11. Mr. Roblin was still Premier for a year, then resigned. The Conservatives held a leadership convention and Walter Weir, who represented the Constituency of Minnedosa, was elected leader and premier. There were four vacancies in 1968 of which three were won by the Conservatives and one by the NDP, at Thompson. But the Conservatives wanted to make sure they got a big majority, so they called a general election the next year. The voters turned against them, and that brought the NDP to power in 1969, under the leadership of Ed Schreyer.

A year earlier, on the federal scene, Trudeaumania swept the country, and so for the first time in six years and two sessions we had a majority government in Ottawa. Ed Schreyer was elected to parliament for the federal riding of Selkirk. He won the riding of Springfield in 1965; but before the next election, the two ridings of Springfield and Provencher were combined, and since he resided in the Kildonan-Selkirk area, he ran where he lived, and won with a big majority.

He stayed a year in the federal parliament and would have stayed on but, in 1969, the NDP party executives and a lot of people asked him to come back to Manitoba and to seek the leadership of the NDP here. He resigned his seat in Ottawa and won the leadership, and in June that same year defeated the Conservatives, and for the first time in the history of Manitoba we have a Social Democratic government. As the *Free Press* reported, he won the most seats: 28 for the NDP, 22 for the Conservatives, one Social Credit, five Liberals and one Independent. The Member for St. Boniface, Larry Desjardins, joined the NDP. That made 29 members and the NDP had a majority.

Other events in 1969 were we got Medicare but it was just in on April 1st. The payment was $17.00 a month. It was just too much for the small farmer and he could not pay it. But then the NDP changed that to an income-tax basis. Another legislative change was brought in, Autopac. It was a disgrace the way they let the insurance firms treat our young people. People under 25 were paying three times as much as an adult. The firms were overcharging the public, yet each year they raised the premium about 12 percent. Today they pay no more than an adult and beyond that the government has been able to cut the insurance rates by about five percent.

Another important legislation was passed; that of Unicity. The big firms all built out of the city into the suburbs to avoid paying higher taxes. Each municipality promised them tax cuts, leaving the City with very little revenue. The government united the City so that all the municipalities and the City levy the same taxes. So that is fair to all of them. Another important event was that my wife and I celebrated our 50th anniversary on the 18th of May, 1969. We had all our neighbours and family and old friends, about 500, celebrating with us.

We celebrated our Centennial in 1970. The Provincial Centennial of Manitoba was the most important event of all time. The Royal Family visited such places as Churchill and Thompson and The Pas, Beausejour and Steinbach, and visited the Legislature and spoke to thousands of people on the south side of the Legislative Building.

In 1971, the Manitoba government provided funds to help repair old-age pensioners' houses. The same in 1972 and 1973. It was to help the senior citizens as they could not do the repairing themselves and it created a lot of jobs for each locality. The government also gave each taxpayer a school tax rebate of $50. Also, the people that rented houses and apartments did get a rebate of $50, and in 1973 each taxpayer will get a rebate from $50 to $150 and now every senior citizen over 65 will be exempt from paying Medicare, starting April 1st. The government also will be financing more nursing homes, paying for all; patients will not be paying regardless of what financial status they are in. Even more important is there will be brighter, more cheerful living space for seniors needing help, instead of hopeless waiting lists because of such a small number of homes to go to. This, plus the new Home Care Program, should make a very big difference in the years ahead.

— *John James Schreyer*

AND SO ENDS MY GRANDFATHER'S MEMOIRS. The narrative ends in the future tense, looking forward, not back. The optimism in my grandfather's voice is clear, as he outlines what the social democratic government in Manitoba accomplished, and what they are going to. Reading it, a rather dry summation of statistics in some parts, you wouldn't know that he was referring to a government that was lead by his own son. And I, up until this time, never knew just how much my grandfather was behind the things my father and the others in his government had accomplished, almost as if he were whispering in my father's ear the whole time. Almost as if, on these last yellowed pages, he were giving himself a pat on the back. What am I saying? My grandfather didn't need to whisper — and my father didn't need to be told; he already knew what had to be done.

Our memories are beginning to converge at this point, in my grandfather's final entry. I don't remember meeting the royal family — not in 1970, anyway — but I do remember walking down a carpet inside the Winnipeg Arena, holding a cardboard spaceship with the words 'Hello 2070!' emblazoned on it, and, I do believe, visions of silvery-tinselled dancers and 'Age of Aquarius' music. It was Manitoba's Centennial celebrations; for my grandfather 'the most important event of all time'. I was six years old and it was fun indeed. But there are other experiences I associate with my father's career from those early days: I remember picketers in our yard, the Siberia signs, sitting beside my father in a parade, on the back of a convertible and someone coming out of the crowd to punch him. I remember bursting into tears, and the look on people's faces along the side of the road, and my parents pulling me down onto the back seat to hide me from the crowd, so they couldn't see how afraid I was. That wasn't fun.

My grandfather died suddenly when my father was campaigning in northern Manitoba for the 1977 Manitoba general election. That I also remember very well; I stood one row behind my father at the funeral. I saw his bowed head, I watched, with feelings of bewilderment and a little fear, as his tears fell to his feet. I've often seen him get misty-eyed; a Habitat For Humanity dinner for example, when new homeowners talk about their feelings as they enter their own home for the first time, and what it has meant for their family, will always have my dad reaching for a tissue. But I had never seen him weep such tears of sorrow. At the time, I didn't know that he was — among all the things he was — a son. When you are a child, mothers and fathers can be other things — teachers, premiers, taxi drivers — but they are parents above all else; they are not sons and daughters. When you're a child, you assume a parent cannot be afraid of losing a parent, because they *are* a parent. I know better now.

I am glad that my grandfather was a part of my father's first political successes; glad that he didn't witness my father's electoral defeat in 1977 to take his place as the Leader of the Opposition. I am sorry that he was not there to see his son become the governor general of Canada. My grandfather's family narrative is couched within a chronicle of Canada's more *political* history; prime ministers and premiers, party politics and the good fight — but I am sure he would have been pleased, and proud, because, now I know, he loved this country more than anything.

Optimism for the future. Things weren't always good; crops were still bad — prices worse — even at a time of patriotic celebration. But there was always something to celebrate. And there was always — always — hope. Canada had given my grandfather that, I hope Old Anton had felt the same way. Hello 2070. I wonder if my two girls will think to come to this place in 2070. They will be brand-new senior citizens themselves, by then; a concept I cannot get my head around, because even though I now know that I will not live forever, I want my children to be forever young. I have no idea where they will end their years, but now I hope — more than ever before — that they will find their way back here sometime along the way, like I did.

I am counting down the days now, in a flurry to get things done. Yesterday I took my girls and Emelyn back to the Beausejour-Brokenhead Museum, another thing I had been wanting to do all summer. The other day, my Aunt Lillian told me that she had donated the trunk that my great-grandfather Anton had brought when he came with his family to Manitoba. I wanted to see that, too. But when we got there the museum was closed for grounds work, so instead we bought some flowers and lay them on the graves of my grandparents, John James and Elizabeth. My grandfather's sister *is* buried next to him. I want so much to stay a while, but there will be no quiet time, with the girls.

Instead we drive to the farm, past the row of grain samples, the ghost house and the Cromwell sign. Emi sees our farmhouse a mile away. We get out of the car for one last look, and I find an old piece of fuschia-coloured sidewalk chalk in the drive. It is a reminder of our existence here. We had had a lot of fun playing with the big box of chalk. So many colours; we never even used half of them. I grab the piece of chalk and draw a big heart on the barn door: *Emi and Blaise were here*. I snap a picture of them by the door, another of them standing in the empty wheat field by the house. I take one of Emelyn and the girls; she takes one of the three of us. Okay girls, time's up. Let's go. And we're gone. I don't tell the girls that this is the last time they'll see the farm — at least for now. I don't want them to know. As we drive down the highway, I am preoccupied by the little white lie I am perpetrating on my girls, and I am not thinking of what lay ahead of us, in the road.

"Mama, look!" Emi shouts.

I suck in my breath, startled. I brake. "What is it, Emi?" I almost hit a deer once, a frightening experience.

"The Mightyhead."

Emelyn laughs. I let my breath go and relax. "Good girl."

We continue north to Lake Winnipeg for our last swim. The wind is up and the waves are high. Emi's swimming lessons have really built up her confidence over the last few months; she and I head into the waves eagerly. Emi no longer clings to me, demanding to be carried. She and I punch the waves when the big ones roll in . . . "Pow! Bam!" we say. Emi is fearless now. She even rode a pony the other day, at the summer fair in my parents' neighbourhood — after Blaise.

From a final round of visits to uncles, aunts, and cousins; to packing boxes that will be mailed across the ocean — our lives are a flurry of the urgent activity that I tried hard to avoid for these last days, but I hadn't factored in the US Department of Homeland Security. The reality of our daily lives is starting to pull us back into its grasp. For one thing, husband and Daddy are waiting for us back in Hong Kong (Darrel had returned there shortly after his parents returned to Yorkshire), Emi continues with kindergarten, I have my own work to get back to. Life goes on. The wheat is gone, and the garden on our farm is now empty, but we still have our memories. In these last few days, Emi and I talk a lot about the things we did and the people we met; it is a most enjoyable activity. We are not going to be sad to go, regretting the things we have not done. We are going to celebrate the fact that we could come in the first place, that we saw so much, and had so darn much fun. And learned so much about so many of us. My daughters have eaten perogies, they have ridden on ponies, they have run fearlessly into the waves of Grand Beach on a windy day, they have stood in the good earth of Manitoba, they have walked among rows of golden wheat, they have fended off grasshoppers without success, and they have prayed for rain. I give myself a pat on the back for a mission accomplished. And we'll come back again. There is no reason for tears.

It is late in the evening when we arrive back at my parents' home. I put my sleepy girls to bed, then head to my father's office to check the email. I notice that the voicemail message light on the telephone is blinking. I press a button and I sit, drowsy, and listen half-heartedly to a stranger's voice. I hate phones, and don't spend much time on them. I don't expect calls, either. The woman is calling from the office of St. Mary's cemetery. She apologizes for the delay in returning my call. I turn to the phone; I am listening now — go on.

"We have searched the burial records for an Anton Schreyer, aged 15, died in 1896, and for a Catherine Schreyer, aged 26, died in 1918." A pause follows. "There is no record of their burial. But the records we have prior to about 1920 are incomplete, I'm afraid. I'm sorry."

I press the button again, and listen to the voice repeats its message. So that's that. I am disappointed, but only a little. I wish I could pay my respects somewhere, but I don't think it makes a difference anymore. *I just wanted you to know that you haven't been forgotten.* I press another button on the telephone and the blinking light disappears. Then I go to bed on the floor between my sleeping daughters, imagining that my own message has been heard and understood.

My last day. I get up before the girls wake, let Emelyn know I am leaving, then drive off in the morning quiet. There is one more thing I want to do, something that I have been meaning to do all summer. I return to the windswept cemetery to say hello again to my great-grand-parents, Old Anton and Caroline. I am alone this time; I want to do this right. It seems odd to me, at first, that I should want to spend my last few moments by the Brokenhead with my great-grandparents, and not my grandfather John James and grandmother Elizabeth. After all, it is my grandfather's words that unlocked the biggest treasure of all; a chance to see his world grow, through his eyes. It is my world, too. Nevertheless, it is to the cemetery just north of Ladywood that I go on my last full day in Canada. I bring some flowers from my mother's garden and place them on the grass. The wind is whispering and I can hear a combine in the distance. I hear geese, too, but I do not look to see which way they are flying. It doesn't make a difference; they'll be back.

Hello, Great-grandpa Anton and Great-grandma Caroline. It's me again, Karmel — a mother. I know you wondered about the future. I know you had doubts. When your son died and your daughter died, you may have asked yourself if you had done the right thing. You often wondered what the future had in store. Maybe you even wished for a chance to see it, somehow. Well, we are the future you wondered about. My daughters are living the future you couldn't even imagine. But we are also living the same things you did: war and sickness. Grasshoppers. Death. Life. When I look at my daughters I can tell you that the future will be good. Yes, I believe the future will be good. This is my hope. So don't worry. Sleep well.

I cannot understand it, but tears are falling down my cheeks, and I let them come, don't try to wipe them away. *I am going to bring you back. We will not forget you, I promise. My daughters will know you — will know you all. They know you even now. They will come back. They will think about you. And you will come back to us. Thank you for your courage. Thank you for your strength. Thank you for the freedom you have given us. We will not forget. Come back to me. I am going to bring you back. . . .*

> For I know that my Redeemer lives, and at last he will stand upon the earth; and after my skin has been thus destroyed, then from my flesh I shall see God, whom I shall see on my side, and my eyes shall behold, I and no other.
>
> — *Job 19:25–27*

I am not sure how long I spend there. The wind has dried my tears, and I start to hear the world around me once again; the wind, the combine, an occasional car passing by on the highway. I look around, and my eyes rest on a boulder, surrounded by flowers, in the corner of the graveyard. I raise myself and walk over to it: *The St. Peter and St. Paul Parish Community remembers and honours the ancestors who not only brought faith to this community some 100 years ago, but through their daily example, showed us that we could live in harmony with our neighbours and the world. Thanks be to God. This memorial is placed where the early faith community erected its first church building. Dedicated June 27, 1999.*

I get back in the car, ready to turn south towards Beausejour, but turn north instead. This will be my last drive alongside the Brokenhead. I turn around at the intersection of Highway 317 and Highway 12, by the other boulder I'd often passed this summer and wondered about. But I stop and get out of the car this time, and see that the big rock is a memorial in honour of the postmasters of Deneross, from 1938 to 1970. I think about Old Anton, postmaster just down the road. From what my father told me, my grandfather's father had perhaps been more suited for postmaster than for pioneer farmer. He never did bushwork, my father had said. "Aside from clearing his own land for farming, he never went into the bush to work — not at all." But I think I know why; I imagine Old Anton must have been afraid, every time he watched his son and grandsons heading out. How brave he was to let them go. I think about the old man, and then I think about my young girls, and realize that the sentiment carved in the rock in the cemetery is just as fitting now, in Hong Kong; in Discovery Bay where we live — in my daughter's school ... *but through their daily example, showed us that we could live in harmony with our neighbours and the world.*

I turn the car around and head south. I pass through Brokenhead. I pass the cemetery again. I pass through Ladywood, pass the old Gables' General Store and the old church across from it. I pass the farm and note that there was rain here last night; it washed our pink chalk farewell message off the barn door. Already we are gone without a trace, I think, but then I look at the row of stunted, brown corn stalks and with a smile I realize that the thought is not altogether true. And then, just as I am driving by the Baker's fields, I notice a van parked at the side of the road. It is Clarence Baker, inspecting the sunflowers. His wife is in the van reading a book. I stop my vehicle on the other side of the road, wipe some more tears from my eyes with my shirt sleeves, and jog across the highway. He is happy to see me, and I am thrilled to see them both. Clarence shows me the head of a sunflower, heavy with seeds. He is pleased. Farming is still in his blood.

"But how are the rest of your crops," I ask. I had been reading all summer in the papers about despairing Canadian farmers. I expected to hear some bad news.

"It's the best year yet," is Clarence's surprising reply.

"But what about the drought? The grasshoppers?"

"Well, for us right here. It's the best year ever," he says. "We're lucky I guess."

My time here is not over yet. I am invited to follow Clarence and his wife to their son Andy's house for a visit. First we pick up Alyssa, and then over to her uncle's house one country-block down. I meet Andy's wife Jan, who tells us that Andy is not in because he's busy cleaning out a neighbour's grain bin. They need the extra space because their cereal grain crops are the best they have ever been. "We just got lucky this year," Andy's wife tells me, reiterating her father-in-law.

I see a tall boy come out of the house, followed by his younger cousin, the lovely Alyssa, who had gone inside to get him. He's one of these new Baker Boys I had heard about. Well, look here: a young girl who can dance *en pointe* and drive a tractor — and who is not afraid to do either; and a fine young man, who works the land alongside his father. I can see the future after all — and the future looks good.

I am a mother. In my mind I count the difference between this young man's age and my daughters'. And he has brothers, too. I smile; these are reasons to celebrate.

There's always hope, anyway.

CHAPTER 28

Wings

If you've heard the wild goose honking,
If you've seen the sunlit plain,
If you've breathed the smell of ripe grain, dewy, wet,
You may go away and leave it, say you will not come again.
But it's in your blood, you never can forget.

— in *The Second Chance,* by Nellie McClung

ON THE PLANE TO HONG KONG, while my daughters sleep, I have time to reflect upon our summer. I am reminded of a line from *Grain,* by Robert Stead: "I have often thought life is like a thresher, pouring out its cloud of straw and chaff and dust, and a little grain. A little hard, yellow, golden grain, that has in it the essence of life. . . ." I jot down a list; the golden grains of my summer. It is a collection of familiar notions, I realize, but I have decided that it is a comfort to have things in print. And it makes things easier to pass down. So here's what I learned by the banks of the Brokenhead:

Work hard. Have a passion. Opportunities are yours to make.
Love your spouse. Give generously.
Be proud of your children. And be proud of your parents, too.
Be optimistic, but learn to be brave; there will always be setbacks.
Be funny when you can; laughter is the best medicine.
Celebrate life.
Celebrate anything.

AFTERWORD

SINCE I WROTE THIS BOOK in the fall of 2003, many things have happened. For starters, while Emelyn, Emi, Blaise, and I were flying back to Hong Kong, a lab worker in Singapore was being diagnosed with SARS. It came about as a result of cross-contamination; the lab worker had been studying the West Nile virus. He survived. Canadian Beef was allowed back onto American plates in the summer of 2005. Saddam Hussein is on trial. Farmers around the world are in dire straits. And the world is bracing for the flu pandemic of the century.

On a more personal note, Blaise has started nursery school. Emi is in grade two and learning Putonghua. Aunty Emelyn is still with us. My husband is still building Hong Kong International Airport. I am still working on a long-overdue novel, set in Indonesia. Steve had the lead role in an independent short and is taking acting classes. Dave Chomiak, my father's best friend, left the health portfolio in the fall of 2004. He is now Manitoba's Minister of Energy, Science and Technology, Minister Responsible for Manitoba Hydro — and Minister Responsible for the Gaming Control Act.

Last month, I learned that my father had decided to run in the snap 2006 federal election in Canada, in the riding of Selkirk-Interlake, which includes Beausejour. Electoral boundaries get redrawn from time to time, but it is, more or less, the same area he represented as a member of parliament 40 years ago. Never thought I'd see the day. Good thing he didn't write those memoirs when I told him to.

I don't think I cried when his government was defeated in the Manitoba election of 1977, but I've shed a tear or two this time. I am joyful, because my father has reminded me that it is important to do what one feels one must, despite odds and opposition. I was glad for the opportunity to defend him — in cyberspace, this time, instead of a schoolyard. I am joyful because, this time, I told him that I am proud of him, and because I could tell he was pleased that I did. I am joyful because he has shown me, once again — and when I didn't think he could anymore — that there is nothing to be afraid of. Except global warming. (Actually, I can think of one other thing, but I am hoping it will no longer exist after 2008.) These are reasons to celebrate, and so I do. I am.

The election's on Monday.

Karmel Schreyer
Friday, January 20th, 2006
Discovery Bay, Hong Kong
(a Special Administrative Region of the People's Republic of China)

ACKNOWLEDGEMENTS

THIS BOOK IS A COLLABORATION, and it pleases me to be sharing the author's credit. Thank you, Grandpa Schreyer, for writing down the story of your life, so that my children and my cousins' children, and the rest of us, can better know you and your family and the world you lived in. And thank you, Cousin Bev, for having undertaken the task of turning Grandpa's fading longhand into typewritten pages.

I am grateful to my parents for their unending support — moral, logistical, and otherwise, and also to Sharon Butala, Silver Don Cameron, Peter Gordon, and Steve Washen for their editorial advice and words of encouragement. Thank you also to Ron Jackson, for permission to reproduce parts of his text on the geological history of the Rural Municipality of Brokenhead; and to Roseanne Greenfield Thong, for permission to reproduce the stanza from *Round is a Mooncake.* If I have neglected acknowledgement of any other passages I do apologize and when advised shall be pleased to rectify this in future editions. I want to again pay my respects to all the writers of 'prairie' fiction I mentioned in Chapter 1: Martha Ostenso, Frederick Philip Grove, Robert Stead, Gabrielle Roy, Margaret Laurence, Laura Ingalls Wilder, and, of course, Nellie McClung. (If at least one student of Canadian literature spends some enjoyable hours spotting the literary references in this book, I will die happy.) I also wish to acknowledge the women I write with: Lavinia, Becky, Nancy, Roseanne, Sarah, Victoria, Vivian, Cecilie, Dania, Leela, Marjorie, and Robin. Your sisterhood has meant a lot to me. To my editor, Alan Sargent, thank you for your meticulous editing as well as your determined detective work.

To my daughters Emi Celeste (Emi-poo) and Blaise Lily (Blazer-loo), thank you for providing much of the material for this book, as well as the motivation to write it. Thank you for being my ever-willing partners in the adventure of my motherhood. To D.P., thank you for your consistently wise words, your right-on editorial comments, your encouragement, and your love. To Emelyn Marquez, thank you for enabling me to embark on this journey, with my daughters by my side.

To all my Schreyer aunts and uncles and cousins — and to my Schulz aunts and uncles and cousins (a smaller bunch, but equally fascinating) — I want to thank you for being a part of this story. I hope it will make you smile and remember. I also owe a major debt of gratitude to the Baker Family, which has figured greatly in the lives of Schreyers for over a hundred years. I hope it continues for at least a hundred more; perhaps this can be arranged.

And, finally, I want to thank Cousin Greg, who graciously gave up his home for a summer so that Cousin Karmel could live her dream.